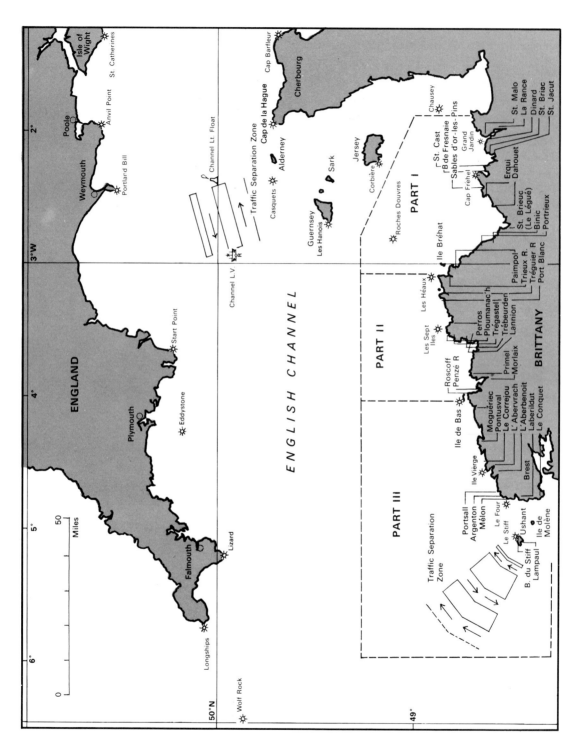

Chart 1. English Channel, western part; showing areas covered in this book. *Based on Admiralty Chart No 2675.*

NORTH BRITTANY PILOT

From St Malo to Ushant

K Adlard Coles
Revised by the RCC Pilotage Foundation
Edited by Donald Beswick
Fifth Edition

ADLARD COLES LIMITED
GRANADA PUBLISHING
London Toronto Sydney New York

Adlard Coles Ltd
Granada Publishing Ltd
8 Grafton Street, London W1X 3LA

Published in Great Britain by
Adlard Coles Limited 1984
Fifth Edition

Partly based on
Harbours and Anchorages of the North Coast of Brittany
by H G Hasler, first published by Adlard Coles Limited in 1952
Second Edition 1965
Third Edition 1972
Second impression 1973
Third impression 1976
Fourth impression 1976
Fifth impression with amendments 1977
Fourth Edition 1980

British Library Cataloguing in Publication Data
Coles, K. Adlard
    North Brittany pilot: St Malo to Ushant.—
    5th ed. rev.
    1. Pilot guides—France—Brittany
    I. Title   II. Beswick, Donald
    III. RCC Pilotage Foundation
    623.89′29′441   VK845

ISBN 0 229 11696 5

Photoset by CG Graphic Services, Aylesbury, Bucks
Printed and bound in Great Britain by
Richard Clay (The Chaucer Press) Ltd, Bungay, Suffolk

Acknowledgements

Almost all the charts in this book are based on the official French charts, with the kind permission of the Directeur du Service Hydrographique & Oceanographique de la Marine. The exceptions are based on Admiralty Chart numbers 2644, 2668 and 2675, with the permission of the Hydrographer of the Navy. The charts themselves are painstakingly drawn in short time by W G Wilson of Imray Laurie Norie and Wilson, and to him full thanks are due. Appreciation is also expressed to Professor A N Black for allowing his method of calculating tidal heights to be adopted, and for his help in correcting the proofs.

Details of tidal movement, buoys, beacons and lights have been checked against *Reeds Nautical Almanac*; *Tide Tables, European Waters*; *Channel Pilot*; and *List of Lights Vol A*; together with supplementary information contained in the RCC portfolios on foreign ports.

Help has also come, as usual, from sources too many and varied to mention. Suffice it to say that it has all been useful and much appreciated. Finally, the finished book would have been a poor shadow of itself but for the original work on which to build.

Foreword

In 1976 an American member of the Royal Cruising Club, Dr Fred Ellis, indicated that he wished to make a gift to the Club in memory of his father, the late Robert H Ellis MD, and of his friends the late Peter Pye and John Ives who were both prominent members, and as a mark of his esteem for Roger Pinckney, a past Commodore of that Club.

An independent charity known as the RCC Pilotage Foundation was formed and, with the approval of Dr Ellis, the funds provided by him were transferred to the Foundation. At the request of K Adlard Coles, as its first operation the Foundation undertook completely to revise *North Brittany Pilot.*

I was asked to edit the 4th and 5th editions and I am privileged to continue the work of my predecessors and to have their sound basis on which to build. I am also indebted to the Publishers and to Messrs Imray Laurie Norie and Wilson for their helpful co-operation.

Since these revisions were undertaken, the foundation received a further gift by will and, in conjunction with the Publishers, has revised the *North Biscay Pilot* and also written a new book called *The Atlantic Crossing Guide*.

Donald Beswick
October 1983

Notices to Mariners

This edition has been corrected against Admiralty Notices to Mariners to 20th October 1983.

Contents

List of Charts and Diagrams

Preface to Fifth Edition

This fifth edition of *North Brittany Pilot*, with all the charts re-drawn, has again been completely revised by Donald Beswick for the RCC Pilotage Foundation and I have been invited to repeat the brief history of how the book came into being.

It makes a somewhat personal story. Before the Second World War my wife and I did most of our cruising in the Baltic, and it was not until 1946 that as newcomers we started sailing on the French coast, which included a lively night passage from St Malo to Lézardrieux before many of the lights had been restored after the war. A year or two later I started to compile information for a book on the coast of Brittany, similar to my book *Creeks and Harbours of the Solent* which had been published in 1933. However, at the end of 1949 I was invited to race my boat *Cohoe* in the 1950 Bermuda and Transatlantic races as a member of the RNSA entry, an opportunity of a lifetime. At that time my wife and I lived at Bursledon in Hampshire where we knew H. G. ('Blondie') Hasler well. So as publisher I asked him whether he would write the book himself, to which he kindly agreed.

His work was first published in 1952 under the title *Harbours and Anchorages of the North Coast of Brittany*. As might be expected of the author it was a masterly volume, incorporating his own characteristic and original approach to the subject. This edition, for which I was responsible as publisher, had particularly clear charts printed in black, with blue for shoals and red for light sectors, area boundaries, etc. It was not until 1965 that a second edition was published. Hasler had been unable to undertake the revision so, by arrangement with him, I took over the work. In this new edition I followed his system and in fact referred to his book for much of my own pilotage. A major change which I made was the introduction of photographs of approaches and leading marks as, for example, the series of pictures taken through the intricate Portsall Inner Passage. Working with the aid of large scale French charts and sailing in boats of much less draught than Hasler's *Petula*, I was able to add a considerable number of small harbours and anchorages, some of which were previously known only to local yachtsmen; the alterations involved the addition of over 100 pages to the book which we retitled *North Brittany Harbours and Anchorages*. A third edition was published in 1972 and the title abbreviated to *North Brittany Pilot*.

Acknowledgements to individuals for their generous help have been made in previous editions, but I would like to repeat in general terms my gratitude to the Royal Cruising Club and fellow cruising men and friends who have contributed information and given me so much encouragement.

The fourth edition was published in this format in 1980, after the revision by the RCC Pilotage Foundation. I am proud to leave the work in their capable hands.

Adlard Coles

Cruising in Brittany

Brittany is rich in deep water and small secluded anchorages, and has held a particular fascination for British yachtsmen ever since Frank Cowper demonstrated that foreign cruising does not necessarily require a large yacht. It is a wonderful coastline in its indentations and in its contrasts between rugged rocks and sands. North Brittany is the nearest foreign shore to the western part of the south coast of England and, with a fair wind, it is only a 24 hour sail from our overcrowded but rather lovable Solent to the peaceful river of Tréguier where a different world is entered – a completely contrasting coastline and a foreign country with different customs and outlook. From Falmouth to L'Abervrac'h the distance across the Channel is even less.

The features of the Brittany coast are the rocks, the inlets, the large tidal range and the strong tidal streams. So the navigator, unfamiliar with local conditions, has several factors to contend with:

(a) The numerous rocks which are difficult to identify except in clear visibility.
(b) The strong tidal streams especially between St Malo and Les Sept Iles, which at spring tides will quickly raise severe overfalls on many parts of the coast, if the wind rises contrary to them. The streams also set towards rocks in certain positions.
(c) The Atlantic swell, particularly between Ile de Bas and Ushant which becomes very steep against a westerly running stream. A big swell may also restrict visibility so that landmarks and buoys can only be seen when one is perched at the top of each sea.
(d) In summer there is often a haze which makes it difficult to identify leading marks at a distance, and fog is by no means uncommon. If when approaching the coast of Brittany visibility becomes poor, whether from fog or rain squalls, it is best to return to the open water of the English Channel, even if one has to ride out a gale there. The coast can only be approached safely if one is certain of position and certain of picking up the leading marks or outer beacons.

It would be irresponsible not to mention the possibility of these dangers as, although North Brittany is near to us, the navigation is more difficult than farther afield on the coast of the Bay of Biscay, and there is often no margin for mistakes. A stranger to the coast should at first be content with the straightforward deep anchorages and only attempt the comparatively out of the way ones after he has gained experience, and even then only in the right conditions.

The relieving factors are that the coast is extremely well marked by beacon towers, beacons and buoys, and that at neap tides the streams are moderate. Even at spring tides there are many days when the seas are smooth, the weather is sunny, the visibility is clear and there are no exceptional hazards if proper care is taken in navigation.

From the yachtsman's point of view there are three pictures of North Brittany. The first is at low water spring tides, when a maze of rocks are uncovered and glorious stretches of yellow sands. The second is at high water spring tides, when most of the rocks have plenty of water over them and, with the aid of large scale charts, it is often possible to depart from the recognised channels. The third is at low water neap tides. Here the picture in the approach is more moderate, but there is about 3 m or more water above chart datum, which is then deep enough to provide anchorage in many of the most interesting and pictorial harbours such as Bréhat, Ploumanac'h and Ile Grande, which may be termed neap tide anchorages.

Many of the best harbours in North Brittany such as Roscoff dry out at low water. It is a great advantage to have a yacht equipped with legs or constructed with suitable bilge keels, so that she can take the bottom; but there is rarely any difficulty in lying alongside the quay. Booms, dinghy, anchors and chains can be placed on the side of the yacht against the quay and, as a precaution, a halyard can be secured to a ring ashore to ensure that the yacht will not fall outwards as she takes the bottom. Some modern yachts have very short keels and fall by the bows as the tide recedes. This is uncomfortable but not dangerous, providing that she still heels towards the quay and is secured by a halyard. Such yachts should be berthed heading in-wards towards the shore end of a jetty, as the slope of the bottom usually rises from the outer end of the quay towards the inner end which dries out further. Good fenders are required and the modern type of long plastic ones with a line at each end are excellent, as they act as elastic rollers between the yacht and the quay.

In drying harbours yachtsmen should if possible avoid mooring against the seamost ladder, as this position is often needed by fishermen.

Where a sea lock gives access to a fresh water dock or river, e.g. Morlaix, there is heavy turbulence and a strong current when the gates are opened and the fresh and salt water mix. Yachts should remain secured until this dies down. Where the dock remains salt, being periodically filled from the sea, e.g. St Malo, this does not happen to the same extent.

The coastline of North Brittany, composed of rocks and sand, alters little but there are frequent changes in lights, fog signals, beacons and buoys, and sometimes in their names and positions. The navigator must be prepared for alterations, as they continue even while a book is being compiled and printed. See also page 16.

Lights. Particulars of lights are given each year in *Reed's Nautical Almanac*, and in the Admiralty *List of Lights, Volume A*, published every year or two. Alterations are published weekly in Admiralty *Notices to Mariners* and are also shown on new charts corrected up to the date of sale. Particulars of light buoys are given in the *Channel Pilot* and also on large scale charts. The French Government *Feux et Signaux de Brume*, which is loose leaf and rather expensive, gives full particulars of lights and light buoys and beacons. Replacement pages and small amendments are published from time to time. Particulars of radio beacons are given in *Reed's Nautical Almanac* and in the Admiralty *List of Radio Signals Vol 2.*

Passports. These are essential, except for members of a professional crew. They are required for production to the Douane, when cashing travellers' cheques, Euro-cheques, or collecting post and, not least, should it be necessary to re-enter the UK by public transport.

British Customs. Customs declaration C1328 must be completed before departure and parts II and III retained for delivery to Customs on return.

French Customs and Requirements. Regulations, which can be expected to be strictly enforced and which carry penalties, impose restrictions on: (1) Pursuing any paid activity on land. (2) The arranging of skippered or bare-boat charters, without first paying import charges and taxes. (3) Cruising in French waters without carrying a Certificate of Registry or an international certificate of ownership. (4) The carrying of drugs, whatever the quantity (medicaments?), and (5) The carrying of goods other than (a) personal effects, (b) authorised goods intended for personal use within the limits of duty free allowances and (c) foreign currency in excess of the authorised amount (5,000FF in 1982). If the restrictions imposed by these regulations are complied with, no 'Q' flag or other formalities are required on arrival in Brittany. There is no need to enter at a port with a Douane, no need to report departure, freedom to berth anywhere, subject to local restrictions and, freedom to stay in French waters and canals for an aggregate of six months in any period of twelve consecutive months. If the restrictions are not being complied with, then entry must be made at a port with a Douane and a 'Q' flag must be flown until cleared. The Douane have the right to make random inspections anywhere and, as well as calling for the Certificate of Registry or other approved document, they will require proof that the boat and the goods on board conform to the regulations.

Harbour dues. These are now the rule in Brittany.

Ensign. A French courtesy ensign should always be worn.

French Charts. These are accurate and finely engraved, although naturally a British yachtsman finds Admiralty charts easier to read. They may be obtained by post from Service Hydrographique de la Marine at 29283 Brest Cedex, France; payment can be made through any bank. They can also be bought at the Librairies Maritimes at various ports, although sometimes the selection may be limited.
When using French charts it is necessary to keep in mind the following differences:
(a) they have no compass roses and are intended to be used with a protractor.
(b) Small rocks which do not cover at HW are marked with a 'T' on older charts.

3

This is a useful convention, as such rocks are often difficult to make out on British charts.

(c) Some latitude scales are in degrees, minutes and seconds of arc, not in degrees, minutes and decimals of minutes as in Admiralty charts, so that they do not read directly in miles and decimals of a mile. Care must be taken, when transposing these scales to miles, to remember that a mile is 60 seconds. Some of the large scale charts and some of the older ones are not graduated, but they have a graticule based on the main landmark, the Lat and Long of which are given under the title.

(d) It is a good plan to put a circle round each beacon or buoy which may otherwise be overlooked in a mass of soundings and other useful details.

Echo Soundings. The modern echo sounder is a great advance on the older method of measuring depth by lead and line. It is particularly useful on the Brittany coast, as it enables a navigator to feel his way into secluded anchorages where the bottom is sand or gradually shelving rocks. Echo sounders must not, however, be relied upon to give warning of steep-to rocks, where at one moment a yacht may be in deep water and the next on top of them.

Fresh Water. Most commercial jetties can supply water by hose. The smaller towns and villages often have public water taps near the landing place. Restaurants or cafés will usually oblige by filling jerrycans. A yacht intending to stay some time in French waters would find it useful to carry a length of hose with a universal tap adaptor, since hoses are not always available.

Fuel. Note the following translations:

Petrol	..	..	.. Essence (f)
Diesel oil ..	..	..	Gasoil (m) (pronounced Gaswahl)
Paraffin	..	..	.. Pétrole (m)

There are no arrangements for the supply of petrol or diesel oil to yachts at reduced prices. The pumps on the quays at most harbours can only supply petrol and diesel oil to fishermen and commercial users through the customs officer.

Paraffin (*pétrole*) can be bought at *drogueries* or sometimes at *épiceries*. Ask for refined (*raffiné*) paraffin for a primus, as the inferior grade quickly chokes the jets. It is not so easily obtained as Camping Gaz which is available anywhere, and an accessory can be bought to connect the cylinder to a Calor gas regulator. There are no facilities for refilling Calor gas cylinders, but the screw connections on French Butagas cylinders are interchangeable with those on 10 lb Calor Gas. These can be obtained in most ports subject to the payment of a deposit, similar to that on a Calor Gas cylinder.

Methylated spirits (*l'alcool*) may easily be obtained at a *pharmacien* or at a *droguerie*. It is colourless in France.

Yacht Clubs. The large yacht clubs of France are hospitable to foreign yachtsmen belonging to recognised clubs, and put all facilities at their disposal. The smaller clubs, of which there are now a great number, are equally helpful within the limits of their smaller premises, and a visitor need not hesitate to call and ask for local advice. There are centres and sailing schools in almost every harbour and sheltered bay, and many plans for the further improvement of facilities.

Currency. Sterling cheques can no longer be cashed on production of British Bank £50 cheque cards. Travellers' cheques are still negotiable. New cheque guarantee cards are available from UK banks and one is recommended to approach one's own bank for details. Travellers' cheques can sometimes be cashed at hotels and shops where money is spent. French banks are closed on Saturdays, Sundays, Monday and all holidays. Non-French currency may be carried on board but if more than the permitted amount (5,000FF in 1982) is carried it must be declared to the Douane.

Post Offices. These are normally open every weekday, and for a time on Sunday mornings. Post-boxes are painted blue or yellow, and are often recessed into the wall of a house.

Telephones. STD telephones are well provided in kiosks (*cabines*) also in Post Offices where one's call is metered and paid for at the counter, and where the charge appears to be less. To ring a UK number dial 19, then pause until a low pitched continuous note is heard, then dial 44, followed by the UK STD code and number, but omitting the first 0 of the code. Thus for London dial 1 and not 01.

Colorado Beetles. These pests, once common in northern France, are now rarely seen in Brittany, but may still fly on board or arrive by other means. Their bright yellow and black colouring is unmistakable, and they should be destroyed at once, as strong measures are in force in Britain and the Channel Islands to prevent them from immigrating.

History. For those who are not well acquainted with the French coast the following notes may be useful:

France, like Great Britain, is subdivided into ancient kingdoms, each of which contains a number of *départements* corresponding roughly to British counties. The coast of Brittany stretches from Mont Saint Michel round Ushant and down as far as the Loire, and its *départements*, taken in order, are Ille et Vilaine, Côtes du Nord, Finistère, Morbihan, and Loire Atlantique. Only the first three concern us here.

Historically, the connection between Great Britain and Brittany is very close. Brittany, whose ancient name was Armorica, was originally peopled by the race of Dolmen-builders, whose stone monuments (*dolmens, allées couvertes, menhirs, cromlechs*

5

and *lechs*) are still to be seen everywhere. Next came the Gauls, later to be conquered by Caesar and incorporated in the Roman Empire.

Then early in the fifth century, fleets of English settlers began to arrive, flying from the Picts and Scots. Later in the same century large numbers of Irish settlers came in, and the Saxon invasion of England increased the flow of refugees to such an extent that they soon occupied the whole of the Brittany peninsula, which became known as 'Lesser Britain' and spoke the British tongue, identical with that now spoken in Wales and until the seventeenth century, in Cornwall.

These early settlers brought Christianity to what was then a pagan country, and many Breton legends are no more than distorted accounts of the work of these 'saints' in spreading the gospel.

The early colonisers formed settlements of two kinds: civil communities called 'Plous', and religious settlements called 'Lanns'. A glance at the map will show the extent to which these two words still occur in the names of towns and villages. Many other towns are named after the missionaries themselves, such as St Malo, St Servan, St Brieuc, St Pol de Leon and St Lunaire.

The new kingdom of Brittany soon ceased to owe any allegiance to Britain, and became more or less independent until 1491, when it came permanently under the French crown. During this time it suffered continual warfare, first at the hands of raiding Norsemen and Danes, and later from civil war between the great feudal families, usually supported by either France or England. At the end of the sixteenth century it is described as having been almost depopulated by war and plague.

During the Revolution the Breton peasantry made a stand against the Terror, and Brittany is still the stronghold of Catholicism in France.

Fifty years ago the western half of Brittany still spoke the Breton tongue almost exclusively, but this is now slowly on the way to extinction. The rest of France has discovered the charm of Brittany, and many of its coastal villages now rely more on holiday-makers than on fishing. Nevertheless, it is still common for the people to speak Breton amongst themselves, particularly in the extreme north-west, and the correct pronunciation of Breton place-names is often nearer to English than French practice.

A surviving Breton custom is the *pardon*, a religious gathering centred around a particular locality. *Pardons* take place on the same date each year, and some of the better-known ones are mentioned later in this book.

Sailing Directions

The book is divided into three parts, as indicated on Chart No 1 (frontispiece). Each part starts with general information, then goes on to a description of the individual ports and anchorages; these are arranged as far as possible in the order in which they would be encountered when sailing down-channel.

Chausey, Cancale and the coast east of St Malo have been omitted as they are covered elsewhere, but St Malo is described as it is a principal port of entry whether one is cruising east or west. At the other end of the book the scope has been extended westward to fill the gap between Ushant and Brest, where *North Biscay Pilot* begins.

Charts

The charts reproduced here are of three general kinds:

(a) A small scale chart of the western part of the English Channel, showing the scope of the book (frontispiece).
(b) Three medium scale charts covering the north coast of Brittany in sections, and showing the positions of the harbours and anchorages mentioned.
(c) Thirty-two large scale charts showing details of the main anchorages and their approaches.

Of these, only the large scale charts are intended to aid navigation. In addition adequate charts of the coastline and seaward approaches, together with the latest light list and tide tables, are essential.

Depth of Water and Unmarked Dangers

The charts in this book have been kept as simple as possible, but are designed for the navigator who likes to use secondary entrances as well as the main channels of approach. Most of these channels are well marked by leading lines, buoys and beacons. In addition to the normal leading lines shown on the official charts, H. G. Hasler put in many leading lines and lines of bearing of his own, and this convention has been followed since. Most of these have been labelled with a letter, for ease of reference.

Even when under power, however, it may be necessary to depart from a chosen line on occasions, such as when passing another vessel; while for a sailing vessel beating to windward the question of following a leading line does not arise. The aim throughout has been to simplify the charts to such an extent that the owner of a small boat can sit at the helm with the book beside him and beat to windward through the approach channels single handed, if necessary.

In effect, the charts suggest how far, and in which direction, a small craft may depart from the given lines in suitable weather and state of tide. The method used has been to apply a shaded tint to areas which have a depth of less than 2 m or which contain unmarked dangers with less than 2 m over them. If the shaded area shows soundings or drying heights, it indicates that nothing in the immediate vicinity of the figures is any higher; but if no figures are shown, it is to be assumed that the area is dangerous to enter at all states of tide and, indeed may contain small rocks which never cover, but which are too small to be shown on the scale of the chart.

Areas which are left plain white carry 2 m of water or more except where lesser soundings are shown. If such lesser soundings mark a small isolated danger, they are surrounded by a line and shaded; otherwise they may be taken as indicating a general shallowness in the vicinity.

In seaward areas and approach channels, no soundings over 2 m are normally shown. This is in order to make the charts as easy as possible to read.

In the anchorages, a few soundings are usually shown, whether over 2 m or not, so that scope of chain and swinging room can be estimated, but in all cases soundings should be taken and the depth at low water calculated. See pages 14 and 42.

All soundings are in metres relative to chart datum.

Chart datum is LAT which is explained on page 13, so that it is only necessary to point out here that at MLWS there is usually at least 1 m more water than at datum (so that 2 m will then be 3 m or more) and at least 3 m more water at MLWN (so that 2 m will then be 5 m or more).

Leading Lines. These often do not follow the centre of the navigable channel. Except where otherwise stated, it is considered safe to follow such lines exactly, but where they can be seen from the chart to pass very close to a danger on one side, it is advisable to borrow slightly towards the other.

Leading marks often cover only part of the approach, after which course has to be altered to a new transit. Care should be taken not to overstand on a transit which eventually leads over dangers. It is frequently easier for a stranger approaching a harbour to navigate by the nearer buoys and marks, as the recognised leading marks are often difficult to pick out even in clear weather. They may be far away and indistinct in haze.

The sailing directions in this book provide for either method, including a description of each mark and how far to port or starboard it is left when following the line.

As a general rule, it is much easier to pick up the leading marks when leaving harbour than when entering. It is therefore a good plan to get to know some of the more difficult secondary channels as exits, before trying them as entrances.

Sketch Views. These are all copied from original drawings made by H. G. Hasler in 1950 and 1951. In some places where substantial alterations have occurred since the drawings were made, the views have been omitted.

Each of the views in this book is labelled with the position from which it was taken. In order to have full advantage from them, it is desirable to pass close to the given positions.

A word of caution may not be out of place to those who are visiting these anchorages for the first time. It is not safe to follow the tracks of other craft instead of relying on one's own navigation. They may themselves be strangers and on a wrong course, or local boats which know every rock in the district and are dodging between unmarked dangers. Fishing boats, in particular, are the most dangerous of guides, as they frequently draw less water than yachts of the same size, and seldom follow the safest channel, unless it happens to be the shortest.

System of Buoyage. The International Association of Lighthouse Authorities (IALA) has drawn up the 'Combined Cardinal and Lateral System' (IALA Maritime Buoyage System, Region A) which now applies to the waters covered by this book. Full details of the scheme are published in the *Channel Pilot* and elsewhere. The French have adapted their traditional system to conform where possible and their navigational marks are summarised on page 16.

Magnetic Variation, Courses and Bearings. All bearings, courses and light sectors expressed in the 360° connotation are True, and are from ship or seaward as the case may be. Cardinal points are used to give general directions. To convert to magnetic, variation must of course be added. Broadly speaking, for the area covered by Part One of this book, add 6°; for Part Two add 7°; and for Part Three add 8°. This holds good for the early 1980s, but it is essential to consult the relevant charts and publications for accurate conversion to magnetic bearings.

Clock Times. All times, time differences and time corrections are expressed in the four figure connotation and 24 hour clock as used in the Royal Navy, e.g. 5 minutes past ten in the forenoon is 1005; 25 minutes past two in the afternoon is 1425.

Lights and Fog Signals. Details of all lights and fog signals are given in each section, but they are subject to frequent alteration. The authorities for these are:

(a) The *Admiralty List of Lights Vol A*, for shore lights and light vessels.
(b) The *Channel Pilot*, or charts, for light buoys.
(c) The French *Feux et Signaux de Brume Série C*, for both.

Radio Navigational Aids. Details of Marine Radiobeacons and Air Radiobeacons of use to shipping are given in the text where appropriate and on the charts. These are also subject to frequent alteration. The authority for these is the *Admiralty List of Radio Signals Vol. 2*.

Traffic Separation Routes. A Separation Zone exists NW of Ushant at the extreme western end of the area covered by this book, and another exists outside its scope, NW of the Casquets light. These have been shown on Chart No. 1, since yachts sailing from Poole or ports east of Poole direct to NE Brittany will pass through or close to the zone off the Casquets. These zones are monitored by their respective traffic controls on channel 11, VHF, in English.

Radar as a Navigational Aid. Particular caution should be adopted when using radar for navigation on the North Brittany coast. If approaching the coast from seaward, offshore dangers may be encountered before the main shore features show up on the screen, or before they can be relied on to give an accurate indication of one's position. Whilst many of the offshore dangers are marked by buoys, these outer buoys do not, as a rule, have radar reflectors. They cannot, therefore, be relied on to produce echoes. Certain of the inshore buoys are fitted with radar reflectors, particularly when they mark dangers close to harbour approaches.

Lobster/Crab Pots and Buoyed Fishing Lines. These are to be found throughout the waters covered by this book, even in deep water and approach channels, especially in secondary channels. They usually have two floats on the surface, the end one with or without a flag. The lines are often of buoyant rope and present a considerable hazard, especially when laid in narrow channels on the line of leading marks. A good look-out is essential. Occasionally one sees a coil of surplus rope close to the inner float, which would badly foul a propeller. Particular care needs to be taken when motoring, and night passage making under engine must be hazardous.

Abbreviations

B – black
bg – bearing
cheq – chequers
Dir – directional
E – east
ev – every
F – fixed
Fl – flashing
Fl() – flashing (Group)
G – green
Gy – grey
HW – high water
Iso – isophase
LAT – lowest astronomical tide
LFl – flashing (long)
LH – Lighthouse
LW – low water
M – miles
N – north
m – metres
MHWN – mean high water neaps
MHWS – mean high water springs

MLWN – mean low water neaps
MLWS – mean low water springs
MTL – mean tide level
Mo() – morse code
Oc – occulting
Pyr – pyramid
pt
pte } – petit or petite
Pte – pointe
Q – continuous quick flashing
R – red; or *Roche, Rocher*
RoBn – radio beacon
s – seconds
S – south
stbd – starboard
VQ – continuous very quick flashing
VQ() – continuous very quick flashing (group)
Whis – whistle
W – white, or where the context so requires, west
Y – yellow

Tidal Heights and Tidal Streams

The charts in this book are drawn to the same datum as the appropriate French charts. This datum is also used in Admiralty and other British reproduction charts for this coast. It is taken as the Lowest Astronomical Tide (LAT) which can occur at any particular place. This prediction, therefore, applies only to equinoctial tides, but meteorological conditions can cause these levels to occur at other times and even produce tides lower than LAT.

Tidal heights and tidal streams are given in the preamble for each principal port. Time differences for high and low water are actual differences from the standard port, and correction should be made for any difference in zone or local time.

To predict tidal levels to a high degree of accuracy, reference should be made to the data and instructions contained in the *Admiralty Tide Tables Vol. 1*. In using the *Admiralty Tide Tables*, particular care must be taken with French secondary ports based on St Helier. The time correction for the French port, applied to GMT St Helier, corrects also for the difference between GMT and the standard zone time for the secondary port. For example find the time of low water at Ile Bréhat on Tuesday 13 June 1978:

Low water St Helier 1726 GMT
Correction for Ile Bréhat +0018 (add 18 minutes)
Low water Ile Bréhat 1744 Zone −0100
Low water Ile Bréhat 1644 GMT
Low water Ile Bréhat 1844 French double summer time

A simplified method of predicting tidal levels has been devised for the coast covered by this book. It is based on the principle that HW and LW heights can be found by taking the Mean Tide Level (MTL) for the port and adding or subtracting the half range of the tide for the day at that port. It assumes certain constants, which may not apply strictly, in all places; but it should provide a sufficiently accurate method of calculation for practical purposes. Detailed instructions, and tables are set out on the next pages.

A rough and rapid method of estimating the height of tide for any place at any given time is by the well known 'twelfths' method. Having arrived at the range of the tide for the day, divide by twelve then adjust as follows: first hour's rise or fall 1/12th of range, second hour 2/12ths, third hour 3/12ths, fourth hour 3/12ths, fifth hour 2/12ths, and sixth hour 1/12th of range.

To predict tidal streams to a high degree of accuracy, reference should be made to the tidal data given on the largest scale Admiralty chart available for the area. For rough use, and particularly for planning passages, reference can be made to the tidal chartlets published by the Admiralty and by Imray, Laurie, Norie & Wilson Ltd.

Tide Tables

From the tide tables in use take the time and height for HW Brest. (Note that this will normally be in French Standard Zone −0100 = BST.)

From the Tidal Data for the port take the time difference between Local High Water and High Water Brest, the Port Index (taking care to note whether 'A' or 'B') and the mean tide level (MTL).

1. Calculate the time of Local High Water.
2. Calculate the time interval, before or after the nearest Local High Water to the time when the height is required.

HW Brest (m)	5·3	5·4	5·5	5·6	5·7	5·8	5·9	6·0	6·
Tide Index	−4	−2	0	1	2	3	4	5	6

+Port Index

TOTA

	A	B	0–1	2–3	4–5	6	7	8	9	10	11	12	13	14	15	16	17
Add to MTL	0000	0000	0·8	0·9	1·1	1·2	1·3	1·4	1·5	1·6	1·7	1·8	1·9	2·1	2·2	2·3	2·5
	0020	0020	0·8	0·9	1·0	1·2	1·3	1·3	1·4	1·5	1·6	1·8	1·9	2·0	2·2	2·3	2·5
	0035	0040	0·7	0·9	1·0	1·1	1·2	1·3	1·4	1·5	1·6	1·7	1·8	1·9	2·1	2·2	2·4
	0050	0100	0·7	0·8	0·9	1·1	1·1	1·2	1·3	1·4	1·5	1·6	1·7	1·8	1·9	2·1	2·2
	0100	0110	0·7	0·8	0·9	1·0	1·1	1·2	1·2	1·3	1·4	1·5	1·6	1·7	1·8	2·0	2·1
	0110	0120	0·6	0·8	0·9	1·0	1·0	1·1	1·2	1·3	1·3	1·4	1·5	1·6	1·8	1·9	2·0
	0120	0130	0·6	0·7	0·8	0·9	1·0	1·0	1·1	1·2	1·2	1·3	1·4	1·5	1·6	1·7	1·9
	0130	0140	0·5	0·6	0·7	0·8	0·9	0·9	1·0	1·1	1·1	1·2	1·3	1·4	1·5	1·6	1·7
	0135	0150	0·5	0·6	0·7	0·7	0·8	0·9	0·9	1·0	1·0	1·1	1·2	1·3	1·4	1·5	1·6
	0145	0200	0·5	0·5	0·6	0·7	0·7	0·8	0·8	0·9	0·9	1·0	1·1	1·1	1·2	1·3	1·4
	0150	0210	0·4	0·5	0·5	0·6	0·6	0·7	0·7	0·8	0·8	0·9	1·0	1·0	1·1	1·2	1·3
	0200	0220	0·3	0·4	0·5	0·5	0·5	0·6	0·6	0·7	0·7	0·8	0·8	0·9	0·9	1·0	1·1
	0210	0230	0·3	0·3	0·4	0·4	0·4	0·5	0·5	0·5	0·6	0·6	0·7	0·7	0·7	0·8	0·9
	0225	0240	0·2	0·2	0·3	0·3	0·3	0·4	0·4	0·4	0·4	0·4	0·5	0·5	0·6	0·6	0·7
	0235	0250	0·2	0·2	0·2	0·2	0·2	0·2	0·3	0·3	0·3	0·3	0·3	0·4	0·4	0·4	0·5
	0245	0300	0·1	0·1	0·1	0·1	0·1	0·1	0·1	0·1	0·1	0·1	0·2	0·2	0·2	0·2	0·2
Subtract from MTL	0250	0310															
	0300	0320	0·1	0·1	0·1	0·1	0·1	0·1	0·1	0·1	0·1	0·1	0·2	0·2	0·2	0·2	0·2
	0310	0330	0·1	0·2	0·2	0·2	0·2	0·2	0·2	0·3	0·3	0·3	0·3	0·3	0·4	0·4	0·4
	0315	0340	0·2	0·2	0·3	0·3	0·3	0·3	0·4	0·4	0·4	0·4	0·5	0·5	0·5	0·6	0·6
	0325	0350	0·2	0·3	0·3	0·4	0·4	0·4	0·5	0·5	0·5	0·6	0·6	0·7	0·7	0·7	0·8
	0335	0400	0·3	0·4	0·4	0·5	0·5	0·5	0·6	0·6	0·7	0·7	0·8	0·8	0·9	0·9	1·0
	0340	0410	0·4	0·4	0·5	0·6	0·6	0·6	0·7	0·7	0·8	0·8	0·9	0·9	1·0	1·1	1·2
	0350	0420	0·4	0·5	0·6	0·6	0·7	0·7	0·8	0·8	0·9	0·9	1·0	1·1	1·1	1·2	1·3
	0400	0430	0·5	0·5	0·6	0·7	0·7	0·8	0·8	0·9	1·0	1·0	1·1	1·2	1·3	1·4	1·5
	0405	0440	0·5	0·6	0·7	0·8	0·8	0·9	0·9	1·0	1·1	1·2	1·2	1·3	1·4	1·5	1·6
	0415	0450	0·6	0·7	0·8	0·9	0·9	1·0	1·0	1·1	1·2	1·3	1·4	1·5	1·6	1·7	1·8
	0425	0500	0·6	0·7	0·8	0·9	1·0	1·1	1·1	1·2	1·3	1·4	1·5	1·6	1·7	1·8	2·0
	0450	0520	0·7	0·8	0·9	1·0	1·1	1·2	1·3	1·4	1·4	1·5	1·6	1·8	1·9	2·0	2·2
	0515	0540	0·8	0·9	1·0	1·2	1·2	1·3	1·4	1·5	1·6	1·7	1·8	2·0	2·1	2·2	2·4
	0545	0600	0·8	0·9	1·1	1·2	1·3	1·4	1·5	1·6	1·7	1·8	1·9	2·1	2·2	2·3	2·5

Interval before local HW

3. Along the top of the table below, select the nearest height of High Water Brest and read off the Tide Index immediately below this.
4. Add this to the Port Index = Total Index.
5. Select the vertical column headed with the Total Index.
6. Read off the time interval before or after HW Brest in column 'A' or 'B' as appropriate. (The 'A' column applies to ports east of Les Sept Isles, where the tides are not symmetrical.) Run along this line to the column selected in 5 and read off the height difference.
7. Add or subtract this to or from the MTL, as indicated in the margin, to obtain the approximate height of tide above datum at the time required.

•2	6·3	6·4/5	6·6	6·7/8	6·9	7·0/1	7·2/3	7·4/5	7·6/7	7·8/9	8·0/1
7	8	9	10	11	12	13	14	15	16	17	18

NDEX

18	19	20	21	22	23	24	25	26	27	28	29	30	31	B	A	
2·7	2·9	3·1	3·3	3·5	3·7	4·0	4·3	4·6	4·9	5·2	5·6	6·0	6·4	0000	0000	
2·6	2·8	3·0	3·2	3·4	3·7	3·9	4·2	4·5	4·8	5·2	5·5	5·9	6·3	0020	0020	
2·5	2·7	2·9	3·1	3·3	3·5	3·7	4·0	4·3	4·6	4·9	5·3	5·6	6·0	0040	0040	Add to MTL
2·3	2·5	2·7	2·9	3·1	3·3	3·5	3·7	4·0	4·3	4·6	4·9	5·2	5·6	0100	0055	
2·2	2·4	2·6	2·7	2·9	3·1	3·4	3·6	3·8	4·1	4·4	4·7	5·0	5·4	0110	0105	
2·1	2·3	2·4	2·6	2·8	3·0	3·2	3·4	3·7	3·9	4·2	4·5	4·8	5·1	0120	0115	
2·0	2·1	2·3	2·4	2·6	2·7	3·0	3·2	3·4	3·6	3·9	4·1	4·4	4·7	0130	0125	
1·8	2·0	2·1	2·2	2·4	2·5	2·7	2·9	3·1	3·3	3·6	3·8	4·1	4·4	0140	0135	
1·7	1·8	1·9	2·0	2·2	2·3	2·5	2·65	2·8	3·0	3·3	3·5	3·7	4·0	0150	0145	
1·5	1·6	1·7	1·8	1·9	2·1	2·2	2·4	2·6	2·7	3·0	3·1	3·4	3·6	0200	0155	
1·3	1·4	1·5	1·6	1·7	1·9	2·0	2·1	2·3	2·4	2·6	2·8	3·0	3·2	0210	0205	
1·1	1·2	1·3	1·4	1·5	1·6	1·7	1·8	1·9	2·1	2·2	2·3	2·5	2·7	0220	0215	Interval after local HW
0·9	1·0	1·0	1·1	1·2	1·2	1·4	1·5	1·6	1·7	1·8	1·9	2·0	2·2	0230	0230	
0·7	0·7	0·8	0·9	0·9	1·0	1·0	1·1	1·2	1·3	1·4	1·5	1·6	1·7	0240	0240	
0·5	0·5	0·5	0·6	0·6	0·7	0·7	0·8	0·8	0·9	0·9	1·0	1·1	1·2	0250	0250	
0·2	0·2	0·2	0·3	0·3	0·3	0·3	0·3	0·4	0·4	0·4	0·5	0·5	0·5	0300	0305	
														0310	0315	
0·2	0·2	0·2	0·3	0·3	0·3	0·3	0·3	0·4	0·4	0·4	0·5	0·5	0·5	0320	0325	
0·4	0·5	0·5	0·5	0·6	0·6	0·6	0·7	0·7	0·8	0·9	0·9	1·0	1·0	0330	0335	
0·6	0·7	0·7	0·8	0·8	0·9	0·9	1·0	1·1	1·2	1·2	1·3	1·4	1·5	0340	0345	
0·9	0·9	1·0	1·0	1·1	1·2	1·3	1·4	1·5	1·6	1·7	1·8	1·9	2·0	0350	0400	
1·1	1·1	1·2	1·3	1·4	1·5	1·6	1·7	1·8	2·0	2·1	2·3	2·4	2·6	0400	0410	
1·2	1·3	1·4	1·5	1·6	1·7	1·8	2·0	2·1	2·3	2·4	2·6	2·7	3·0	0410	0420	
1·4	1·5	1·6	1·7	1·8	1·9	2·1	2·2	2·4	2·6	2·7	2·9	3·2	3·3	0420	0430	Subtract from MTL
1·6	1·7	1·8	1·9	2·0	2·2	2·3	2·5	2·7	2·8	3·0	3·3	3·5	3·7	0430	0440	
1·7	1·8	2·0	2·1	2·2	2·4	2·6	2·8	2·9	3·1	3·4	3·6	3·8	4·1	0440	0450	
1·9	2·1	2·2	2·3	2·5	2·7	2·9	3·1	3·3	3·5	3·8	4·1	4·3	4·6	0450	0505	
2·1	2·2	2·4	2·5	2·7	2·9	3·1	3·4	3·6	3·8	4·1	4·4	4·7	5·0	0500	0520	
2·3	2·5	2·6	2·8	3·0	3·3	3·5	3·7	4·0	4·3	4·6	4·9	5·2	5·6	0520	0545	
2·6	2·8	2·9	3·1	3·3	3·6	3·8	4·1	4·4	4·7	5·0	5·4	5·7	6·2	0540	0605	
2·7	2·9	3·1	3·3	3·5	3·7	4·0	4·3	4·6	4·9	5·2	5·6	6·0	6·4	0600	0640	

French Navigational Marks

The IALA Buoyage System A is very largely based on the lateral and cardinal systems which the French themselves developed, except that the lights for cardinal marks have all had to be changed; otherwise the old lateral and cardinal marks have been adapted to conform with IALA. Former marks which remain, but which have not been given IALA designations, have been painted white. Some light towers have been painted as IALA marks; but some still retain coloured sectors, so that they serve as beacon towers by day and lighthouses by night.

In this book, so far as possible, symbols for the various marks have been designed to show, pictorially, the shapes and colours which a navigator can expect to see and recognise.

Near low water, care needs to be taken not to mistake the portion of between HW and LW as a black band, especially when viewed from a distance. The following are examples of descriptions and symbols used in this book:

Lighthouses (Phares)

(a) In buildings shaped like dwellings, shown e.g.

(b) In masonry towers, shown e.g.

(c) Where a radio beacon is operated: Ro Bn.

(d) In both (a) and (b) the position of the light is at the base of the symbol.
Sectors are indicated by pecked lines radiating outwards.

Beacon Towers (Tourelles)

Masonry towers painted in appropriate IALA colours, otherwise white, e.g.

Beacons (Balises)

Iron, masonry or wooden pole-like structures painted in IALA colours and usually with the appropriate topmark, e.g.

Pyramids (Pyramides)

Conical beacon towers, usually white and quite narrow for their height, like obelisks with flat tops. Mainly used for leading and clearing marks. e.g.

Buoys (Bouées)

(a) *Pillar.* Usually lattice structures. The colours on the latticework are not always easy to distinguish.

16

Where a radar reflector is mounted, it is often larger than the topmark (see page 110). shown e.g. B R B

(b) *Spindle*. Basically can-shaped cylindrical, but much higher in relation to its diameter. Invariably a lateral port mark, e.g. R

(c) *Spar*. A narrow steel cylinder mounted on a float. Usually painted in IALA colours, with appropriate topmark. Not always conspicuous, e.g. G

(d) *Can*. Generally used only as lateral and safe water marks e.g. R

(e) *Conical*. Generally used as lateral starboard marks but occasionally as lateral port marks. G

In relation to all buoys:
Those fitted with lights are shown:
Those fitted with bells are noted 'Bell'
Those fitted with whistles are noted 'Whis'
Those fitted with radar reflectors have:

Daymarks (Amers)	Stone walls or other structures built on dry land as navigational marks, and usually painted white, or black and white.
Withies (Perches)	Small saplings stuck into the mud to mark the edge of oyster beds and the like. Being light and flexible, they are not themselves a danger to navigation.
Leading marks (Alignements)	These fall into the following categories: (a) Natural objects, such as a headland or one edge of a prominent rock. (b) Lighthouses, church spires, old mill towers and the like. (c) Beacon towers or pyramids, usually painted white or black and white. (d) Daymarks, usually painted white, or black and white.
Painted rocks	A few above-water rocks near certain entrances are painted white, red, or red and white, to serve as leading marks or simply to help in identification.

17

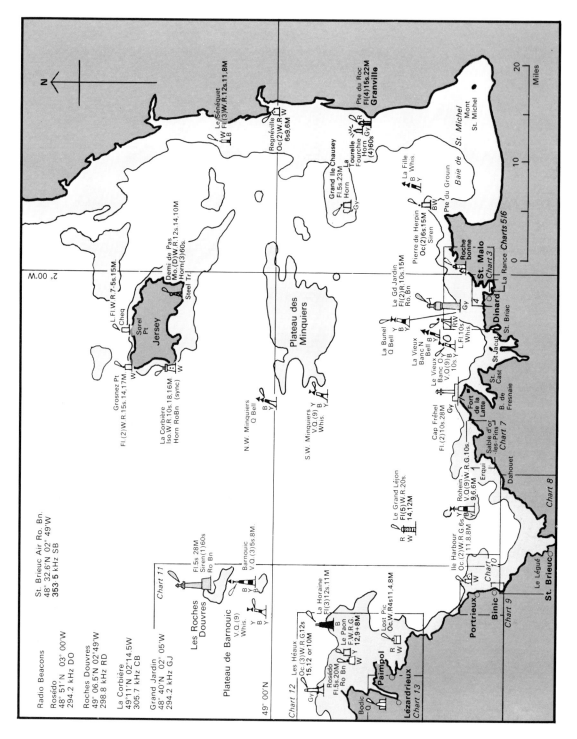

Chart 2. Mont St Michel to Lézardrieux, showing limits of large scale charts in this part of the book. Principal marks only shown. *Based on Admiralty Chart No 2675.*

18

Part One   St Malo to Lézardrieux

Between St Malo and Lézardrieux the coast consists mainly of cliffs and steep rock with small sandy bays, and is encumbered with offlying rocks and shoals, extending in places over 7 miles offshore. Beyond these coastal dangers lie the Iles Chausey, Plateau des Minquiers, Grand Léjon, Roches Douvres, and Plateau de Barnouic, all of which contain sunken rocks and should not be approached close-to without consulting a large scale chart.

The range of tide is very great, and the tidal streams reach 5·5 knots on the NE side of the Ile Bréhat.

LIGHTS AND FOG SIGNALS

Details of the main coastal lights and fog signals are given below. All bearings are given in degrees True. To convert to magnetic, one must of course add variation, which is approximately 6° west during the early 1980s on this part of the coast.

The height of the light structures is measured from the lantern to the base of the structure; elevation is measured between the centre of the lantern and MHWS.

La Corbière (Jersey) Iso WR 10s vis W 18M, R 16M. W from the land to 294°; thence R to 328°; thence W to 148°; thence R to the land. Circular stone tower 19m high; elevation 36m. Signal Station. Fog Horn Mo (C) 60s. Ro Bn: CB 305·7 kHz – 20M.

Le Sénéquet Fl (3) WR 12s vis W 11M, R 8M. R from 083·5° through east to 116·5°; W elsewhere. W circular tower with B base 26m high, elevation 18m.

Regnéville Oc (2) WR 6s vis W 9M, R 6M. R from 063° through east to 110°; W elsewhere. W tower 12m high, upper part R; W dwellings; elevation 12m.

Pointe du Roc Fl (4) 15s vis 22M. Gy circular tower, R top, 16m high; elevation 49m.

Tourelle Fourchie Horn (4) 60s.

Grande Ile (Chausey) Fl 5s vis 23M. Gy square tower 19m high; elevation 39m. Horn 10s.

Pierre de Herpin Oc (2) 6s vis 15M. B and W circular tower 24m high; elevation 20m. Siren Mo (N) 2 ev 60s.

Les Courtis Fl (3) G 12s vis 5M. G tower 21m high; elevation 14m.

Le Grand Jardin Fl (2) R 10s vis 15M. Tall concrete tower; 38m high; elevation 24m. Ro Bn: GJ 294·2 kHz – 10M. Grouped with Rosédo.

Cap Fréhel Fl (2) 10s. vis 28M. Gy square tower 33m high; elevation 85m. Horn 2 blasts ev 60s.

Le Rohein VQ (9) WRG 10s vis W 9M, R 6M, G 6M. R 072° to 105°; thence W to 180°; thence G to 193°; thence W to 237°; thence G to 282°; thence W to 301°; thence G to 330°; thence W to 072°. Cardinal west tower 15m high; elevation 13m.

Le Grand Léjon Fl (5) WR 20s vis W 14M; R 12M. W from 058° to 283°; thence R to 350°; thence W to 015°; thence R to 058°. R circular tower with W bands, 23m high; elevation 17m.

Ile Harbour Oc (2) WRG 6s vis W 11M; R 8M; G 8M. R from 270° to 306°; thence G to 358°; thence W to 015°; thence R to 080°; thence W to 133°; thence G to 270°. W square house with small W tower with R top on its roof; elevation 16m.

L'Ost Pic Oc WR 4s vis W 11M, R 8M. W from 221° to 253°; thence R to 291°; thence W to 329°; thence *obscured* to 105°; thence W to 116°; thence R to 221°. W square tower, R top 13m high; elevation 20m.

La Horaine Fl (3) 12s vis 11M. W octagonal tower 18m high; elevation 11m.

Barnouic VQ (3) 5s vis 8M. Cardinal east octagonal tower. 19m high; elevation 14m. – Unreliable.

Roches Douvres Fl 5s vis 28M. Pink tower on dwelling with dark green roof. 60m high; elevation 60m. Siren 60s. Ro Bn: RD 298·8 kHz – 70M. Penlee Point seq No 4.

Les Héaux Oc (3) WRG 12s vis W 15M; R 12M; G 10M. R from 227° to 247°; thence W to 270°; thence G to 302°; thence W to 227°. Gy granite tower 53m high; elevation 48m.

Le Paon F. WRG vis W 12M; R 9M; G 8M. W from 033° to 078°; thence G to 181°; thence W to 196°; thence R to 307°; thence W to 316°; thence R to 348°. Yellowish tower, 10m high; elevation 22m.

Rosédo Fl 5s vis 20M. W tower 12m high; elevation 29m. Ro Bn: DO 294·2 kHz – 10M. Grouped with Le Grand Jardin.

OFF-LYING BUOYS AND MARKS

In addition to the lighthouses listed above, the following off-lying buoys and marks may be useful when making passages along this coast. They are unlit unless otherwise stated.

Plateau des Minquiers. Not all the buoys marking the perimeter are shown on Chart No 2; it will be seen that some of them are lit.

La Fille (0·5 mile NE of Pierre de Herpin LH). Cardinal north buoy.

Rochefort (6 miles W of Pierre de Herpin LH). Cardinal east and Cardinal west beacons.

Le Vieux Banc (6 miles ENE of Cap Fréhel). (a) On the north side a Cardinal north spar bell buoy and (b) on the west side a Cardinal west pillar light buoy.

Banchenou (5 miles E of Cap Fréhel). Cardinal north pillar light buoy.

Les Landas (6·5 miles SE of le Grand Léjon). Cardinal north spar buoy.

Le Petit Léjon (3·5 miles SSE of le Grand Léjon). Cardinal west bell spar buoy.

Note: for all buoys and beacons in the approaches to Lézardrieux, Paimpol and Bréhat, see under these respective headings post.

AERO BEACON

Saint Brieuc. 48° 32′ 37″ N – 2° 49′ 06″ W. 353·5 kHz. Range 35 miles.

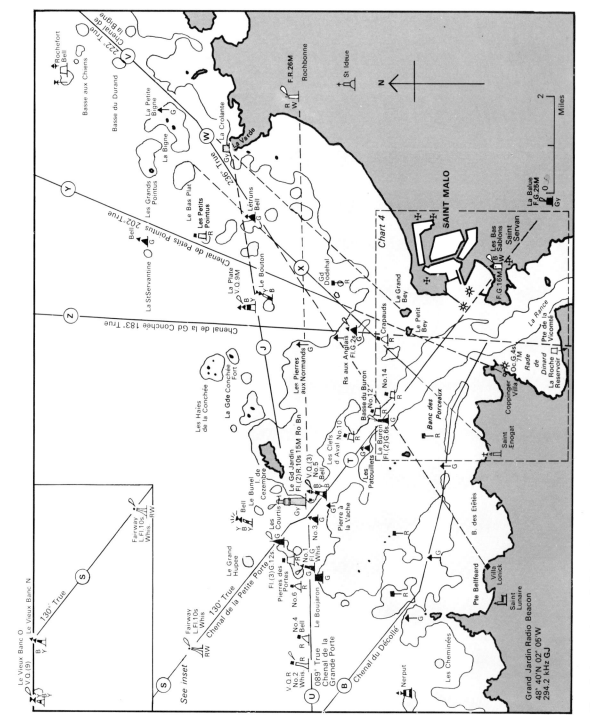

Chart 3. Approaches to St Malo. Based on French Chart No 844.

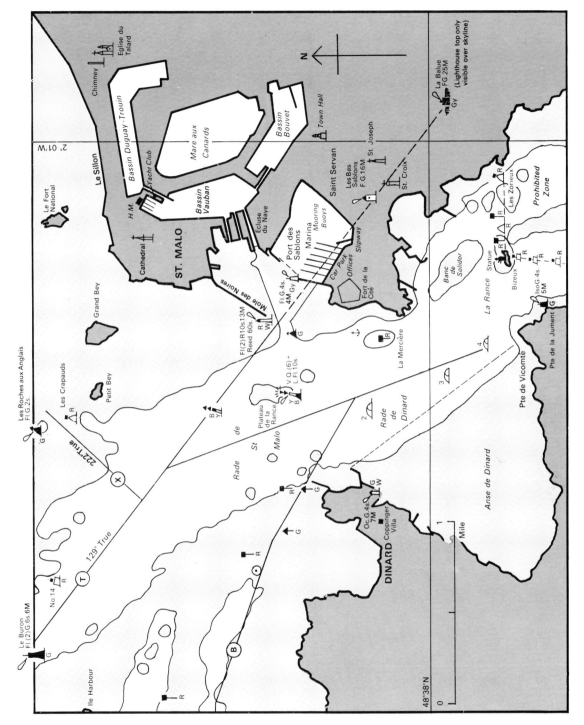

Chart 4. St Malo and Dinard. *Based on French Chart No 5645.*

23

1 St Malo and Dinard

Tidal Data

Tidal Heights
High Water: approx −0020 St Helier, −0515 Dover, +0205 Brest.
Mean Tide Level: 6·75 m. Index 13 A.
Heights of Tide above Datum: approx MHWS 12·2 m; MLWS 1·2 m; MHWN 9·1 m; MLWN 4·2 m.

Tidal Streams

1. In the offing between the Minquiers and Ile Cézembre the ESE-going stream begins about +0555 St Helier (+0100 Dover); and the WSW about −0005 St Helier (−0500 Dover).
2. In the eastern approach northward of Tourelle Rochefort and in the Chenal de la Petite Porte the ENE-going stream (NE in Chenal de la Petite Porte) reaching 3·8 knots at springs, begins at −0510 St Helier (+0220 Dover); and the WSW at +0030 St Helier (−0425 Dover) reaching 2·8 knots.
3. In the Chenal de la Grande Porte the stream turns at the same times as in 2 above, but the directions are east and west and both streams reach 3·8 knots at springs.
4. In Chenal de la Bigne the NE-going stream, reaching 3·8 knots at springs, begins at −0540 St Helier (+0150 Dover) and the SW-going stream at 0000 St Helier (−0455 Dover) reaching 3·3 knots.
5. In the Chenal de la Grande Conchée and Chenal des Petits Pointus the times are the same, but the directions and rates differ, east reaching 2·8 knots and west 1·9 knots.
6. Between St Malo and Dinard, the SSE-going stream begins −0525 St Helier (+0205 Dover) and the NNW-going stream begins HW St Helier (−0455 Dover).

General

St Malo is by far the most important commercial harbour on the north coast of Brittany, but remains an attractive and convenient port of call for yachts. It is possible to anchor in the river abreast the town, but there is little shelter here and yachts usually lock through into the basin, where they can lie alongside floating pontoons or alongside the wall, with all the amenities of a marina close to the town and the *plage*. Alternatively, yachts can, when depths over the sill permit, secure to a visitors' pontoon in the yacht marina at Port des Sablons. This is more expensive, less convenient and in a NW blow less comfortable than a berth in the basin.

Opposite St Malo, across the entrance to La Rance river, is the town of Dinard, mainly a large holiday resort with several adjacent bathing beaches. There is an anchorage in the Rade de Dinard abreast the town, but unless a yacht is prepared to take the ground, this is rather inconvenient at springs.

La Rance is a charming river and above the barrage (see page 40) is navigable at low water level almost to St Suliac, 5 miles from the entrance. There are several good anchorages on the way. Above St Suliac the river dries at chart datum, but when the water level is high enough it is navigable for a farther 2 miles to Port St Hubert, where there is a pool in which a yacht can lie afloat, even at low water.

When the water level has risen sufficiently it is possible to continue over the drying river bed to L'Ecluse du Châtelier. The bridge here swings to pass masted vessels, so yachts can lock through into the Canal d'Ille et Rance and proceed up to Dinan. From Dinan it is possible for small craft drawing less than 1·4 m and needing less than 2·3 m headroom, to pass by canal and river to Redon, and thence down the Vilaine to the Bay of Biscay. Before planning this passage, it is necessary to find out whether the canal system will be open at that time; it usually closes for maintenance for about a fortnight in late August and early September.

The seaward approaches to St Malo are complicated, but splendidly marked. There are two channels which can be taken by day or night at any state of the tide, and three more which can be used in daylight except near LWS.

Approaches

By day: the following can be used for fixing position during the approach:

Cap Fréhel (10 miles west of the Ile de Cézembre) a high headland with steep cliffs, with a lighthouse (tower 30 m high, elevation 85 m), a disused light tower, and a disused signal station (see photograph, page 48 and view on page 53).

Le Grand Jardin lighthouse: a tall concrete tower (29 m high, elevation 24 m) standing about 0·4 miles WSW of the Ile de Cézembre. This has a radiobeacon: GJ 294·2 kHz – 10 miles.

Ile de Cézembre: a prominent island 32 m high with several rounded summits.

La Grande Conchée: rock with fort on it situated east of Ile de Cézembre.

Rochefort: E and W Cardinal marks, standing at the E and W ends of a group of drying rocks 2·5 miles E of **Rochebonne** lighthouse.

Many of the leading lines described below are rather difficult for a stranger to pick up, but the channels can equally well be used by locating the outer marks and then steering compass courses with allowance for tide, checking off the numerous buoys and beacons as they appear.

By night: both the **Chenal de la Grande Porte** and the **Chenal de la Petite Porte** are excellently lit, and should not be difficult in reasonable visibility.

25

Les Courtis lighthouse at high water bearing about W by S. It is left on the starboard hand when entering by the Chenal de la Petite Porte. Behind the lighthouse, just to the left of it, is Pierre des Portes Lateral port beacon tower situated on a wide reef of rocks extending as far as the lighthouse. The distant marks are for the other channel – Chenal de la Grande Porte.

By day and by night: approach can be made to either channel by homing on safe courses, on **Le Grand Jardin** Radiobeacon (see Chart No 3 on page 22).

Those wishing to use secondary approaches, navigable by day only, or to sail outside the two main channels should buy the large scale Admiralty Chart No 2700, or better still French Government Chart No 5645; these show detail which cannot be reproduced on small scale.

CHENAL DE LA PETITE PORTE

This is the principal approach. A yacht needs plenty of speed to cope with the strong cross tide in this channel, except at slack water. The least depth is 7·3 m as far as the **Rade de Dinard.** If approaching from the NW, note **Le Vieux Banc** (dries). It is marked by two buoys, one of them lit. See inset on Chart No 3.

By Day   Approaching from any direction, first make a position about 150 m to the NE of the fairway light-and-whistle safe water mark buoy which is moored about 2 miles NW of **Le Grand Jardin** lighthouse. From here, the leading marks will be in line: **Le Grand Jardin** lighthouse in line with **La Balue** lighthouse (square tower with black lantern, 31 m high, elevation 69 m, standing on the skyline behind the town, bearing 130° True (line **S**). This line leaves the unmarked **Grande Hupée** rock (least depth 1·2 m) 0·1 mile to port; **Le Bunel** Cardinal west bell buoy 0·3 mile to port; and **Les Courtis** lighthouse (lateral stbd 19 m high, elevation 13 m) 0·2 miles to starboard. When this lighthouse tower bears 280° True, quit line **S** and steer

Grand Jardin lighthouse at high water bearing about NE by E with Ile Cézembre in background. The lighthouse is left on the port hand as also the Lateral port beacon to the right of it.

170° True for 0·15 mile then alter course to follow line **T**, which is marked by **Les Bas Sablons** lighthouse (white square tower 14 m high, upper part black, elevation 20 m) in line with **La Balue** lighthouse (elevation 69 m) bearing 129° True.

This line leaves the following marks on the sides shown:

No 3 Lateral starboard buoy 0·15 miles to starboard.

Le Grand Jardin lighthouse 150 m to port. A Lateral port beacon stands about 40 m SW of the lighthouse and must also be left to port.

No 5 Cardinal east buoy 50 m to starboard.

No 8 Lateral port buoy 0·125 miles to port.

No 10 Lateral port buoy 0·15 miles to port.

Le Buron light tower surmounted by a cylinder 110 m to starboard.

No 12 Lateral port buoy 100 m to port

No 14 Lateral port buoy 120 m to port.

The channel now approaches the **Plateau de la Rance**, a shoal containing drying rocks, which may be left on either hand:

(a) To pass to the eastward of it, continue along line **T** leaving the Cardinal north buoy marking the NE side of the shoal 60 m to starboard. When this buoy is abeam, hold on for 0·15 miles, sufficiently to leave **Plateau de la Rance** to starboard before altering course to 170° True for 0·2 miles. Then steer for the lock gates when they bear 070° True leaving the end of the **Mole des Noires** about 80 m to port. Alternatively, when the buoy is abeam, alter course to leave the end of the mole 0·15 miles to port. Then approach the St Malo lock gates when they bear about 070° True. If bound for **Port des Sablons** bear to starboard when the marina breakwater light is abaft the beam and check the depth of water shown on the tide gauge before crossing the sill. (See page 38.)

(b) To pass to the westward of it, when **St Malo Cathedral** tower bears 085° True, quit line **T** and steer 160° True, leaving the Cardinal south light buoy which marks the southern end of the **Plateau de la Rance** about 0·1 mile to port, and so into the **Rade de Dinard.**

By Night   Approaching from any direction, it should be easy to fix position by the main coastal lights: **Cap Fréhel, Les Courtis, Grand Jardin, Pierre de Herpin** and **Grande Ile, Chausey.** Then make a position close NE of the fairway light-and-whistle (safe water mark) buoy, which is moored about 2 miles NW of **Le Grand Jardin.** From here, follow line **S** by keeping **Le Grand Jardin** (Fl (2) R 10 s) in line with **La Balue** (the upper of two fixed green lights south of **St Malo**), bearing 130° True and leaving **Les Courtis** (Fl (3) G 12 s) 0·175 miles to starboard. Line **S** can often be picked up while still a long way to seaward. It leaves the unlit **Vieux Banc** bell buoy (Chart No 2) only about 18 m to starboard, and the fairway light-and-whistle buoy about 36 m to starboard. From the deck of a small yacht, **La Balue** dips behind **Le Grand Jardin** tower at some point along this line. When this happens, borrow a few yards to the westward and keep **La Balue** touching the west side of the tower. This line also clears all dangers. There are fixed red lights on pylons 0·7 and 1·2 miles SW of **La Balue.** When **Les Courtis** bears 280° True at which position **Le Grand Jardin** should be ahead distant 0·3 miles quit line **S** and steer 170° True for 0·15 miles then pick up line **T**; the fixed green lights of **Les Bas Sablons** and **La Balue** in line bearing 129° True intensified 127° to 130° True. Follow this line closely leaving:

> **Le Grand Jardin** lighthouse 150 m to port.
> **No 5** Cardinal E light buoy 50 m to starboard.
> **Le Buron** light tower (Fl (2) G 6 s) 120 m to starboard.

If passing to the east of the **Plateau de la Rance**, continue along line **T** until the unlit buoy which marks the north side of the shoal is abeam to starboard, distant 60 m. Hold on for 0·15 miles then steer 170° True until the light on the end of the **Môle des Noires** (Fl (5) 20 s) bears 080° True. Then alter course to approach the lock on the transit of the three FR lights over and behind the lock.

Alternatively, keep on transit **T** until the Cardinal south light on the buoy marking the south of **Plateau de la Rance** bears 250° True.

Le Buron lateral starboard light tower is left about 110 m to starboard when approaching by Chenal de la Petite Porte. Here with left edge in line with Lonic Villa and Ile Harbour to starboard (line **W**).

Then steer midway between the buoy and the mole end light until the latter bears 080° True. Then approach the locks as before.

If passing to the west of the **Plateau de la Rance**, when the tower of **St Malo** Cathedral bears 085° True quit line **T** and steer 160° True leaving the Cardinal south light-buoy, marking the south end of the shoal, 0·1 miles to port, and so into the **Rade de Dinard.**

Alternatively, if the cathedral cannot be seen, quit line **T** when the light buoy bears 150° True.

CHENAL DE LA GRANDE PORTE

This channel has a least depth of 6·5 m as far as the **Rade de Dinard**. If approaching from the NW, note **Le Vieux Banc** (dries), which is beyond the limits of Chart No 3, but is shown on the inset of Chart No 3. It is marked by two buoys, one of them lit.

By Day   First make a position 70 m south of No 2 Lateral port light-and-whistle buoy. From here, **Le Grand Jardin** lighthouse will be in line with (and obscuring) **Rochebonne** lighthouse (white square tower, red top 16 m high, elevation 40 m bearing 089° True). Line **U**. Follow this line which leaves the following marks on the sides shown:

> **No 4** Lateral port buoy 60 m, to port.
> **Boujaron** Lateral starboard beacon tower, 250 m to starboard.
> **No 6** Lateral port buoy, 140 m to port.

la Grande Conchée · les Haies de la Conchée · Ile Cézembre

Entrance of Chenal de la Grande Conchée. La Grande Conchée fort is left about 0·3 mile on the starboard hand. The photograph is taken with Ile Cézembre bearing about SW by W at about half-tide.

No 1 Lateral starboard buoy, 40 m to starboard.
Pierre des Portes port beacon tower, 0·15 miles, to port.
Les Courtis Lateral stbd LH 0·225 miles to port.
No 3 Lateral starboard buoy 0·1 miles to starboard.

When **Le Grand Jardin** lighthouse is 240 m distant, alter course to follow line **T** with **Les Bas Sablons** lighthouse (white square tower 14 m high, upper part black, elevation 20 m) in line with **La Balue** lighthouse (square grey tower 31 m high, elevation 69 m, the top only appearing on the skyline). Thence proceed as described under *Chenal de la Petite Porte: By Day*, above.

By Night   While still west of No 2 Lateral port light and whistle buoy VQ bring **Le Grand Jardin** (Fl (2) R 10 s) into line with **Rochebonne** (Fixed R) bearing 089° True (line **U**). (When exactly on the line, Rochebonne will be obscured by the tower of Le Grand Jardin. It is best to keep it touching one side.) This line leaves **No 2** Lateral port light-and-whistle buoy 70 m to port, **No 1** Lateral starboard light-and-whistle buoy 40 m to starboard, and **Les Courtis** (Fl (3) 12 s) 0·225 miles to port. When just more than 0·1 mile from **Le Grand Jardin** lighthouse, the leading lights for line **T** will come into line: the fixed green lights of **Les Bas Sablons** and **La Balue** in line bearing 129° True. Alter course to follow this line and proceed as described under *Chenal de la Petite Porte: By Night*, above.

CHENAL DE LA GRANDE CONCHÉE

By Day   This channel carries a least depth of 0 m (i.e. 6·7 m at half tide). It is the principal route used by the hydrofoils and other shallow draft fast ferries which ply between St Helier and St Malo via the east side of the Minquiers. Approaching from the north, first identify the **Ile**

Cézembre, then **Les Haies de la Conchée** rocks about 4 m high which lie about 1 mile ENE of the island. They are situated over 0·25 miles NNW of **La Grande Conchée**, which is easily identified as it has an old fortress on it, and form the NE corner of the group of rocks and dangers on this side.

Make a position from which these rocks bear 270° True distant 0·4 miles then steer to make good 183° True along line **Z** which is marked by the conspicuous fort on **Le Petit Bey** just open to the east of a white painted reservoir at **La Roche**, 0·7 miles SSW of Pointe de la Vicomté.

This line leaves the following marks on the sides shown:

La Grande Conchée (4 m high) with a fort on it, 0·3 miles to starboard.

La Plate Cardinal N beacon tower, 0·2 miles to port.

Le Bouton Cardinal S buoy, 0·25 miles to port.

Les Pierres aux Normands Lateral starboard beacon.

Grand Dodehal Lateral port beacon, 0·5 miles to port.

Les Roches aux Anglais Lateral starboard beacon, 0·1 miles to starboard.

Les Roches aux Anglais Lateral starboard buoy, close to starboard.

After proceeding a farther 0·15 miles past this buoy alter course to make good 222° True to follow line **X** heading for the eastern side of the **Baie des Etêtes** and leaving **Les Crapauds** Lateral port buoy to port. Then, when **Les Bas Sablons** lighthouse comes in line with **La Balue** lighthouse bearing 129° True (line **T**) alter course to follow this line and proceed as *Chenal de la Petite Porte: By Day*, above.

By Night From the northward identify **La Plate** Cardinal N. This light has a range of 9 miles. Bring this on to a bearing of 180° True and steer to make good a course of 180° True towards the light leaving **La St Servantine** unlit bell buoy 0·75 miles to port then steer so as to leave the light 0·2 miles to port on a course of 186° True. This course should then be heading for **Les Roches aux Anglais** Lateral starboard buoy Fl G 2 s. Leave this close to starboard. After proceeding a farther 0·15 miles past this buoy, alter course to make good 222° True to follow line **X** and leaving **Les Crapauds** unlit Lateral port buoy 60 m to port. When the fixed green lights of **Les Bas Sablons** and **La Balue** come in line bearing 129° True (line **T**) alter course to follow this line and proceed as described under *Chenal de la Petite Porte: By Night* above.

CHENAL DE LA BIGNE

By Day Only   This channel has a least depth of 0 m (i.e. 6·7 m at half tide), and is the most direct entrance from the eastward.

First make a position from which **Rochefort** shoal marked by Cardinal E and W beacon towers bears 280° True, distant 0·7 miles. From here pick up the leading marks for line **V: La Crolante** beacon tower in line with the north-western edge of **Le Grand Bey** (the larger of two islets close NW of **St Malo**) bearing 222° True. This line leaves **Les Chiens**, an unmarked rock that dries 0·6 m, 0·1 mile to starboard; **Le Durand** shoal, with a least depth of 0·6 m, 0·1 mile to starboard; and **La Petite Bigne** Lateral starboard beacon, 80 m to starboard.

After 0·4 miles farther, alter course to 236° True and follow line **W** keeping **Le Buron** black beacon tower in line with **Lonick Villa**, a house standing on the right edge of a wood near **Pointe Bellefard**, a point with a white stripe painted on it. This house is not easy to identify from this position.

This line leaves **La Crolante** beacon tower 0·1 mile to port (there is a range off **La Varde** point where red flags are flown when firing is in progress) and leads straight to **Les Létruns** Lateral Starboard bell buoy, which should be left close to starboard. Continuing along line **W**: when **La Plate** Cardinal N beacon tower bears 300° True; alter course to 222° True and follow line **X** heading for the eastern side of the **Baie des Etêtes**.

This line leaves:

Le Bouton Cardinal south buoy, 0·5 miles to starboard.
Grand Dodehal Lateral port beacon, 0·2 miles to port.
Les Roches aux Anglais Lateral starboard buoy, 0·1 mile to starboard.
Les Crapauds Lateral port buoy, to port. Then, when **Les Bas Sablons** lighthouse comes in line with **La Balue** lighthouse bearing 129° True (line **T**) alter course to follow this line and proceed as described under *Chenal de la Petite Porte: By day* above.

CHENAL DES PETITS POINTUS

By Day Only   This channel has a least depth of 0 m (i.e. 6·7 m at half tide). First make a position from which **Rochefort** shoal, marked by Cardinal E and Cardinal W beacons, bears E, distant 1·25 miles. From here, steer so as to make good 202° True along line **Y** keeping the conspicuous fort on **Le Petit Bey** just open to the east of **Coppinger**

Villa, a prominent house in the NE part of **Dinard**. This line leaves the following marks on the sides shown:

> **St Servantine** Lateral starboard buoy, 0·2 miles to starboard.
> **Les Petits Pointus** Lateral port beacon, 150 m to port.
> **Les Létruns** Lateral starboard bell buoy, 0·5 miles to port.
> **La Plate** Cardinal north beacon tower, 0·35 miles to starboard.
> **Le Bouton** Cardinal south buoy, 0·2 miles to starboard.
> **Les Pierres aux Normands** Lateral starboard beacon 0·5 miles to starboard.
> **Grand Dodehal** Lateral port beacon 0·2 miles to port.

As soon as this latter beacon is abaft the beam alter course to 222° True to follow line **X** and proceed as described under *Chenal de la Bigne*, above.

CHENAL DU DECOLLE

This channel is still shown as line **B** on Chart 3 but it has fallen out of use and is described as dangerous due to the continuing encroachment of the **Banc des Porceaux** into the channel at the east end, and the rear leading mark for the western entrance **Amer Pival** having become obscured by trees. Directions are therefore not included. It afforded no advantage in distance over the *Chenal de la Grande Porte*.

ILE DE CÉZEMBRE

Two old forts stand on this rather desolate island, dominating the approaches to St Malo. There is a landing slip which dries 3·3 m in the middle of the south side of the island, and a temporary anchorage in 2·7 m sheltered from the west, in a position from which the eastern corner of the island bears about 285° True distant 0·1 miles. The easiest approach to this anchorage is made by sailing along line **Z** (see under *Chenal de la Grande Conchée*) until **La Plate** Cardinal north beacon tower is in line with **La Crolante** beacon tower bearing E (line **J**). Follow this line westward as far as the anchorage.

ST MALO

Anchorages

1. In calm weather there is a reasonable temporary anchorage with the buoy marking the N corner of the Plateau de la Rance bearing about 280° True. This is out of the main strength of the tidal stream, but it is well to keep as far inshore as possible, as a certain amount of commercial traffic uses this channel.

The Mole at St Malo. The entrance to L'écluse du Naye and, to the right, the entrance to Port des Sablons with, at extreme right, Les Bas Sablons lighthouse.

2. There is a temporary anchorage with the centre of the **Fort de la Cité** bearing about 100° True, and **La Mercière** red beacon bearing about 180° True. The least depth is 3 m sand.

Prohibited Anchorage

Vessels may not anchor in or near the channel leading from the light buoy, which marks the southern end of the Plateau de la Rance, to St Malo lock. See below under *La Rance* for prohibited zone near barrage.

Docks

The docks consist of three main basins, in which a least depth of about 5·4 m is maintained, and Mare aux Canards, which serves mainly as a reservoir. All four are at the same level, and are reached by way of locks which lie ENE of the end of the Môle des Noires. The names of the basins are shown on Chart No 4, but the Bassin Duguay-Trouin is still commonly called by its old name of Bassin de St Malo, and

General view of the approach to St Malo from the leading line, line T on Chart No. 4. On the left, Le Petit Bey, then Le Grand Bey. In the centre the Citadel and cathedral spire and, on the far right, Les Bas Sablons lighthouse, just open to the west of La Balue lighthouse.

the Bassin Bouvet by its old name of Bassin de St Servan. Entry is made at the lock (Ecluse du Naye).

Entry Procedure

The port is open for a period of $1\frac{1}{2}$ hours either side of HW at St Malo, both by day and by night. Passage through the locks, or past the traversing bridges which separate the main basins, can be made only during these periods. (The bridge-keepers are allowed to work their bridges at other times, but will claim a heavy overtime for doing so.) When the tides are making, both gates of the lock are usually opened for a period of about $1\frac{1}{2}$ hours just before HW. This is the best time for a yacht to pass through, but it is wise to keep plenty of way on, and to be ready for a strong set just outside the lock. The cross currents may attain 4 knots just before HW, on an 11 m tide, when passage through can be dangerous and it is best to wait for slack water.

Unless the lock is very crowded, a yacht should secure against the side on which the lock-keeper is standing. The lock attendants will pass down heaving lines for the shore ends of the warps.

Signals

Light signals for regulating the passage of vessels through the lock, both by day and night, are exhibited on a mast by the side of the lock.

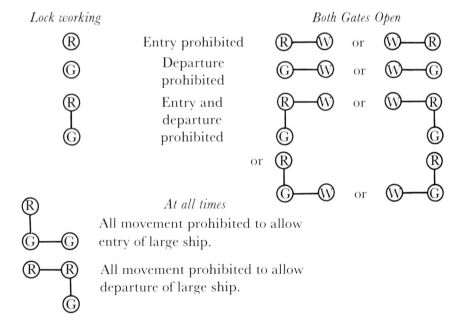

When signals prohibit entry it is necessary to lie off clear of the fairway, or temporarily on a mooring, but be ready to respond when the correct signal is made. When both gates are open and the signal is exhibited for entry, the current may at first be so fierce that entry is dangerous and the lock master warns yachts away by loud-speaker. While waiting entry use moorings on port hand, but they dry 2·1 m LAT.

Docks and Facilities

Yachts proceed to the northern end of the **Bassin Vauban**. Speed limit 5 knots. Berthing is allocated as follows: Boats less than 7 m on W side of No 1 pontoon. Boats between 7 m and 10 m on E side of No 1, on both sides of No 2, and on W side of No 3 pontoon. Boats between 9 and 12 m on E side of No 3 pontoon. Boats above 11 m, **Quai St Vincent** (near town walls) **Quai de Bajoyer** (by Yacht Club) or **Quai de L'Esplanade** in the **Bassin Dougay Trouin**. Access to the latter is through a lifting bridge over a busy thoroughfare. Signal – one long blast. The St Malo Yacht Club is an active centre for yachtsmen. It has a bar and *poste restante*. The Harbour Master's office is at the N end of the Bassin Vauban. He does not now give information personally, but has a notice board on which is posted the day's heights for the Rance basin and the times of operation of the barrage. There is a stock of give-away literature, on signals and opening times for the lock and a programme of the times, during the summer season, when the water in the Rance basin will be maintained (a) at the higher level and (b) at the lower level, on local tides and services, and pro-forma order forms for duty free purchases.

Water taps and electricity sockets (4 amps, no heating) are on the quays and pontoons. Bins are provided for rubbish and there is a drum for waste oil opposite HM's office. The garage for petrol etc is over the bridge behind the Yacht Club. Showers & WCs by HM's office. There are excellent shops and bonded stores may be obtained without formality from R & G Dekyspotter, 22 boulevard Théodore Botrel, 35400 St Malo. There are several shipwrights and engineers. French charts and publications can be obtained at the Librairie Maritime 5, Rue Broussais. There is a casino and many hotels among which the Hôtel de L'Univers appears popular among yachtsmen. The restaurants are innumerable: the Duchesse Anne is nearest the quay and the cooking is good at an appropriate price. As well as at the banks, travellers' cheques can be cashed at the principal hotels restaurants and at some shops where purchases are made. St Malo is a compact closely built town; but a short walk from the club takes the visitor to the northern *plage* which is totally different in character, being a seaside resort with a front facing the sands extending for nearly 2 miles from St Malo to Paramé with hotels pensions and restaurants.

Vedettes leave the slip just east of the root of the Môle des Noires at frequent intervals for Dinard and, with sufficient rise of tide, for Dinan. Hydrofoil and fast ferry services, weather permitting, run daily to the Channel Islands from a berth in the Avant Port. Regular drive-on-off vehicle and passenger ferry services operate from the ferry terminal on the south side of L'Ecluse du Naye.

Historical

The foundation of St Malo is a single rock, which originally stood in the middle of a salt marsh, but became an island in 1709 through an incursion of the sea. Later the causeway (Le Sillon) was built to connect it to Paramé, and the docks have slowly developed in the sheltered area to the south of it.

The town itself started with a monastery founded in the sixth century by a monk named Aaron, who was succeeded by St Malo (or St Maclou) himself. St Malo was actually Bishop of Aleth, the Gallo-Roman town which became St Servan. As the centuries passed, a powerful walled town grew up on the isolated rock, and Aleth declined.

The inhabitants, known as *Malouins*, were famous seamen, corsairs and explorers. They successfully resisted four English sieges, and even maintained themselves between 1390 and 1594, as an independent republic owing no allegiance to France or Brittany. *Ni Francais, ni Bretons, Malouins seulement.*

Among the famous Malouins of history are Jaques Cartier, the discoverer of Canada, and Chateaubriand, who was born in the house which is now Hôtel de France and is buried on Le Grand Bey.

During the sixteenth and seventeenth centuries the walled town took on its present form, with immensely heavy fortifications, and streets of fine granite mansions for the rich sea captains and merchants.

Towards the end of the Second World War most of the centre of the old town was demolished, but is now restored, as far as possible to its former condition.

ST SERVAN – PORT DES SABLONS

Approaches: as for St Malo

Anchorages

1. Off **Fort de la Cité**. See page 34.
2. Three mooring buoys have been laid in the dredged area close eastwards of the new mole at Les Bas Sablons, for temporary mooring whilst waiting sufficient tide to cross the sill, and enter the yacht harbour.

A rocky mole 250 m long to the northwards of **La Cité** has been constructed and a sill from the end of this to the root of the ferry berth has been built making the **Anse des Bas Sablons** into a harbour for nearly 700 yachts. This sill dries 2 m above chart datum leaving depths inside of 2·5 m at the outer berths and less elsewhere. The

Port des Sablons. General view of marina from SE.

dredged area to the north-west of the mole is being enlarged but drying sands still extend from near the root of this to the north-west.

A yacht intending to enter the harbour should keep to the northward of the end of the mole until it has been calculated that there will be adequate water over the sill or, when it is functioning, the illuminated panel, giving depth over the sill, can be seen. White figures indicate metres, red decimetres and 'O' – No entry.

The westernmost pontoon with eighty berths for craft up to 15 m LOA is allocated to visitors. The outer berths on this pontoon can be uncomfortable in a north-westerly blow. Further berths for craft up to 20 m LOA are available on swinging moorings.

There is a landing slip in the southern corner of the harbour against the western side of which it is possible to dry out for a scrub, but it should first be inspected at low water to locate a rocky patch on the bottom.

A light is exhibited at the end of the mole (2 lts Vert Fl G 4 s). When movement of ships is expected, a white light between the two green, indicates that departure of yachts is prohibited.

Water and electricity is laid on to the pontoons. The water may not be used for washing down.

The harbour office is near the root of the easternmost pontoon where there is a bar-brasserie, w.c.s, showers and public telephones. An indoor swimming pool has been built on the eastern side of the harbour. There are extensive car parks.

St Servan town centre is only about half a mile from the marina where there are shops, banks, hotels and restaurants; and all the facilities of a large town.

The village of **Solidor** is only a short walk from the marina. This has small shops and restaurants. It overlooks its small harbour and anchorage which are dominated by the massive **Tour de Solidor**, built at the end of the fourteenth century.

DINARD

Approach. See under St Malo, *Chenal de la Petite Porte*

Anchorage

The best time to visit Dinard is at neap tides, as at springs the bottom drops steeply from the edge of the drying bank into depths of 7 m (i.e. 18 m at HWS). The holding ground, however is good.

It is best for a yacht to anchor as far in towards the **Anse de Dinard** as her draught will allow. Suitable anchoring positions can be chosen using Chart 4, and at neap tides small craft will be able to stay afloat much farther in, in a position from which the small fixed green light on the *Cale des vedettes* bears about N, distant 0·1 miles or, with the aid of soundings, even nearer to the landings.

There are two tansits, refer to Chart No 4, which may help in selecting an anchorage by day or night:

Le Grand Jardin lighthouse (Fl (2) R 10 s), touching the eastern side of the **Pointe de Dinard**.

Le Buron light tower (Fl (2) G 6 s), touching the eastern side of **Pointe de Dinard**.

There is a row of yacht moorings in the northern part of the **Anse**, near the edge of the bank. An area close to the Club, with a narrow entrance channel, has been dredged and forms a small wet basin. Many small local yachts lie in this basin or on drying moorings near the town. Of recent years the number of moorings has greatly increased, and there are also many NW of **Pointe de la Vicomté**.

The harbour facilities consist of the **Quai de la Perle** (dries 6 m), and several small slips at the north end of the bay which are used by the *vedettes*. The most northerly of these does not dry.

Facilities

The town is chiefly a residential and holiday resort, with excellent shopping facilities. There is a large yacht club, well known for its hospitality to British yachts, and a casino. Dinghies may conveniently be left on the endless mooring lines near the yacht club or at a slip. Cans can be filled with fresh water at the yacht club, but for large quantities it is necessary to go alongside the quay near high water. There are many hotels and restaurants. Dinard has an airport and railway station.

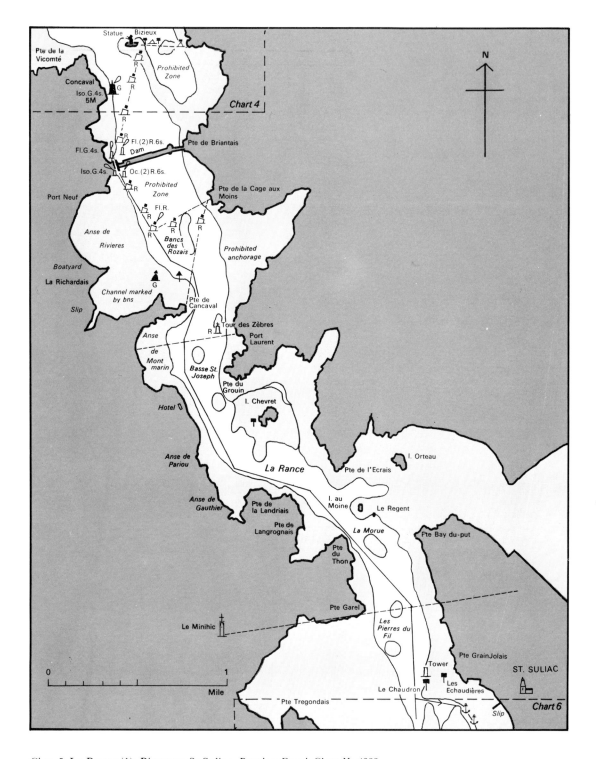

Chart 5. La Rance (1): Bizeux to St Suliac. *Based on French Chart No 4233.*

40

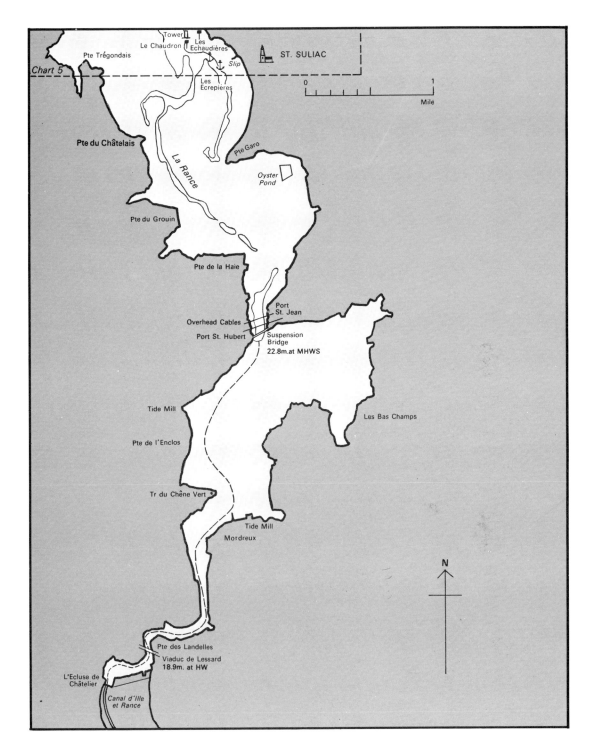

Chart 6. La Rance (2): St Suliac to L'Ecluse du Chatelier. *Based on French Chart No 4233.*

41

2 La Rance

Before entering the River Rance it is necessary to consider the effects on its navigation caused by the construction of the hydroelectric barrage near the entrance. This makes little difference to the depths at chart datum.

The water level above the dam changes by amounts comparable with the changes in tide level outside, but not at the same time. Normally the rate of the streams are also comparable with what they were before; very strong at springs and in emergency substantially faster rates are permitted for short periods. Starting at or after high water there is a stand for an hour or two, at a level at or rather above the level of HW outside. Then the ebb begins suddenly. At neaps the level ceases to fall before it reaches LW outside, but at mean tides and springs the level may fall to or below LW outside. After a stand the level rises and continues to do so rapidly until about or after the time of HW outside.

It is thus possible to pass through the lock and sail in the river without special directions, providing the deep water (white areas on Charts No 5 and 6) is adhered to. However, it is preferable to visit St Malo first to obtain a copy of the programme from the Port Master's office (see above, p. 36). This shows the periods when the level will be 4 m and 8·5 m above chart datum in the river during daytime from 15 June to 15 September, together with other relevant information. The programmes are also available at the **dam** and at **Le Châtelier** or the information will be given by telephone (Dinard (99) 46–14–46) from any post office. If it is desired accurately to ascertain how far the level will fall for anchorage purposes, the information is available on the HM's notice board or by telephone as above. It is not possible, accurately, to interpolate for intermediate heights. It is recommended that, before anchoring, soundings are taken whilst the water is at the higher level. The difference, between the day's height for this and the succeeding low water level, is then subtracted from the sounding to find the minimum depth. Alternatively, anchor whilst the water is at the lower level, allowing a suitable margin, as would normally be done at LW.

The variation in height is not more than 4m per hour, or 1m in 15 minutes, except when necessitated in exceptional circumstances, when the maximum can be 1·4 m in 10 minutes. Rapid changes such as these cause fierce currents.

BIZEUX TO ST SULIAC

There is a prohibited zone to the north and south of the barrage which is shown on Chart No. 5. Yachts should keep to the west side of the river between **Pointe de la Vicomté** and the lock leaving the lateral port buoys marking the prohibited zone and the floating barrier to port.

Approaching the lock on the west side of the barrage.

The lock is worked from 0700 to 2100 (French civil time) during the season when the tide or basin levels are 4 m above datum or more. For entry from seaward yachts should arrive 20 minutes before, and from the basin between 40 and 20 minutes before the exact hour. Be ready to give draught and masthead height in metres. Vessels awaiting the lock may moor to the dolphins outside, two to the N and three to the S, the outer one in each case being marked with a red triangle on a white background. There is a least depth of 1·25 m at the N and 2·20 m at the S dolphins. In busy periods vessels without masts should enter after those with masts if proceeding upstream and first if proceeding downstream. This is because the lifting road bridge spans the north end of the lock and can be lowered without waiting for the lock to clear. Within the lock ropes hang down to hold. There is very little swirl, and it is not necessary to make fast securely.

Traffic signals are shown *at the lock:*

Cone, hoisted point down	=	Entry permitted from seaward.
Ball, hoisted	=	Entry permitted from La Rance.
Cone and ball hoisted	=	No entry from either direction.

Signals. Signals *on the centre of the dam* indicate the flow through the turbines: white cone over black cone, points up (green over white by night) indicate flood stream; black cone over white cone, points down (white over green by night) indicate ebb stream; no signal, no stream. Similar signals over the eastern end of the dam indicate the flow through the sluices there.

A boat which takes the first locking out of St Malo, from 2 to 1½ hours before HW, should find no difficulty in reaching **Le Châtelier** lock before the water level falls.

After passing through the barrage lock there are three Lateral port buoys and a floating barrier to be left to port. These mark the south side of the prohibited zone, which may be dangerous owing to the currents associated with the barrage and sluices. Anchorage is prohibited for a mile south of the dam on account of submarine telephone cables.

The river above the barrage is unlit, except for the lateral port buoy at the SW corner of the prohibited zone, and it would not be easy for strangers to navigate at night. If the channel is correctly followed it carries a least depth of 2·4 m nearly to St Suliac, plus the level at which the basin is maintained above datum.

There is a certain amount of traffic in the river, mostly *vedettes* running between St Malo and Dinan, and the number of yachts is increasing.

After clearing the SW prohibited zone a yacht can sail anywhere the depth of water permits at the level maintained above chart datum plus or minus the depths shown on your chart.

To keep in the deepest channel after passing the prohibited zone steer to pass 100 m east of **Cancaval** Lateral starboard beacon leaving to port the **Bancs des Rozais**. When approaching **Cancaval** beacon leave it and **Pointe de Cancaval** 100 m to starboard, and **Les Zèbres** Lateral port beacon 0·15 miles to port.

When the **Pointe de Cancaval** comes into line with **Pointe de la Briantais** (on the east side of the dam) bearing 358° True, alter course to follow this line. Having passed the **Basse St Joseph**, a small shallow patch to the north-west of Pointe du Grouin, steer to pass about 200 m from the hotel on the west bank, 150 m from the **Pointe de la Landrais**, and 100 m from the **Pointe du Thon**. From here steer so as to make good a course of about 137° True leaving **la Morue** (dries 3 m) to port and **Les Pierres du Fil** (dry 1·2 m) to starboard. (Note the latter are roughly in mid-stream, and on a line formed by **Le Minihic** spire and the southern side of **Pointe Garel**.)

Then steer so as to leave **Le Chaudron** lateral port beacon (and the concrete tower containing a tide gauge) 100 m to port. If bound for **St Suliac**, cut in about 100 m to the south of this beacon, leave **Les Echaudières** Lateral port beacon 50 m to port, turn to starboard and bring up in the anchorage described below.

ANCHORAGES

Anchorage is prohibited for a mile south of the barrage. At **La Richardais** there is a landing slip, a yacht yard, a small restaurant and shop. A yacht able to take the ground may be able to follow the winding drying channel, marked by beacons, and find room to dry out without breaking the regulations. Elsewhere it is possible to anchor almost anywhere in the river on the edges of the deep channel after taking soundings as mentioned on page 42. It is advisable to ease as close to the land as draught and low water level permit, in order to avoid the strength of the stream, particularly off headlands. Many of the bays are crowded with local moorings, many of which dry.

1. **Anse de Montmarin**. At the southern end of the bay in 4 m or closer in when programme permits. Good landing slip 0·15 miles south, near the conspicuous hotel.

2. In the pool north or east of **Ile Chevret**.
3. **Anse de Gauthier**. In 3·6 m near the edge of the channel in the centre of the bay.
4. Off the bay between **Pointe de Langrognais** and **Pointe du Thon**. Moorings have been laid in this area, including some with heavy chains, but if anchoring it is best to take soundings and lie as far into the bay as possible as the current is astonishingly fast when the water level is being altered. The bay itself dries out. Slip and yacht yard. Restaurant at **Le Minihic** 0·5 mile uphill walk.
5. **St Suliac**. Between **les Ecrepières** and local moorings to SE of **Les Echaudières** lateral port beacon. It is a small, sleepy country town with PO and a few shops. Hotel stated to give excellent meals. There is good dinghy landing at the slip.

ST SULIAC TO L'ECLUSE DU CHATELIER

Most of the estuary from **St Suliac** to **Port St Hubert** suspension bridge dries out as shown on Chart 6 on page 41. This shows, in dotted line, the approximate track carrying the best water which, in summer months is marked by a continuous line of Lateral port buoys which should be given a berth of about 50 m, as also between **Port St Hubert** and **Mordreux** as some sand banks are developing. Alternatively, with a rise in level above datum of about 7 m, a yacht can sail straight up the middle of the river over the shoals as far as **Port St Hubert**. Here the river is spanned by overhead cables and the suspension bridge. The clearance under the bridge is 22·8 m at MHWS and even more under the cables.

There is a pool over 0·25 mile long in the narrows off **Port St Hubert** which provides the only deep water anchorage in this part of the river. Anchor near the sides of the fairway (which are very steep).

Approaching the suspension bridge at Port St Hubert.

Beyond the pool the river dries out very high at low level and the channel may be taken as drying 7 m above datum up to **Le Châtelier** lock. The time during which the depth above datum is more than 8·5 m is the period during which the channel is taken to be open and, the lock is worked when there is a minimum of about 1·5 m. The channel is narrow and winding and it is necessary to keep close to the line. Do not overlook the buoy at the corner 0·7 miles SSW of **Mordreux** and then keep close to the buoys. 0·5 mile before **Le Châtelier** is reached the river is spanned by the **Viaduc de Lessard** which has a clearance of 18·9 m at high water. Above the viaduct the channel, now dredged, is marked by port and starboard beacons.

On the banks of the river there are one or two villages, of which the largest is **Mordreux**. There are landing slips at **Port St Hubert, Port St Jean, Mordreux** and **L'ecluse du Châtelier**, amongst other places.

Anchorages

Drying anchorages at Pointe de l'Enclos and Mordreux.

CANAL D'ILLE ET RANCE

The bridge at **Le Châtelier** swings to allow passage of masted vessels. The sill is 6·34 m above datum. Mooring lines are provided which should be kept taught as the lock fills and afterwards until the turbulence subsides. For opening times see notices in HM's office at St Malo or telephone (99) 46–21–87.

Between **Le Châtelier** and **Dinan**, the best water in the first reach is found by turning easily to port on leaving the lock and steering to pass between the first pair of red and black posts, before the first bend, thereafter between the red posts and the towpath. Take care not to mistake a broken red post at the first bend for a black post.

The port of **Dinan** is formed by that part of the canal running through the town, and has quays on either side which are used by barges and *vedettes* from St Malo and by small motor yachts. There are also short (6 m) finger pontoons on the starboard hand. The maximum draft in the canal to Rennes is now 1·3 m. There is no point in continuing to Nantes, as there is now no difficulty in joining the Vilaine near Redon. There are sixty-five locks from sea to sea, counting the barrages at both ends, and it is necessary to help in working them.

Cap Fréhel from about east by north and Amas du Cap.

3 St Briac

Tidal Data

See under St Malo.

General

Lying 7·5 miles SE of Cap Fréhel, this small natural drying harbour is liable to be confused with St Brieuc, 25 miles farther west. St Briac harbour is formed by the mouth of the River Fémur. The sand bottom dries 1·3 m–6·2 m LAT, with rocky outcrops along each bank. There are no berths alongside and a yacht must dry out in the middle of the harbour.

Approach

By Day   First identify **La porte des Ehbiens**, a small rock which lies 0·65 miles 020° True from the large tower on Ile des Ehbiens. From a position about 0·2 mile N from La porte des Ehbiens (do not approach nearer than 0·1 mile as drying rocks extend northward) bring the Lateral port beacon on **Les Perronais** (200 m SW of **Ile du Perron**) in transit with the Lateral port beacon **Bal de la bouche** (which appears as the third) bearing 125° True. If they can be identified, this line is also made by the **Moulin de la Marche** being almost hidden by the **St Briac** light structure. Follow this line. On close approach leave **Les Perronais** beacon to port and thereafter make good a mid-channel course between the beacons.

By Night   From seaward to the NW pick up the directional light at **St Briac** bearing between 122° and 129° True. This has a green sector to the south, a red sector to the north and a white sector over the channel bearing 125° True. Steer to keep in the white sector. On close approach visibility will be necessary to identify the channel beacons as in *By Day* above.

Anchorages

In fair weather in about 1 m LWS south of Ile du Perron; or pick up a vacant mooring in this area. Yachts which can take the ground can find better shelter on or outside the moorings in the next bay or complete shelter to port beyond the two pairs of beacons, but care is needed to avoid gullies.

Facilities

A yacht club, hotels and shops.

4 St Jacut

Tidal Data

See under St Malo.

General

The village stands on a peninsula between **Baie de l'Arguenon** and **Baie de Lancieux** both of which dry. On the eastern side of the peninsula are the small drying ports of **Le Chatelet** and **La Houle-Causseul**. The former has a jetty 70 m long which at the outer end dries 8 m. The latter has a slip which dries 5·8 m at the outer end and 11 m at the inner.

Approach (By Day Only)

First identify **La porte des Ehbiens** rock (see under *St Briac*, above). From a position 100 m E of this steer to bring it on a stern bearing of 344° True then steer to make good 164° True leaving **Platus** beacon tower 80 m to port, **Roche Gautrat** 0·15 miles to starboard, and **La Charbotier** beacon 0·5 mile to starboard. When this is abeam alter course for **La Houle-Causseul** to the N or for **Le Chatelet** to the S.

Anchorages

These are exposed and drying.

Fort de la Latte is conspicuous and identifies the point of the same name on the west side of Baie de la Fresnaie.

5 St Cast

Tidal Data

Tidal Heights – see St Malo.

Tidal Streams

Off Cap Fréhel the ESE-going stream begins at −0520 St Helier (+0130 Dover) and the WNW-going stream begins at −0020 St Helier (−0435 Dover). Both streams attain between 3·5 and 4·0 knots.

General

The Anse de St Cast lies immediately south-east of the **Pointe de St Cast**, which itself is 4 miles south-east of **Cap Fréhel**. The port of St Cast is 1 mile north of the village of **L'isle St Cast**, and has been developed as a holiday resort catering for yachtsmen. A mole with a slip 80 m long alongside, has been constructed south of the beacon on **Roche Cannevez**.

Approach (By Day Only)

The outer approach may be made either from the north or the east avoiding the **Bourdinot** rocks, which are just over 0·5 mile north-east of **Pointe de St Cast** and are marked at the northern end by a Cardinal east spar buoy. The harbour is entered either north or south of **Le Bec Ronde** and **Le Feuillatre**. A Lateral starboard buoy off the end of the mole marks the end of the works.

Anchorages

South of the mole moorings have been laid for local boats. Anchorage is possible between 1 m below and 1 m above datum on sand; but holding ground is doubtful. In deeper water the bottom is rocky. There is a good anchorage about 0·15 mile south of **Pointe de la Garde**, 1 mile to the south, with a landing slip and yacht club adjacent, sheltered from south through west to north-west.

Facilities

Shops, chandlers and customs. Water, petrol, diesel at the root of the mole.

6 Baie de La Fresnaie

Tidal Data

As for St Cast.

General

A large bay lying about 2 miles SE of Cap Fréhel. Most of it dries and there is a large oyster bed near the mouth. The French chart 5646 shows a line bearing ESE from **Pointe de la Latte** south of which is labelled **Zone Dangereuse**. It contains **Port-Nieux**, a small drying harbour, which lies on the NW side of the bay about 1 mile from its head.

Approach (By Day Only)

The approach from the northward is straightforward, having identified the conspicuous **Fort de la Latte** on the western headland.

Anchorages

There is an anchorage in 3 m sand and mud, very good holding ground, with **Fort de la Latte** bearing 010° True, distant 0·6 mile. It is presumed that the **Zone Dangereuse** does not refer to anchorages such as this.

Port-Nieux has a quay and a small jetty, with berths alongside which dry 7·8 m. As the neap tide rise does not exceed 9 m, keel boats would risk being neaped here when the tides are taking off. There is a small landing slip near to the above anchorage on **Pointe de la Touche** which at the end dries about 3·5 m.

Facilities

None, but is is said that a visit to Fort de la Latte is well worth a scramble up the cliffs.

7 Sables d'Or-les-Pins

Tidal Data

As for St Cast.

General

A holiday resort in a small bay 4 miles SW of Cap Fréhel. The bay contains two small drying harbours. In the eastern corner is **Port Barrier** which is sheltered by a jetty and with a quay which dries 5·5 m at the north and 6·5 m at the south. In the western corner are **Les Bouches d'Erqui**, a small natural harbour immediately west of a large sand dune where several small streams run into the bay and which dries 5 or 6 m.

Approach (By Day Only)

Identify **Ile St Michel** with a diminutive chapel on the summit. There is an unmarked drying rock shaped like an inverted saucer just over 0·5 mile NE of Ile St Michel. The bay should be entered to give this a wide berth and approach could be made with the help of Chart No 7. Follow line **J** (see under *Chenal d'Erqui*) until **Plurein** belfry bears 180° True and is just open to the west of the left hand large hotel on the *plage*. Alter course to follow this line (**M**) which leaves **Roche Plate St Michel** 0·4 mile to starboard and **Rocher Bernard** 0·2 mile to port.

Anchorages

Port Barrier was built for loading stone from neighbouring quarries and the outer end of the jetty is partly demolished and the access is becoming more and more difficult due to the encroachment of shingle. There is a jetty at **Les Bouches d'Erqui** which is reserved for fishing boats. There is stated to be a good anchorage in offshore winds SE of **Rocher Bernard** with about 3 m ordinary LWS but beware of **Rocher Fournel**, a cable offshore farther SE which dries 11 m.

Facilities

Sables D'Or-les-Pins has all the amenities of a popular holiday resort.

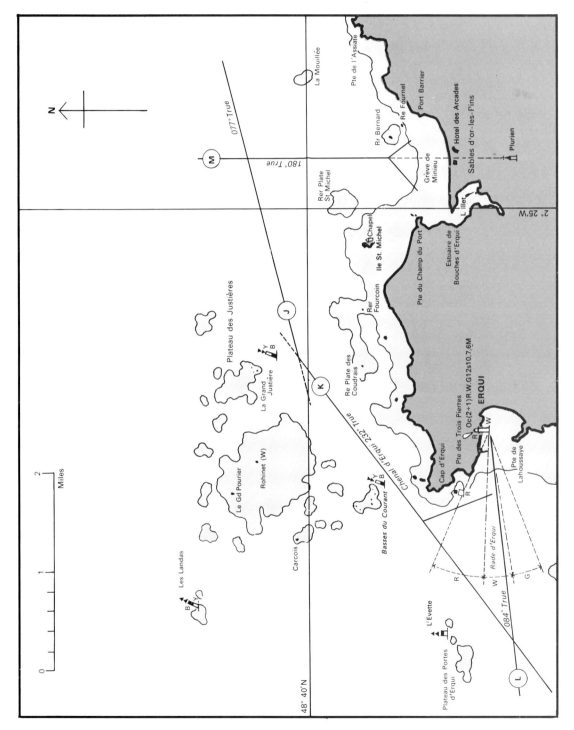

Chart 7. Chenal d'Erqui. Based on French Charts Nos 833 and 5724.

N

Plateau des Justières

Les Landas

B Y

Le Gd Pourier

Rohinet (W)

La Grand Justière

Y B

Carcois

Re Plate des Coudrais

077° True

180° True

M

La Mouillée

Pte de l'Assiate

Rer Plate St Michel

Rr Bernard

Re Fournel

Port Barrier

Hotel des Arcades

Sables d'or-les-Pins

Grève de Minieu

Plurien

2° 25'W

Chapel

Ile St. Michel

Rer Fourcoin

Estuaire de Bouches d'Erqui

L Illet

Pte du Champ du Port

J

K

Chenal d'Erqui 232° True

Basses du Courant

B Y

Pte des Trois Pierres

R. Oc(2+1)R.W.G12s10.7,6M

ERQUI

Cap d'Erqui

W

R

R

Pte de Lahoussaye

084° True

R

W

Rade d'Erqui

G

L'Evette

B Y

Plateau des Portes d'Erqui

L

48° 40'N

Miles

0   1   2

8 Chenal d'Erqui

Tidal Data

Tidal Streams

In the **Chenal d'Erqui** the ENE-going stream begins at −0540 St Helier (+0150 Dover) and the WSW-going at HW St Helier (−0455 Dover). Both reach 3·8 knots at springs.

General

This channel lies between **Cap d'Erqui** and the off-lying rocks which extend 3 miles to seaward of it. It can be regarded as having a least depth of 3·5 m, and should offer no difficulty in daylight and clear weather.

Approaching from the east, having passed north of **Cap Fréhel** and of **Amas du Cap**, the large rock which lies about 0·4 miles from it, close the shore until the southern edge of **Amas du Cap** (HW mark) is touching the end of **Cap Fréhel**, bearing 077° True (line **J** – see view). Follow this line of bearing to the westward, leaving the **Plateau des Justières** Cardinal south spar buoy 0·5 miles to starboard.

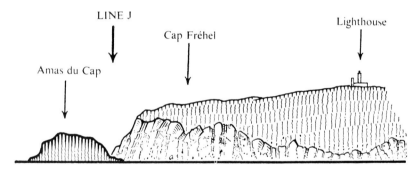

LINE J   Cap Fréhel   Lighthouse

Amas du Cap

Chenal d'Erqui. From a position on line **J** and half a mile south of the plateau des Justières buoy at LW.

When this buoy is just abaft the beam, and Cap d'Erqui bears 222° True alter course to make good 232° True (line **K**), leaving the **Basses du Courant** Cardinal south spar buoy 100 m to starboard, **Cap d'Erqui** 0·3 miles to port and **l'Evette** Cardinal north beacon tower 0·4 miles to starboard. If continuing to westward: when **Erqui** lighthouse (red and white circular tower 10 m high on the head of the jetty) bears 084° True, alter course to make good 264° True so as to keep it on that bearing astern (line **L**). This line passes well north of **Plateau des Jaunes**, a group of above-water and sunken rocks lying 4 miles WSW of Erqui, just off the western edge of Chart No 7.

9 Erqui

Tidal Data

Tidal Heights
High Water: approx −0020 St Helier, −0515 Dover, +0205 Brest.
Mean Tide Level: 6·2 m. Index 12 A.
Heights of Tide above Datum: approx MHWS 11·2 m, MLWS 1·2 m, MHWN 8·5 m, MLWN 3·9 m.

Tidal Streams

1. For **Chenal d'Erqui** see above.
2. About 5 miles west of **Erqui** the ENE-going stream begins at −0600 St Helier (+0130 Dover) and the WSW at −0010 St Helier (−0505 Dover). Both streams reach 2·8 knots at springs.

General

A small drying harbour 0·75 miles south of Cap d'Erqui. It now consists of two parts, the old harbour to the east which is partly sheltered by a jetty, on the end of which stands a red and white circular lighthouse 10 m high, and to the west of this the new *port de pêche* protected by a new rocky mole and having a landing slip 80 m long. The village at the harbour and the town 0·5 miles to the south of it makes a pleasant holiday resort and there is an active sailing club.

Approach

By Day   If approaching from the eastward, sail along line **K** (see under *Chenal d'Erqui*, above) until **Cap d'Erqui** is abeam to port distant 0·3 miles. Then follow the coast round keeping about this distance offshore and leaving **Les Trois Pierres** Lateral port buoy to port. When Erqui lighthouse bears 090° True course may be shaped to enter the old harbour. Beware of a strong eddy running past the end of the jetty, before and at high water.

If approaching from the north, leave **Landas** Cardinal north spar buoy (see Chart No 7) to port and **L'Evette** Cardinal north beacon tower, at least 0·2 miles to starboard.

If approaching from the west, pass 1·25 miles south of **Le Rohein** lighthouse (white tower with black top, elevation 13 m), which is just off the limits of Chart No 7 to the westward, and steering to make good 084° True for Erqui lighthouse, and leaving **Plateau des Jaunes** (on the centre of which is a rock which never dries) 0·5 mile to southward and **Plateau des Portes d'Erqui** (on which stands **L'Evette** Cardinal north beacon tower) over half a mile to northward.

By Night   The best approach is from the west. The southerly white sector of **Le Grand Léjon** light leads between the **Roches de St Quay** and **Le Rohein**, after which course should be altered to between 081° and 093° True to keep in the white sector of **Erqui** light, Oc (2+1) WRG 12 s. The recommended anchorage is on the dividing line between the white and red sectors, with Cap d'Erqui bearing 355° True.

Harbour and Anchorage

There is an anchorage in about 3 m LAT sand and mud, good holding ground, with the lighthouse bearing about 100° True and Cap d'Erqui bearing 355° True. This position is sheltered from NE through to SE but is open to the west, especially to north-west. This anchorage is a long row from the harbour and there is sometimes an uncomfortable swell there. The bottom is gently shelving, so on an ordinary spring tide it is possible to anchor closer to the harbour if soundings are taken and if the weather is sufficiently settled to allow only a margin of 0·5 m or so under the keel at LW. At neaps a yacht drawing 2 m can lie in a position nearly 0·1 mile east of the harbour entrance. The old harbour jetty has a quay 78 m long and the new mole a landing slip 80 m long. The new harbour is for the exclusive use of fishing boats and the inner harbour under the lee of the breakwater is busy during the season with small fishing and hire boats and there are many chains on the bottom which dries in most parts 3 hours after HW. Erqui is a doubtful bet as a harbour, but the anchorage is good under suitable conditions and, near high water a yacht can anchor temporarily close to the harbour whilst her crew go ashore for shopping or a meal. Land at the slip in the old harbour or on the rocks off the sailing club.

Facilities

The sailing club is just westward of the root of the old jetty and is the centre of active dinghy racing and sailing. Efficient *madame du port*. A l'Abri des Flots, which is the second restaurant on the left, is excellent, but in season it is best to book a table in advance. There are good shops and a garage for petrol in the town, but this involves a $\frac{1}{2}$ mile walk from the port, unless one is given a lift in a car. Water by courtesy from restaurant.

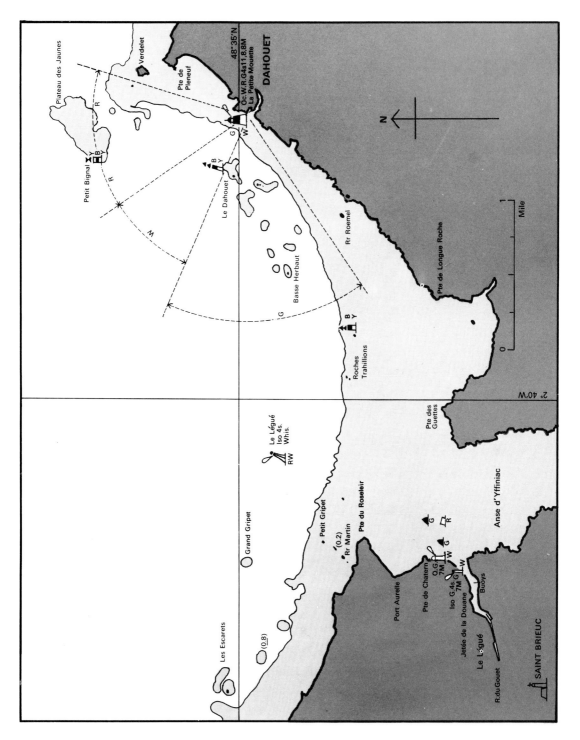

Chart 8. Le Légué and Dahouet. Based on French Chart No 833.

10 Dahouet

Tidal Data: approx as for Erqui.

General

The Port de Dahouet is a small drying harbour lying in a gap in the cliffs 5 miles SW of Erqui. In strong onshore winds the seas break as much as 0·2 mile offshore and entrance is dangerous.

Approach

By Day Approach from the north or west. First identify **Verdelet**, a conical island about 0·25 mile NW of **Pointe de Pleneuf**. Then make for a position just north of **Dahouet** Cardinal north buoy, from which **Verdelet** bears 050° True about 1·5 miles. With sufficient rise of tide and leaving Dahouet buoy to starboard make good about 120° True to leave a red stake to port and **La Petite Mouette** lighthouse at the entrance about 50 m to starboard. When this is abeam steer to make good 158° True until two white stakes to port come into line, then turn to leave them close to port. (These are on the extreme edge of a wall 3 m high and a watch should be kept for floating warps attached

Port de Dahouet. Entrance. La Petite Mouette beacon tower to be left about 50 m to starboard.

57

to them.) The quay wall will be seen immediately to port. Keep between this and the centre of the harbour.

By Night **La Petite Mouette** lighthouse has a directional light. This has a red sector to the north and a green sector to the south with a white sector over the safe approach, between 114° and 146° True. Nevertheless entrance by night would be dangerous for a stranger.

Anchorages

The harbour is very crowded with fishing boats and small yachts, in the outer harbour fishing boats berth two and three abreast alongside the quay. The inner harbour, which is to port beyond the customs house, provides maximum shelter. The inner harbour is packed with moorings but the wall may be clear and it may be possible for yachts to lie alongside.

Facilities

Customs, boat yard, small chandlers, poor shops locally, better at Le Val André. Winter laying up (floating at springs) is possible.

11 Le Légué (St Brieuc)

Tidal Data

Tidal Heights
High Water: approx −0030 St Helier, −0525 Dover, +0215 Brest.
Mean Tide Level: 6·2 m. Index 12 A.
Heights of Tide above Datum: approx MHWS 11·5 m, MLWS 1·2 m, MHWN 8·5 m, MLWN 3·9 m.

General

Le Légué is the port of St Brieuc, and lies about 1 mile from the mouth of the river Le Gouet at the head of the Baie de St Brieuc. During strong northerly weather the sea breaks right across the head of the bay and no attempt should be made to enter, but the approach is sheltered by land during prevailing west and south-west winds and, with sufficient rise of tide, is easy.

Approach

By Day   From the north see below under Paimpol, Portrieux and Binic. **Le Légué** landfall light-and-whistle safe water mark buoy lies 1·5 miles NE of **Pointe du Roseleir**. From this position make good 202° True with sufficient height of tide, to leave No 1 Lateral starboard buoy off **Pointe du Chatern** close to starboard, thence proceed along the buoyed channel to the lock gates. Vessels can secure to the wall on the south side immediately outside the lock whilst waiting for the gate.

Pointe de Roselier from the eastward when approaching Le Légué.

By Night   From seaward pick up **Le Légué** breakwater light (Iso G 4 s). This has an elevation of 6 m and a range of 7 miles. Steer so as to bring this on a bearing of 208° True and **Le Rohein** Cardinal west beacon tower light astern. This leads to **Le Légué** landfall light and whistle safe water mark buoy (Iso 4 s). From thence, with sufficient height of tide and good visibility, make good 202° True to pick up unlit No 1 Lateral starboard buoy which leave to starboard. Thence proceed as *By Day* above. There are in total twelve Lateral starboard and six Lateral port buoys of which four and two respectively are lit. In addition the **Jetée de la Douane** has a Lateral starboard light.

Anchorages

In settled weather with the wind offshore, a small vessel awaiting her tide can anchor in suitable depth south of **Le Légué** landfall buoy.

The lock, which opens between 1 hour before to 1 hour after high water, measures 85 m long 14 m wide and the sill is 5 m above datum. Inside the lock there are two interconnected basins. No 1 is to port about 0·3 mile from the lock and No 2, which is formed by a canalised part of the **Rivière du Gouet**, is entered through a swing bridge about 0·5 mile from the lock. For a short stay a yacht is directed to a berth in Basin No 1. For a longer stay it is probable that it would be given a berth in Basin No 2. On leaving, fresh water from the river continues to flow into the lock for some time after the gates have opened and it is advisable to have the stern warp ready first.

Facilities

There are cranes of up to 2 tons capacity and mobile cranes are available. Fresh water is laid on the quays. There is a boatyard in Basin No 2. There are some shops,

Near approach to Le Légué left to right, Tour de Cesson on hill on left of entrance and white lighthouse to right.

including a small supermarket, close to Basin No 2. There are larger shops at St Brieuc, which is a cathedral town with several fine old timber houses.

Although Le Légué appears to have potential, it was formerly a commercial port and a base for a fleet of *goëlettes*, the fine two-masted topsail schooners that fished off Iceland and Greenland. It now caters for small tankers, bulk carriers and general dry cargo ships, as well as a number of resident fishing boats. There is no provision for yachts inside the lock, except perhaps to lay up in Basin No 2.

Historical

The Baie de St Brieuc is an area of shallow water which has greatly increased in size during the last 2,000 years. At the time of the Roman Empire, forests and cultivated land existed where there is now nothing but drying sand. The Tour de Cesson was built by Jean IV in 1395 and was blown up by Henri IV.

St Brieuc, which stands on high ground a mile to the south-west, is an old cathedral town, named after the Celtic monk who arrived with his disciples in the fifth century, and converted the district to Christianity. Much of the cathedral is thirteenth and fourteenth century.

12 Binic

Tidal Data

Tidal Heights
High Water: approx −0030 St Helier, −0525 Dover, +0215 Brest.
Mean Tide Level: 6·2 m. Index 12 A.
Heights of Tide above Datum: approx MHWS 11·5 m, MLWS 1·2 m, MHWN 8·5 m, MLWN 3·9 m.

General

Binic is an artificial harbour at the mouth of the Rivière d'Ic. It consists of an outer harbour which dries 4 m at the entrance and 5 or 6 m inside which provides good shelter in winds from north through west to south, and a wet basin which was formerly the Vieux-Port, access to which is through a dock gate 10·5 m wide, the sill of which is 5·5 m above datum. In the basin the depths vary between 5·5 m and 7·5 m.

Approach

By Day   The outer approach from the eastward is clear except for **Basse Gouin**, a rock with a depth of 1·6 m LAT which should not affect yachts otherwise than as an anchorage. This is about 1·5 miles ENE of the entrance. With sufficient rise of tide the inner approach is straightforward.

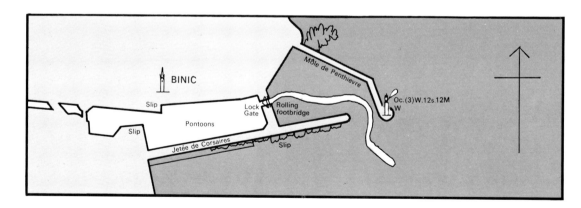

Chart 9. Binic. Diagram showing the harbour. *Based on French Chart No 5725.*

For the approach from the northward see under *Paimpol* and *Portrieux*, *Approaches*, below. When **La Ronde** Cardinal west beacon tower bears 090° True with sufficient rise of tide, alter course for the entrance. This leaves a Cardinal east spar wreck buoy and **L'Ours Seul** isolated danger beacon each about 0·25 mile to starboard.

By Night   From westward only, as in *By Day* above. The breakwater light (Oc (3) 12 s) has an elevation of 12 m and a range of 12 miles.

Anchorages and Moorings

The nearest anchorage in which a yacht can stay afloat at springs is with the lighthouse on the end of the northern mole (white circular tower elevation 12 m) bearing about 270° True distant 1·25 miles, but see note on Basse Gouin, above. From here course may be shaped to enter the port when the tide serves. If there is space, a yacht may berth in the Avant Port alongside the eastern mole which dries 4·2 m sand and mud. Alternatively, if early on the tide, there is space to anchor in the

Binic. The harbour entrance.

Facing west, looking towards the inner harbour and entrance to the basin, just to the left of the church. The end of the southern mole is seen on the left of the picture.

centre. The dock gate is not operated between about 0100 and 0530, nor when the tides are of an index of about 7 (HW St Helier 8·5 m) or less. Otherwise it is opened between one and one-and-three-quarter hours before HW and must close at HW or within 10 minutes or so. For a day or two either side of neaps the gate may not open at all. The Harbour Master will furnish a time table on request and one is exhibited outside his office. There is a rolling bridge across the E end of the lock which is operated by the Harbour Master.

There are marina type pontoon berths in the harbour and there are berths reserved for visitors, alongside the mole immediately to port inside the basin. There are also berths alongside the north wall.

Facilities

Fresh water is laid on the pontoons, but not the visitors' berths, although a spare resident's berth may be taken temporarily for this purpose. There is also a water point on the north quay, immediately outside the lock. Application for this should be made to the Harbour Master. There are shops of all kinds. Mechanic, sailmaker, chandlery and fuel in the town. Many hotels, restaurants and cafés.

Despite the restricted access to the basin, in all respects this harbour is preferable to Le Légué from the yachtsman's point of view and the Harbour Master is most obliging.

Historical

Binic was the first Breton port to fit out a vessel for the Newfoundland cod fisheries, which had previously been a Basque monopoly. The Binic *terre-neuviens* commonly sold their fish in Marseilles before returning home for the winter. The old town is now surrounded by villas and hotels and is a minor holiday resort, with good bathing beaches each side of the harbour. There are also good sands at Grève des Rosaries, about 3·5 miles south-east, where there is a sailing school and club.

13 Portrieux: Roches de St Quay *Inner Passage*

Tidal Data

Tidal Heights
High Water: approx −0030 St Helier, −0525 Dover, +0215 Brest.
Mean Tide Level: 6·2 m. Index 12 A.
Heights of Tide above Datum: approx MHWS 11·5 m, MLWS 1·2 m, HMWN 8·5 m, MLWN 3·9 m.

Tidal Streams

1. The offshore streams to the NE off **Le Grand Léjon** turn SE at −0600 St Helier (+0130 Dover), and NW at +0020 St Helier (−0435 Dover). Both streams reach 3·8 knots at springs.
2. In the **Rade de Portrieux** the SE-going stream begins at +0600 St Helier (−0105 Dover), and the NW-going stream at −0015 St Helier (−0510 Dover). Both streams reach 3·8 knots at springs.

General

Portrieux is a small drying harbour lying to the west of the Roches de St Quay and is separated from them by the Rade de Portrieux, a deep water anchorage which can be entered either from the north or south. The northern entrance carries more water but for a stranger is navigable by day only.

Approaches From the north, see under *Paimpol*, below.

Northern Entrance

By Day   This entrance has a depth of at least 4·2 m as far as the Rade de Portrieux. First identify **Madeaux** Cardinal west beacon tower and make a position from which it bears 090° True, distant 0·5 mile. From here, the **Moulières de Portrieux** (alias **Port de Portrieux**) Cardinal east beacon tower will be in line with **Le Four** white beacon tower bearing 168° True. (Line **N** on Chart No 10.)
　　Follow this line which leaves **Ile Harbour** lighthouse (a white house with a small light tower on its roof) 0·6 mile to port, and **Moulières de St Quay** Cardinal north beacon 0·3 mile to starboard. When **Herflux** Cardinal south beacon tower comes into line with **La Longue** Cardinal south beacon tower alter course to follow line **P**

65

for 0·3 mile, leaving **Moulières de Portrieux** beacon tower 0·2 mile to starboard. Then follow line **Q**, which is formed by **Le Four** white beacon tower in line with **Pordic** belfry, bearing 182° True. This line leaves **Les Noires** Cardinal west pillar buoy 0·25 miles to port and **Pierre Alien** rock (dries 2 m LAT) a cable to starboard. When **Les Moutons** Cardinal east spar buoy has been left on the starboard hand; and **Portrieux** lighthouse (a white tower elevation 11 m on the end of the old jetty) bears 270° True, course may be altered to enter the harbour, if the tide serves, leaving **Les Moutons** buoy to starboard.

It is said that the local yachtsmen sometimes dodge the strength of the tide up to 3 hours after HW by passing inside **Moulières de St Quay** and **Moulières de Portrieux** on the transit of **la Hergue** white pyramid and **Le Pommier** (white painted rock off headland just N of **Pointe de Plouha**) at 317° True (line **R**, see *Southern Entrance* below). Note that this line touches the edge of the rocks off **Pointe de St Quay** and leads close to dangers on the west side.

Southern Entrance

By Day   This entrance carries a least depth of 1·4 m (= 2·7 m MLWS) along line **R**, but as it passes close to a 0·3 m patch it would be safe for a stranger to regard it as having a least depth of 0·3 m (= 1·5 m MLWS).

First identify **La Ronde** Cardinal west beacon tower, taking care not to confuse it with **La Longue** Cardinal south beacon tower, which lies 1 mile farther east.

Make a position from which **La Ronde** bears 035° True, distant 0·5 mile, and **La Roselière** Cardinal west pillar buoy bears 090° True, distant 0·3 mile. From here, the leading marks for line **R** will

Le Rohein lighthouse from the southward on a hazy morning at below half-tide. It is a useful mark half-way between Erqui and Portrieux.

La Longue, near low water, taken close up from the SW, when navigating by chart between shoals outside the regular channels.

66

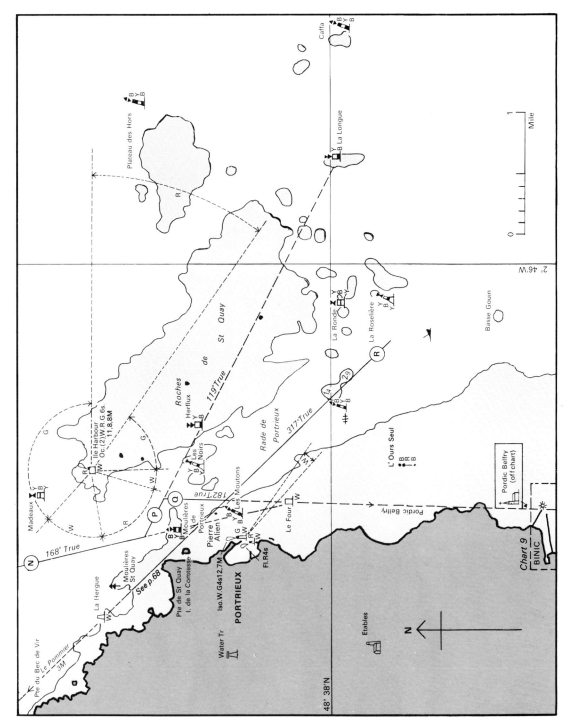

Chart 10. Portrieux. Based on French Chart No 5725.

La Ronde at low water taken close up from out of the channel from the SE.

Portrieux lighthouse and harbour. A new mole has been added to the south.

be in line: **La Hergue** white pyramid in line with **Le Pommier** (see Chart No 10), a small steep rock (painted white on its SW side) which lies 100 m from the headland just N of **Pointe de Plouha**, bearing 317° True. (Neither of these marks is very easy to pick up at this distance, but line **R** can be followed well enough by keeping the **Pointe de St Quay**, on which is a white signal station, bearing 317° True.) This line leaves a Cardinal east spar buoy marking a wreck about 0·2 mile to port and **Le Four** white beacon tower about 0·4 mile to port.

When **Portrieux** lighthouse, a white and green tower (elevation 11 m) on the end of the old jetty, bears 270° True, course may be altered for the harbour. When steering towards the lighthouse there may be a strong cross stream and **Les Moutons** Cardinal east spar buoy must be left to starboard.

By Night   The southerly white sector of **Grande Léjon** (Fl (5) WR 20 s, see Chart No 2), leads between the Roches de St Quay and **Rohein** Cardinal west light beacon tower. When **Binic** breakwater (Oc (3) 12 s) bears 250° True steer as if entering Binic. When **Portrieux** old jetty light (Iso WG 4 s) changes from green to white, alter course so as to keep in this white sector, between 306° and 312° True, which leads straight to the harbour entrance, over a bottom which dries 1·2 m LAT in the approaches. Enter between this light and the light on the new mole (Fl R 4 s).

If bound for the anchorage, when **Ile Harbour** light (Oc (2) 6 s) bears 355° True alter course so as to keep it on the bearing until **Portrieux** green light (Iso 4 s) bears 270° True, when course may be shaped for the anchorage. By this route, the least depth is 2 m as far as the anchorage.

Anchorage and Harbour

Anchor with **Portrieux** lighthouse bearing 270° True, and as far inshore as possible in order to keep out of the main strength of the tide. Note **Les Moutons** (dry 2·5 m LAT), marked by a Cardinal east spar buoy, which are only 100 m, north of this line of bearing. The bottom is sand and mud, good holding ground. At neap tides a small yacht will be able to stay afloat close southwards of the harbour entrance.

There are good berths alongside the jetty and the quay, on hard sand drying from 4 m to 7·1 m LAT. Small craft with legs may prefer to lie out in the harbour, also on hard sand. The new mole has improved protection.

Facilities

Portrieux and St Quay are now mainly holiday resorts. There are a number of hotels and restaurants and reasonable shopping facilities. Water and petrol at garage at the end of the jetty. There is a keen sailing club, with premises built by members, on the east side of the harbour. The harbour is used by small fishing boats, and there are now many shallow-draught yachts and dinghies there, all of which dry out.

Historical and Surroundings

In former times several of the big *terre-neuviens* would spend the winter here, with their bows well up the beach inside the harbour.

About 0·75 mile west of **Le Pommier** mentioned above under *Southern Entrance: By Day* is the tiny drying harbour of **Portz-Moguer**. This is itself of little interest to yachtsmen but it has a conspicuous white tower daymark which is an important rear leading mark for two channels in the approach to Bréhat and Paimpol.

14 Paimpol

Tidal Data

Tidal Heights
High Water: approx −0030 St Helier, −0525 Dover, +0155 Brest.
Mean Tide Level: 5·4 m. Index 12 A.
Heights of Tide above Datum: approx MHWS 10·3 m, MLWS 0·6 m, MHWN 7·6 m, MLWN 3·3 m.

Tidal Streams

1. For tidal streams in the outer approaches from northward see Ile Bréhat, page 98 below.
2. For tidal streams in the outer approaches from the southward and eastward off **Le Grand Léjon** see under Portrieux, above.
3. In the northern entrance of **Chenal du Dénou**, the SE-going stream begins −0420 Brest (+0050 Dover), and the NW-going stream begins +0135 Brest (−0540 Dover). Both streams reach 2·8 knots at springs.
4. At the eastern entrance of the **Chenal de la Jument** the SSW-going stream (and the SSE-going stream between **La Jument** and **Le Dénou**) begins −0405 Brest (+0105 Dover). The NNE-going stream off the entrance of **Chenal de la Jument** and the NNW-going stream between **La Jument** and **Le Dénou** begin +0120 Brest (−0555 Dover). These streams reach 3·8 knots at springs.
5. In the outer anchorage SSE of **Ile St Riom**, the SE stream begins about −0435 Brest (+0105 Dover) and the NW-going stream about +0105 Brest (−0610 Dover). Both streams attain 1·9 knots at springs.
6. In the anchorage off **Portz-Hévenne** in the **Chenal de la Trinité** the SW-going stream begins half an hour earlier than the SSE and SE streams referred to above.

General

The Anse de Paimpol is a large, shallow harbour which dries at MLWS except for a system of deep, winding channels in the northern and eastern parts. These channels offer fairly sheltered anchorage except in easterly winds, but they are mostly a long way from the shore. The outer channels appear difficult on the chart, but add 5·4 m for mean tide level and it will be seen that at half tide there is plenty of deep water. Add 7·6 m for high water neaps and one can sail almost anywhere except across the rocks marked by beacons.

The Port of Paimpol, at the head of the harbour, may be approached towards high water; in spite of the soundings shown on the chart, the channel of approach is said to dry 4·8 m LAT only (i.e. to have a least depth of 2·7 m at MHWN). The port consists

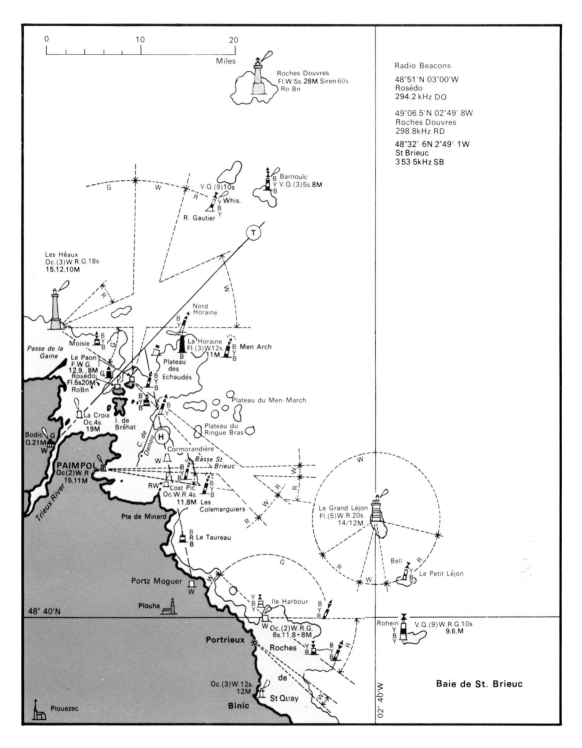

Chart 11. The outer approaches to Lézardrieux and Paimpol. *Based on Admiralty Chart No 2668.*

of two interconnected wet docks, entered through a lock. These docks provide a convenient and fairly peaceful berth in which a yacht can stay afloat with excellent facilities nearby.

Approaches to Anchorage

By Day from the North

First make a position with **La Horaine** lighthouse, an octagonal black light tower, bearing 195° True distant 3 miles (This can easily be mistaken for a sail.) From this position there is a choice of two initial approaches: (1) The outer approach and (2) the Chenal de Bréhat.

(1) Outer approach

From the above position steer to make good 150° True. (If arrival at Paimpol is planned at or before HW there will be considerable lift from the tide.) Follow this course for 8·25 miles, leaving **Men Arch** Cardinal east spar buoy 0·3 mile to starboard. When the conspicuous day mark at **Portz-Moguer** comes into line with the belfry of **Plouha** church, bearing 212° True, distant 8·5 and 10 miles respectively, alter course to follow this line for 0·75 mile then alter course to pick up **Chenal de la Jument** (line **Z**, Chart No 12b). The leading marks for this channel are **Paimpol** church spire (taking care not to confuse with **Plounez** to the south and **Ploubazlanec** to the north) in line with the summit of **Pointe Brividic**. (This is a woody hill in line with **Paimpol** town bearing 260° True.) Follow this line, leaving **Basse St Brieuc** Cardinal east spar buoy 1·6 miles to port, **Colemarguiers** Cardinal east spar buoy 0·75 mile to port, **Les Charpentiers** Cardinal east beacon tower 0·25 mile to starboard, **L'Ost Pic** lighthouse, square tower red top, 0·75 mile to port, **Gouayan** Lateral port beacon tower 0·3 mile to port and **Roche Gueule** Lateral port conical buoy 200 m to port and **La Jument** beacon tower 150 m to port.

(2) Chenal de Bréhat

Navigation of this channel by reference to the leading marks calls for good visibility of upwards of 12 miles but it can shorten the distance sailed by 5 miles if the **Chenal du Dénou** is also used.

The tide in this channel runs in both directions at up to 5·6 knots

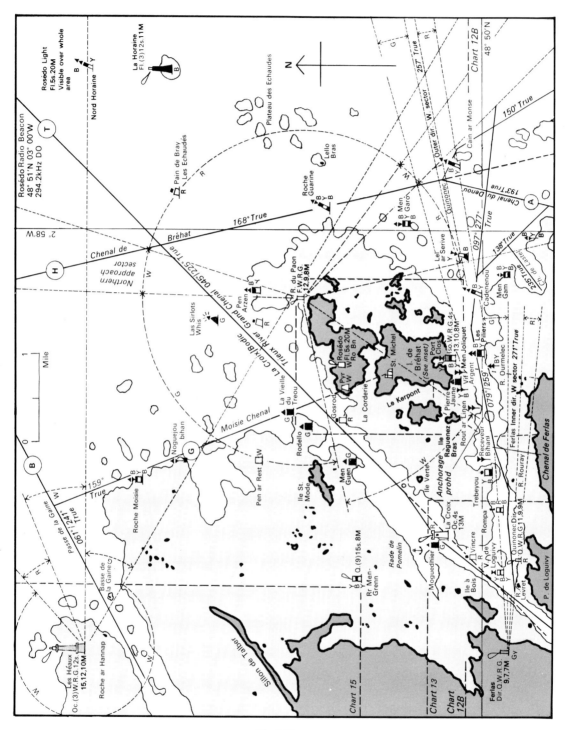

Chart 12a

74

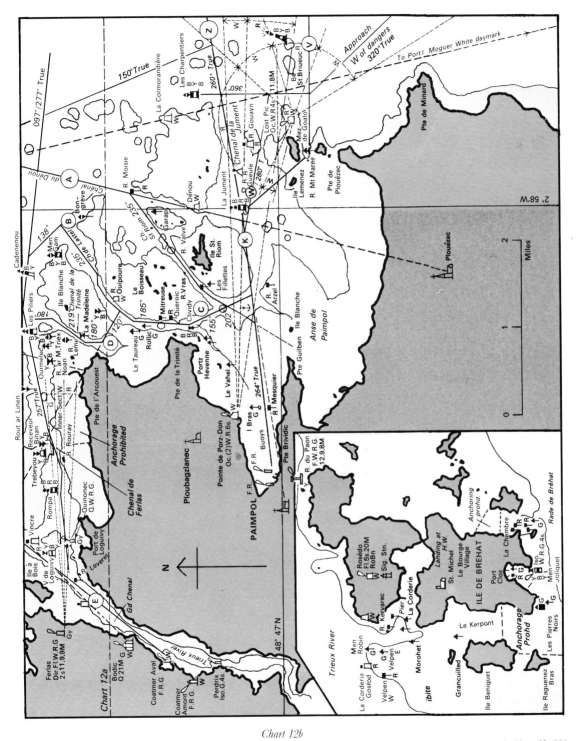

Chart 12b
Chart 12a and b. Approaches to Lézardrieux and Paimpol with Ile de Bréhat. *Based on French Chart No 831.*

75

Approaching Paimpol harbour at high water. The leading line is with the white light structure on the white end of the mole in transit with the rear one at 264° True, but on close approach Lateral beacons and buoys mark the channel.

Looking eastward from the end of the harbour mole towards the approach. This shows the channel at low water, and the buoys and beacons which were passed when entering.

Approaching on line **W** (southern Gouayan) passage. L'Ost Pic lighthouse on the port hand (not to be approached within 0·2 mile on its NE side). The yacht will then leave Mets de Goelo island on the port hand and R. Gouayan (formerly RW) beacon tower and La Jument beacon tower Lateral port to starboard.

at springs, giving, if arrival timed at or before HW, an even greater lift than the outer approach. From the above position steer to follow the leading marks for the **Trieux river Grand Chenal**, which are **Bodic** light structure (see sketch Chapter 9) in line with **La Croix** lighthouse (square tower, painted white towards the north-east, with a red top, elevation 15 m) bearing 225° True, line **T**. (See Chart Nos 11 and 12a.) Follow this line which leaves:

Nord Horaine Cardinal north spar buoy 0·8 mile to port.
La Horaine lighthouse 1·5 miles to port.
Pain de Bray Lateral port buoy 0·5 mile to port.

0·25 mile after this is abeam, if the marks can be identified, course should be altered to bring the conspicuous white day mark at **Portz Moguer** (distant 12 miles) in line with the white pyramid **De la Cormorandière**, distant 5·5 miles bearing 168° True. This channel passes between:

Roche Guarine which dries and is marked by a Cardinal east spar buoy (to be left close to starboard).
Lello Bras about 0·5 mile to port which also dries and is unmarked.

Dénou channel. The leading marks for the Chenal du Dénou are Dénou white pyramid in line with Plouézec belfry at 193° True. It is essential to check the bearing as there is a taller white pyramid 1·1 miles ENE of Dénou pyramid, which can easily be confused with it. When Roch Valve (white painted) is abeam to starboard (rather earlier than is shown in this picture) bear to starboard to leave Dénou between 100 and 150 m to port.

In view of the strong tides in this area it is essential not only to be certain of one's position before entering the **Chenal de Bréhat**, but to have reference marks from which to check the set as one proceeds.

This channel then leaves **Men Garo** Cardinal east beacon tower 0·5 mile to starboard.

At this point, again depending on the visibility, there is a choice of two inner approaches to the main channel (line **K**): (a) The Chenal du Dénou and (b) The Chenal de la Jument.

(2a) Chenal du Dénou

With local knowledge it is possible to navigate this channel with a least depth of 5·7 m, but no adequate marks can be given for the bottleneck at **Roch Dénou**, which is about 120 m west of the beacon and outside a 0·6 m patch. It is therefore recommended that it should be regarded as having a least depth of 0·6 m (i.e. 1·2 m MLWS, 3·9 m MLWN).

Steer to leave **Cain ar Monse** Cardinal north spar buoy 0·25 mile to port. From here the leading marks for the channel will be in line; these are **Dénou** white pyramid in line with **Plouézec** belfry, bearing 193° True. Dénou white pyramid is smaller than and 1·1 miles WSW of the white pyramid **De la Cormorandiere**, with which it can be confused. Follow this line (line **A**) which leaves:

Bongrève Cardinal east beacon 0·35 mile to starboard.
Moisie Lateral port beacon 120 m to port.
Garap Lateral starboard beacon 150 m to starboard.
Roche Valve (painted white) 0·15 mile to starboard.

When the latter is abeam, quit the leading line and steer so as to leave **Le Dénou** pyramid between 100 and 150 m to port. It is important to follow the leading marks precisely up to this point, as the channel is bordered by drying rocks.

Continue to make good 168° True until **La Jument** beacon tower (formerly red and white with globe and cross topmark) bears 110° True and the leading marks for the harbour come into line. These are a white hut with red top (elevation 5 m) at the head of the jetty and a small white tower with red top 0·2 miles west of the former, bearing 264° True (line **K**).

(2b) Chenal de la Jument

Steer to leave **Cain ar Monse** Cardinal north spar buoy 200 m to starboard, then steer to make good 150° True for 2·7 miles, leaving the white pyramid **De la Cormorandière** 0·75 mile to starboard and

Les Charpentiers Cardinal east beacon tower 0·55 mile to starboard. When the leading marks for the Chenal de la Jument (line **Z**), which are **Paimpol** church spire (taking care not to confuse with Plounez to the south and Ploubazlanec to the north) in line with the summit of **Pointe Brividic** (a woody hill in line with Paimpol town), are in line bearing 260° True, alter course to follow this line, leaving:

Les Charpentiers Cardinal east beacon tower 0·25 mile to starboard.

L'Ost Pic lighthouse, square white tower red top, 0·75 mile to port.

Gouayan Lateral port beacon tower 0·3 mile to port.

Roche Gueule Lateral port conical buoy 200 m to port.

La Jument beacon tower (formerly red and white with globe and cross topmark) 150 m to port.

Approach from northward to Le Ferlas Channel, by Trieux River Grand Chenal

If the visibility is insufficient to use the Chenal de Bréhat, continue on line **T** leaving the following marks on the sides shown:

Pain de Bray (Les Echaudes) Lateral port buoy 0·6 mile to port.

Les Sirlots Lateral starboard buoy 0·25 mile to starboard.

Pen Azen Cardinal north beacon tower 0·5 mile to port.

Pen Azen Lateral port buoy 0·5 mile to port.

Vieille du Tréou Lateral starboard beacon tower 0·25 mile to starboard.

Rodello Lateral starboard beacon tower (tower covers and only pole beacon shows at HW) 0·2 mile to starboard.

Rosédo white pyramid 0·3 mile to port.

Gosrod Lateral port beacon tower 0·1 mile to port.

Men Guen Lateral starboard beacon tower 0·15 mile to starboard.

Ile Verte 0·2 mile to port.

When about 0·2 mile from **La Croix** lighthouse, quit line **T** and steer for **Moguedhier** Lateral starboard beacon tower for about 0·2 mile, then pick up the marks for line **E**, which are **Coatmer Aval** light structure, a small white tower with grey roof 8 m high, elevation 16 m in line with **Coatmer Amont** light structure, a similar tower, but with a pointed roof 6 m high, elevation 50 m bearing 219° True. This line leaves the following marks on the sides shown:

Moguedhier Lateral starboard beacon tower 120 m to starboard.

La Croix lighthouse 180 m to port.

Vincre Lateral port beacon tower 0·125 mile to port.

Then steer about 180° True to leave **Vieille de Loguivy** Cardinal west beacon tower 100 m to port. Continue this course until the first marks for the Ferlas channel come in line to port. These are **Rompa** Isolated Danger beacon tower and **Les Piliers** Cardinal north beacon tower, bearing 084° True.

Le Ferlas Channel

Steer this course until about 150 m from **Rompa** when course should be altered to make good 095° True leaving **Rompa** about 50 m to port and heading for **Roche Rouray**. After 0·2 mile alter course to make good 070° True and to bring into line the Cardinal south beacons on **Rout ar Linen** and **Vif Argent**. This line leaves **Trebeyou** Cardinal south beacon tower 200 m to port and **Receveur Bihan** Cardinal south beacon 100 m to port.

Continue on this course until **Rompa** is in transit with the right edge of **Roche Levret** astern, bearing 259° True. Then steer to make good the reciprocal 079° True. This line leaves:

> **Rout ar Linen** Cardinal south beacon 100 m to port.
> **Vif Argent** Cardinal south beacon 230 m to port.
> **Roc'h Ourmelec** Cardinal north beacon 0·25 mile to starboard.
> **Men Joliquet** Cardinal west light tower 0·25 mile to port.
> **Les Piliers** Cardinal north beacon tower 0·15 mile to starboard.

At this point there is a choice of five inner approaches to the main channel (line **K**). These range from being short and difficult to long and simple: (i) **Chenal de la Trinité** (or **Chenal d'ille Blanche**) (ii) **Chenal de Lastel** (iii) **Chenal St Rion** (iv) **Chenal du Dénou** and (v) **Chenal de la Jument**.

(i) Chenal de la Trinité

This channel is the most direct route between le Ferlas channel and Paimpol. It passes close between unmarked rocks which dry 1·2 m and 1·1 m LAT and must be regarded as drying 1·2 m (i.e. has a least depth of 2·1 m MLWN and 4·2 m at half tide). First make a position from which **Les Piliers** beacon tower bears 269° True, distant 0·125 miles. From here steer about 180° True for the NW outlier of **Ile Blanche**. When this rock is distant about 0·125 miles and **Men Triex** Cardinal east beacon is abeam to starboard, distant 0·2 mile, alter course so as to keep the extremity of **Pointe de l'Arcouest** bearing 219° True. This course leaves:

Roch Lème Cardinal east beacon 0·18 mile to starboard.
La Madeleine Cardinal west beacon to port, distant 0·12 mile.

When this is abeam make good 180° True until **La Croix** lighthouse (circular tower, white towards the NW, red top, elevation 15 m) is in line with the coast on the NW side of the **Pointe de l'Arcouest** bearing 300° True. Follow this line **D** making good 120° True until **Le Taureau** Lateral starboard beacon is abeam to starboard distant 0·3 mile, when course should be altered to about 200° True to leave **Le Taureau** beacon 100 m to starboard. Then proceed as described under *Chenal de Lastel (b)*, below. When following line **D** it may be necessary for an observer to stand well above water level in order to see **La Croix** over the intervening rocks.

(ii) *Chenal de Lastel*

This channel which leads in from the north-east (see Chart No 12), may be regarded as having a least depth of 1·2 m, and is subject to a cross tide. After passing **Les Piliers** beacon tower bring **La Croix** lighthouse in line with the left side of **L'île Raguenez Bras** bearing 277° True, then steer so as to make good the reciprocal 097° True leaving **Cadenenou** Cardinal north spar buoy 140 m to starboard. When **Men Gam** Cardinal east beacon tower is abeam to starboard distant 0·3 mile, alter course to make good 138° True. This will be heading for **La Cormorandière** white pyramid in transit with **Les Charpentiers** Cardinal east beacon tower. When **Ouipoure** white beacon tower bears 235° True, alter course to keep on this bearing until **Pointe de l'Arcouest** bears 270° True, steer towards it for about 0·1 mile; then steer so as to leave **Ouipoure** white beacon tower 100 m to port. From here, shape a course for **Le Taureau** Lateral starboard beacon until about 250 m therefrom; then make good 185° True, which leaves **Rollic** Lateral starboard beacon 100 m to starboard; **Mitreuse** Lateral port beacon 60 m to port; and **Queroic** Lateral port beacon 130 m to port. Then when **Pointe de la Trinité** bears 335° True alter course to make good the reciprocal of 155° True. This line **C** is also formed by keeping **Ar Zel** Lateral port beacon bearing 155° True, and leaves **Glividy** 200 m to starboard, and so into the main channel (line **K**).

(iii) *Chenal St Riom*

From **Les Piliers** beacon tower, proceed as for **Chenal de Lastel** and continue making good 138° True until the leading marks for the

Chenal Dénou (*Plouézec* belfry in line with **Dénou** white pyramid) come into line bearing 193° True, when course should be altered to keep this transit. When **La Cormorandière** white pyramid comes into line with **Roch Moisie** Lateral port beacon alter course so as to make good 235° True. This line passes midway between **Boisseau** and **Garap** rocks, and then midway between **roch Vras** and the north-western outlier of **Ile St Rion**. Then steer so as to leave **Les Fillettes** Lateral port beacon 75 m to port and then for a point midway between **Ile Blanche** and **Pointe Guilben**, and so into the main channel (line **K**) when the tide serves.

(iv) Chenal du Dénou

Proceed as for **Chenal de Lastel** continuing to make good 138° True from **Men Gam** beacon tower until the leading marks for the **Chenal du Dénou** (**Plouézec** belfry in line with **Dénou** white pyramid) then continue as described in 2(a), above.

(v) Chenal de la Jument

After passing **Les Piliers** beacon tower, bring **La Croix** lighthouse in line with the left side of **L'Ile Raguenez Bras** bearing 277° True, then steer so as to make good the reciprocal 097° True leaving **Cadenenou** Cardinal north spar buoy 140 m to starboard, and **Cain ar Monse** Cardinal north spar buoy 0·35 mile to port. When this bears 330° True alter course to make good the reciprocal and proceed as described in 2(b), above.

Approaches to Anchorage

By Day from South and East

Chenal de la Jument may be joined anywhere if approached from the south-east outside the **Basse St Brieuc** and **Les Calemarquiers** each marked with a Cardinal east spar buoy. An approach can be made to the westward of these dangers from a position between 0·75 and 1·0 mile east of **Pointe de Minard**. Steering about 320° True, course can be shaped to keep **Roch Gouayan** Lateral port beacon tower just open of **L'Ost Pic** lighthouse. When the summit of **Plouézec** is abeam to port and **L'Ost Pic** lighthouse is distant 0·25 mile, course is altered either to follow line **V** or to 360° True for **Les Charpentiers** Cardinal east beacon tower, to avoid the rocks which extend 0·1 mile north-east of the lighthouse.

Line **V** dries 1 m, and if the tide serves steer to pass midway between **Metz de Goelo** and **Roch Mi-Marée** Cardinal north beacon and to pass about 100 m off the west end of **Metz de Goelo** and the east side of **Ile Lemenez**. Then steer 320° True to leave **La Jument** about 100 m to starboard and so join the main channel (line **K**).

If steering for **Les Charpentiers** beacon just before **La Jument** beacon tower and **Roch Gouayan** Lateral port beacon tower come into line course may be altered to make good 280° True along line **W** leaving these both 100 m to starboard and **Roch Gueule** Lateral port buoy 0·2 mile to starboard, and so into the main channel (line **K**) when the tide serves.

Alternatively the northerly course may be held until the leading marks for Chenal de la Jument (**Paimpol** church spire and the summit of **Pointe Brividic**) are in line bearing 260° True, when course is altered to follow this line (line **Z**).

Approach from Anchorage to Port

By Day
The channel dries 5 m LAT and, after arriving at the anchorage by one of the foregoing approaches, if the height of tide permits the harbour can be approached with the white hut with red top elevation 5 m at the head of the jetty in line with a small white tower with a red top elevation 12 m, 0·2 miles west of the former bearing 264° True (line **K**). This line leaves **le Vahel** Lateral starboard beacon 200 m to starboard; **Mesquier** Lateral port beacon 250 m to port; and **El Bras** Lateral starboard beacon 130 m to starboard. Thereafter the channel is marked by Lateral buoys and by a Lateral port and a Lateral starboard beacon where it passes between rocks. The channel tends to be silted towards the northern side and the southern half is preferable although this is closely bordered by oyster beds. Extensive oyster beds are to be found in all drying parts of the bay outside the main channels.

Turn closely round the end of the **Jetée de Kernoa** and secure alongside its western side, avoiding the centre part which submerges at HW.

By Night
From seaward to the East, approach in the white sector of **Portz-Don**, between 269° and 272° True (Oc (2) WR 6 s), which leads north of **La Jument** beacon tower. When the **Paimpol** leading lights come in line (both Fixed Red, the rear being intensified between 261° and 266° True), bearing 264° True, follow this line until just

83

inside the red sector of **Portz-Don**, which is the outer anchorage on line **K**. If the tide serves follow the **Paimpol** leading lights into the inner anchorage or the harbour.

Anchorages

It is possible to anchor in the Anse de Paimpol wherever there is enough water, but some parts of the channel are rather deep for small craft. Of the following positions, only (iii) can be classed as a good cruising anchorage.

(i) On line **X**, with La Jument beacon tower bearing east and the right hand end of Ile St Rion bearing north. Towards LWS care must be taken to avoid the 0·7 m rock some 250 m WSW from this position. This anchorage is not particularly sheltered, and is a very long way from civilisation.

(ii) NNE of Pointe Guilben, at the head of the deep channel. The most sheltered position has a least depth of 0·5 m (i.e. 1·1 m at MLWS). The swinging room is restricted. This anchorage is roughly on the following transits:

(a) Le Vahel beacon and Lande de Portz-Don monument.
(b) Kerity church and the western side of the hillock on the end of Pointe Guilben.

The part of the channel which lies about 0·15 mile ENE of the anchorage is used by fishing boats which moor head and stern across the stream from half ebb to half flood, and fish for garfish and mackerel with handlines. In the upper half of the tide there is quite a good dinghy landing in the sandy bay on the north side of Pointe Guilben, and from here there is a footpath to Paimpol 2·4 km away.

(iii) Off Portz-Hevenne in 2·7 m with Glividi beacon bearing about 190° True, distant 0·1 mile. Anchor slightly to the east of local moorings.

(iv) Small craft can take the ground in Portz-Hevenne, a small drying harbour which is used by fishing and pilot boats. Towards HW the approach may be made by passing either (a) about 100 m north of Morguevreuse beacons, steering 270° True or (b) about 50 m east of Roch Hir beacon steering 355° True. The end of the jetty dries 3·6 m LAT and there are berths along its western side. The local boats lie on legs in the area to the west of the jetty.

Harbour

The berths alongside the western side of the Jetée de Kernoa dry between 4·4 and 5·5 m and the centre portion becomes submerged at HW. There is a grid on the NW side of the lock.

The fuel pumps on this jetty are no longer available to yachts.

The lock is 60 m long 12 m wide, the outer sill is 3·5 m and the inner 5 m above datum. Vessels of 3·6 m draught can pass through into the basins on all tides.

The lock gates remain open, in general for 2 hours, when the height of tide at

Héaux de Bréhat exceeds 8 m, and yachts may be locked through from 1½ hours before to 1½ hours after HW.

When the height is less than 8 m there are restrictions for ships which can only lock in between ½ hour before and ½ hour after HW, and except by special arrangement, the locks do not operate between midnight and 0400. This apparently does not apply to yachts.

Facilities

The harbour is divided into two basins. There are floating pontoons for yachts in both basins and the berth for visiting yachts is at the south end of the first basin (No 2), but other berths can be made available if need be to supplement this.

Showers and other facilities at the former custom house on Quai Neuf. This is the yacht harbour office which it is proposed to extend. Water is available from a hose outside. There are other water points in the basins. The east side of the inner basin (No 1) is used by commercial craft and has cranes. There are yacht yards, marine engineers, sailmaker, and yacht chandlers available, also a dry dock. There are three garages.

Paimpol is a very pleasant old town, with good shops, including photograph processors, Librairie Maritime at Rue de Romsey and an excellent supermarket close to the south of Basin No 2. There are hotels and restaurants to suit all pockets.

Communications are excellent. There is an exciting bus service on the winding road near the coast from Lézardrieux and Tréguier to Portrieux and St Brieuc. The basin is a convenient place in which a yacht can be left temporarily in charge of a caretaker.

Historical

Paimpol is a town of some character and used to be the great base for the Iceland cod-fishing fleet. These craft were either *goëlettes* (topsail schooners) or *dundees* (ketches), and used to be away for the whole six months of summer every year. The cod were taken on hand lines worked from the ship herself, hove-to in deep water. *La Glycine*, the last of the *goëlettes*, made her last voyage to Iceland in 1935.

Pors-Even (otherwise **Portz-Hévenne**) is a pleasant little fishing village, still unspoilt by tourists. Simple provisions can be obtained, but milk and water are rather scarce.

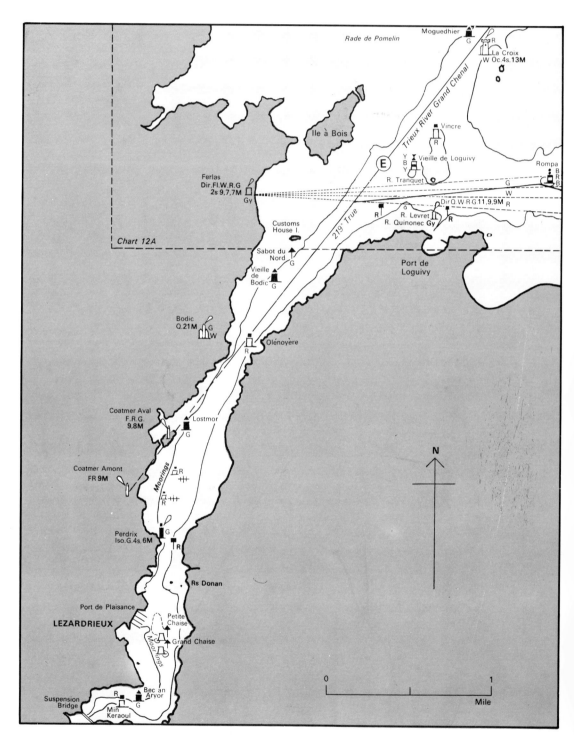

Rade de Pomelin

Moguedhier

G

R
La Croix
W Oc.4s.13M

Ile à Bois

Trieux River Grand Chenal

Vincre
R

E
Y B Y
Vieille de Loguivy

Rompa
B R B

R. Tranquet

Ferlas
Dir.Fl.W.R.G
2s 9,7,7M
Gy

Dir Q.W.R.G 11,9,9M
R
W
G

R. Levret
R. Quinonec Gy
R

Chart 12A

Customs
House I.

279 True

Port de
Loguivy

Sabot du
Nord
G

Vieille
de
Bodic
G

Bodic
Q.21M
G
W

Olénoyère
R

Coatmer Aval
F.R.G.
9,8M

Lostmor
G

Moorings

Coatmer Amont
FR 9M

R
R

Perdrix
Iso.G.4s.6M
G
R

Rs Donan

N

Port de Plaisance

LEZARDRIEUX

Petite
Chaise

Moorings

Grand Chaise

0   1

Bec an
Aryor

Suspension
Bridge
R
G
Min
Keraoul

Mile

Chart 13. Trieux River. *Based on French Chart No 2845.*

86

15 Lézardrieux (Trieux River)

Tidal Data

Tidal Heights
High Water: approx −0030 St Helier, −0525 Dover, +0200 Brest.
Heights of Tide above Chart Datum: approx MHWS 10·3 m, MLWS 0·9 m, MHWN 7·6 m, MLWN 3·3 m.
Mean Tide Level: 5·4 m. Index 12 A.

Tidal Streams

1. For tidal streams in the outer approaches see p. 98 and for Chenal de Bréhat, Le Kerpont and Le Ferlas channels see p. 99.
2. In Grand Chenal and Trieux River. In the outer part of the channel outside **Pen Azen**, the SE-going stream begins at −0405 Brest (+0105 Dover), and the NW-going at +0205 Brest (−5010 Dover). Spring rate reaches 3·75 knots.

    To the SW of **Pen Azen** the SE-going stream turns southwards towards Bréhat and into the Kerpont channel, and the NW-going stream runs northwards towards Plateau des Sirlots.

    Southward of **Gosrod** beacon tower and in the **Trieux River** the ingoing stream begins at the same time as the outer SE-going stream and the outgoing at the same time as the outer NW-going stream. Both streams follow the course of the river. Within the river the streams reach 2 or 2·75 knots at springs and 3·75 knots under Lézardrieux suspension bridge. On the south side of **Donan** rock, before reaching Lézardrieux there is an eddy on the flood stream, so that the stream always runs north here.
3. In the **Moisie** passage at the northern entrance, the E-going stream begins earlier at −0450 Brest (+0020 Dover), and the W-going at +0120 Brest (−0555 Dover). Both streams reach 3·8 knots at springs.

General

Lézardrieux has always been very popular with yachtsmen. The Grand Chenal can be taken by day or night at any state of tide and in any weather, other than with bad visibility or with strong wind over tide conditions, when the approach is rough going. The other approaches require daylight and careful pilotage.

The Trieux river is most attractive and provides excellent anchorages at Lézardrieux and elsewhere: navigation is possible up to Pontrieux, 9 miles from the entrance, where there is a wet dock.

Approaches (See Chart No 12)

By Day from the North

Rosédo radio beacon near the lighthouse (DO 294·2 kHz) is a useful aid in making the outer approach. First make a position with **La Horaine** lighthouse, octagonal tower with diagonal black and white stripes, bearing 195° True distant 3 miles. This can easily be mistaken for a sail. From here steer to follow the leading marks for the **Grand Chenal**, which are **Bodic** light structure (see sketch page 90) in line with **La Croix** lighthouse (square tower painted white towards the north-east, with a red top, elevation 15 m) bearing 225° True (line **T** on Chart No 12). Follow this line which leaves:

Nord Horaine Cardinal north spar buoy 0·8 mile to port.

la Horaine lighthouse 1·5 mile to port.

Pain de Bray (les Echaudés) Lateral port beacon tower 0·6 mile to port.

Les Sirlots Lateral starboard buoy 0·25 mile to starboard.

Pen Azen Cardinal north beacon tower 0·5 mile to port.

Pen Azen Lateral port buoy 0·5 mile to port.

Vieille du Tréou Lateral starboard beacon tower 0·25 mile to starboard.

Rodello Lateral starboard beacon tower (tower covers and only pole beacon shows at HW) 0·2 mile to starboard.

Rosédo white pyramid 0·3 mile to port.

Gosrod Lateral port beacon tower 0·1 mile to port.

Men Guen Lateral starboard beacon tower 0·15 mile to starboard.

Ile Verte 0·2 mile to port.

Pointe du Paon lighthouse on the north of the Ile de Bréhat.

When about 0·2 mile from **La Croix** lighthouse, quit line **T** and steer for **Moguedhier** Lateral starboard beacon tower for about 0·2 mile, then pick up the marks for line **E**: which are **Coatmer Aval** light structure, a small white tower with grey roof 8 m high, elevation 16 m, in line with **Coatmer Amont** light structure, a similar tower, but with a pointed roof 6 m high, elevation 50 m bearing 219° True.

This line leaves the following marks on the sides shown:

Moguedhier Lateral starboard beacon tower 120 m to starboard.
La Croix lighthouse 180 m to port.
Vincre Lateral port beacon tower 0·125 mile to port.
Vieille de Loguivi Cardinal west beacon tower 0·15 mile to port.
Custom House Island 0·1 mile to starboard.
Olénoyère Lateral port beacon tower 100 m to port.

When the latter is abeam, quit the leading line and proceed up the river on any convenient course, noting the marks and obstructions shown on Chart No 13, and in particular the following:
(a) **Perdrix** lighthouse, a Lateral starboard Lighthouse. (b) The prominent **Rochers Donan** which may be left 30 m to port. (c) The Points et Chaussées Depot, the Quay and the Port de Plaisance. (d) **Les Chaises**, a rocky middle ground marked by two white beacon towers with two Lateral starboard beacons to the east of them, which should be left to starboard, if proceeding upstream of the anchorage.

Half a mile above the quay the river turns sharply to starboard and the channel runs between **Bec an Arvor** Lateral starboard beacon tower and **Min Keraoul** Lateral port beacon tower which are to be left to starboard and port respectively. After passing the latter the channel turns to port, passing under the suspension bridge which is 28 m above datum, and leaves to starboard **Beg an Ty Meur** Lateral starboard beacon tower, and to port a Lateral port beacon tower. A further pair of beacons closely follow. Above this the channel is not marked.

By Day from the East

For the leading marks for the Ferlas channel see under Paimpol, above. When **Vieille de Loguivi** Cardinal west beacon tower has been passed, turn into the Grand Chenal and proceed as above.

By Day from the West via the Moisie Channel

The Moisie Channel carries a least depth of 1·3 m and is particularly useful as a short cut from Tréguier to Lézardrieux or Paimpol, but is difficult near low water in hazy conditions if the leading marks cannot be seen. It is also liable to be encumbered with lobster/crab

La Croix lighthouse, and on the skyline to right of it, Bodic. The two in line at 225° True can be followed within 0·2 mile of La Croix lighthouse, when course is altered to starboard to bring in transit the second line of leading lights.

See also photo of Moisie Channel on page 98.

La Croix lighthouse.   Bodic light structure.

pot lines and floats. First make a position from which **Les Héaux** lighthouse (grey granite tower 53 m high) bears 270° True distant 1·75 miles. From here the leading marks on the Ile Bréhat will be in line. These are **Rosédo** white pyramid and **St Michel** chapel, a small building with a red roof and a small red spire at its western end

St Michel chapel.

(see sketch) bearing 159° True (line **G**). Before following this line, check that it passes about 150 m east of **Roche Moisie** Cardinal east beacon tower, then follow it closely. It leaves:

Roche Moisie beacon tower 150 m to starboard (note the shoal northward of the transit in the approach to Roche Moisie).
Nougejou bihan Cardinal east beacon 50 m to starboard.
Pen ar Rest white beacon tower 0·4 mile to starboard.

Then quit the leading line and steer to leave **Vieille du Tréou** 100 m to starboard and proceed as described under *By Day from the North*, above.

By Night from the North

If passing to the west of the **Roches Douvres**, keep in the fixed white sector of **Le Paon**, bearing between 181° and 196° True until the leading lights for the Grand Chenal (line **T**) come into line. These are: **La Croix** (front), Oc 4 s, and **Bodic** (rear) Q bearing 225° True. **La Croix** is intensified 222° to 228° True and **Bodic** from 221° to 229° True.

If passing SE of the **Plateau de Barnouic**, keep in the white sector of **Les Héaux** Oc (3) 18 s, bearing between 247° and 270° True until the leading lights for the Grand Chenal come into line. Note that there are dangers near the edges of both sectors and that, from the deck of a small yacht, **Bodic** light will dip behind **La Croix** tower at some point along this line. When this happens, borrow slightly to westward. When **Men Grenn**, Q (9) 15 s (this is WSW of **Ile St Mode**, and is a mark to a secondary channel, see Chart No 12a), is abeam to starboard, quit the leading line and steer 235° True for about 0·2 mile then bring **Coatmer Aval** and **Amont** lights, both

Approaching Bodic. On line **E** with Coatmer Aval tower (see next picture) on with Coatmer Amont tower (which does not show against the light) at 219° True. Before or when Holléneyres, renamed Olénoyère, Lateral port beacon tower comes abeam, continue up the river navigating by the beacons and buoys.

Coatmer Aval light structure and Lostmor beacon tower are left to starboard.

fixed red in this sector, into line. Follow this line (line **E**) until **Olénoyère** beacon tower is abeam to port, then quit the leading line and proceed as described under *By Day*, above, keeping over to the west side of the channel to avoid the two unlit wrecks and leaving **Perdrix**, Iso G 4 s, about 100 m to starboard. **Perdrix** light in line with **Coatmer Aval** light fixed green sector leads to the anchorage, but passes close to **Roches Donan**.

In the centre of the picture are Donan rocks to be left on the port hand, and to the right Perdrix beacon tower to be left on the starboard hand. Before reaching Perdrix there are two Lateral port buoys to be left to port.

Anchorages

1. The Rade de Pomelin (refer to Chart 12), lying west of Moguedhier beacon tower, offers a reasonable temporary anchorage in 3·5–4·6 m, mud and shells, sheltered from NW through south to east.
2. Loguivi. This little drying harbour lies SSE of Vieille de Loguivi beacon tower, and is used mainly by fishermen and pilots. There is a reasonable anchorage outside the entrance in about 7·5 m sand and shells, but the tide runs strongly and it is open to the eastward. There is also an anchorage 0·25 mile west, between an

The entrance to Loguivi at about half-tide, taken from Le Ferlas channel. The arrows indicate position of the beacons.

above water rock (Roch Lèvret, a mark for the Ferlas channel) and the Lateral port beacon. Small craft which can take the ground may prefer to dry out in the harbour itself, but it is usually very full of fishing boats. The entrance is about 50 m wide, and is made by leaving the Lateral starboard beacon and the above water rock to starboard and the two Lateral port beacons to port. Then head for the west side of the entrance. Loguivi is a small fishing village with few resources, but it may be possible to purchase petrol there and there is a customs office. Boats from here form part of the fleet of French Crabbers that fish for lobster and crayfish off the coast of Cornwall.

3. Ile à Bois. There is a good anchorage to the southward of the Ile à Bois and about 150 m to the NW of line **E**, in about 4·2 m LAT, sand and mud. The edge of the drying bank drops away steeply here, and there is a rock with only 0·1 m LAT just south-west of the outermost drying outlier, and it is advisable to take soundings before letting go.

4. There is sheltered anchorage almost anywhere in the river proper, but it is advisable to avoid the wrecks in Perdrix reach and keep clear of the fairway as commercial ships pass up and down. In 1982, 19 buoys had been laid by the Yacht Club in Perdrix reach and more are planned for the future.

5. Lézardrieux. Just between the quay and les Chaises beacons off the extensive drying area on the west side. Permanent moorings are laid in this area and 5 large steel buoys have been laid on the W side of the beacon towers for use by visitors in fore-and-aft, raft moorings. There is probably room to anchor to the eastwards of moorings or farther up the river. The Marina has some 200 berths, all private, but a vacant berth may be allocated to a visitor, on application to the Marina office.

6. A small anchorage is reported in the bay on the east side of the river immediately beyond the bridge near the Lateral port beacon tower. The position is between the Lateral port beacon tower and the northern shore of the bay on a line with a house ashore, the Lateral port beacon tower and the Lateral starboard beacon tower to the south of it. This is out of the tide (which is strong near the bridge) and is near the restaurant. Soundings should be taken, and care taken to avoid drying rocks off the northern shore and steep shoaling edge on east side. Little swinging room in strong west winds.

7. For other anchorages in this area, see under Ile Bréhat, below.

Facilities

Water and electricity are laid on to the pontoons, and there is a fuelling pontoon at the root of the northernmost pontoon, with petrol and diesel pumps. Yachts can dry out for a scrub on the south side of the quay. The Yacht Club de Trieux and the marina office are in a building near the root of the southernmost pontoon. There is a bar and also showers at the yacht club but the times of opening are restricted. There is a *café du port* near the harbour but the post office and shops are at Lézardrieux, nearly half a mile from the marina. This is a small country town with fair facilities, including eating places and a garage. There is a landing place on the small beach just short of the bridge, which is nearer the town, and there is a water tap at the top of the path. The restaurant *Relais Brenner* is over the bridge on the east side. It is perhaps the best known restaurant among British yachtsmen on the coast of Brittany. The food is notable but expensive.

16 Trieux River – Upper Reaches – Pontrieux

Approaches

By Day   There is no official chart of the 6 miles of river from Lézardrieux to Pontrieux but the river should present little difficulty if a start is made from Lézardrieux at low water, when the course of the channel can be seen before the mud covers. In the first broad reach above the bridge (which is 28 m above datum, giving about 17 m at MHWS), after passing between a pair of Lateral port and stbd beacon towers and a pair of beacons, the best water is towards the west bank, thereafter, in general, it is close to the rocky steep-to banks, on the outside of the bends. If one enters the lock at Pontrieux the return journey will be at HW and it is as well to keep observation astern to assist later. After about three miles the river enters a narrow wooded gorge with a sharp bend to port, which is overlooked by the fine Château de la Roche-Jagu. About a mile and a half farther on there is a junction, keep to starboard here. In the approaches to the lock there are a Lateral starboard and a Lateral port buoy to be left as appropriate. The lock is 65 m long and 11 m wide with the sill 3·5 m above datum. When the height of tide exceeds 8·79 m; both gates of the lock are kept open by day and night. When the height is less than this, the lock will be worked from 1 hour before HW, to 1 hour after, by day only. If waiting for the gate to open, the lock-keeper may secure a yacht to the wall on the east side of the lock.

Above the lock there are commercial quays on the port hand and a rough wall to starboard. The normal depth in the basin is 3·9 m but with silting and leaks in the gates less depths are reported and yachts should berth on the port hand side just short of the Club Nautique.

The Lateral starboard and Lateral port beacon towers in the approach to the suspension bridge, under which the clearance is 28 m above datum. Here the stream attains nearly 4 knots at springs.

96

Anchorage

There is a very sheltered anchorage in about 3 m LWS in the elbow of the bend below the Château de la Roche-Jagu, out of the channel, and with a quay just upstream on the south side.

Facilities

There is a *café du port*. Water may be had from here or from the Club Nautique. Pontrieux is a pleasant country town with the usual shopping facilities. Petrol and diesel are obtainable. On 17 July there is a torchlit religious procession and a fun fair in the town. There are excursions to Château de la Roche-Jagu, which has a programme of theatrical and musical events between 1 June and 31 August. There is a bar and a crêperie.

Tidal Data

Tidal Heights
High Water: approx −0025 St Helier, −0520 Dover, +0151 Brest.
Heights of Tide above Chart Datum: approx MHWS 10·3 m, MLWS 0·9 m, MHWN 7·9 m, MLWN 3·6 m.
Mean Tide Level: 5·7 m. Index 11 A.

Tidal Streams

1. About 2·5 miles WSW of the **Plateau des Roches Douvres** the ESE-going stream begins at −0250 Brest (+0220 Dover) reaching 4·4 knots at springs and the WNW-going stream at +0310 Brest (−0405 Dover) reaching 3·9 knots.
2. Near **Plateau de la Horaine** and the outer approaches off **Ile Bréhat** the SE-going stream begins at −0335 Brest (+0135 Dover) and the NW-going stream at +0235 Brest (−0440 Dover). Both streams reach 3·8 knots at springs.

Moisie channel. Roche Moisie beacon tower at the NW end of the Moisie channel. The photograph is taken when proceeding from Les Heaux eastward to Bréhat. (Pre-IALA).

The streams are strong in the whole area between **Plateau de Barnouic**, **La Horaine** and **Bréhat**, causing severe overfalls when opposed to the direction of the wind, especially where the bottom is uneven.

3. In the **Chenal de Bréhat**, on the east side of the island, the S-going stream begins at −0405 Brest (+0105 Dover) and the N-going at +0205 Brest (−0510 Dover). Both streams reach 5·6 knots at springs.

4. In **Le Kerpont** channel, on the west side of the island, the S-going stream begins at −0405 Brest (+0105 Dover) and the N-going at −0205 Brest (−0510 Dover). Both streams reach 3·75 to 4 knots at springs.

5. In the **Chenal du Ferlas** on the south side of the island the E-going stream begins at −0405 Brest (+0105 Dover) and the W-going at 0205 Brest (−0510 Dover). Both reach 3·8 knots at springs.

General

In spite of its lack of good anchorages at spring tides, this little island at the entrance to the Trieux river is frequently visited by British yachts. The strong tides and off-lying dangers call for careful pilotage, but the island itself is attractive, with its miniature and colourful rocky scenery and its friendly atmosphere, although it is full of visitors during the season.

For a stay, it is best visited at neap tides, when small yachts can stay afloat in the sheltered anchorages. At springs, with care, there is restricted anchorage at La Corderie, otherwise the only reasonable anchorages are in the Rade de Bréhat, exposed to strong tides and open to both eastward and westward.

By reason of its close proximity to other anchorages in the Trieux River and the Anse de Paimpol, the anchorages can be visited when the tide serves.

Approaches

By Day from the North

1. The outer approaches and Grand Chenal (line **T**, Chart No 12) are given under Lézardrieux (Trieux River) on page 88, and Paimpol on page 79.

2. If bound for La Corderie, when **Vieille du Tréou** Lateral starboard beacon tower bears N, alter course to port so as to pass midway between **Gosrod** Lateral port beacon tower (which has 10, 11, and 12 m marks painted on it showing the height of tide above datum) and **Rosédo** white pyramid (see Chart No 12). Then steer to leave **Men Robin** Lateral starboard beacon about 100 m to starboard and then **Roche Kervarec** about 50 m to port and **Moncello Richard** the first Lateral beacon about 100 m to port. Alter course then to port to the anchorage.

Rosédo pyramid and St Michel Chapel, Bréhat, leading marks for Moisie Passage. To the right is Kervarec rock, and the northern entrance of Le Kerpont. The picture is taken from the northward near low water.

3. If bound for Port Clos or La Chambre, there is a choice of four channels:

(a) By the Chenal de Bréhat and Le Ferlas channel (see under *Paimpol, Approaches* page 73 and page 80 above).

(b) By the Outer approach and Le Ferlas channel (see under *Paimpol, Approaches* page 73 and page 80 above).

(c) By the Grand Chenal and Le Ferlas channel (see under *Paimpol, Approaches* page 79 and page 80 above).

(d) By Le Kerpont channel: which provides an interesting and useful short-cut, but can only be used in daylight and near high water. When the slip at the SW corner of Ile Bréhat is covered the passage is clear for 1·8 m draught, this of course has no application of proceeding from northward. The tide runs hard through the channel, but along the fairway. Proceed as for La Corderie but instead of altering to port for the anchorage steer so as to pass between **Morohet** Lateral starboard beacon and **Men ar Fave** beacon which was formerly surmounted by a globe and cylinder, which stands 85 m to the NE. Then leave the following marks on the sides shown: **Granouille** Lateral starboard beacon about 10 m to starboard (this is the narrowest and shallowest part of the channel: when the top of the concrete base of the beacon is awash, there is said to be a least depth of 0·9 m in the channel); the isolated rock on the east side of **Ile Beniguet** 60 m to starboard and the rock off its south-east corner 100 m to starboard. Then follow the deep water round to the north of **Pierres Noires** Lateral starboard beacon, also taking care to avoid the rocks ESE of it, and so out into the Rade de Bréhat.

By Day from Lézardrieux or the Anse de Paimpol

See under *Trieux River Approaches* and *Paimpol – Le Ferlas Channel*, above.

Anchorages

The area in Le Ferlas Channel, and at the southern end of le Kerpont, which is enclosed by dotted lines on Chart No 12b and inset, is a prohibited anchorage, owing to telegraph cables.

1. **La Corderie** (Chart No 12b inset). This small drying harbour is on the west side of the island, and there is anchorage for yachts of about 1·8 m draught in the entrance at springs when La Chambre is not usable at LW. There is good shelter and holding ground within the delightful natural harbour, which dries about 2·4 m to give about 1·2 m at MLWN. The landing jetty is on the north side. Yachts equipped with legs can proceed farther eastward to dry out on the bottom which, except in a few rocky places, is hard sand. Yachts of 1·8 m draught can anchor between the two Lateral port beacons and the Lateral starboard beacon SE of the **Roche Kervarec**, but take soundings to find the best position, as far east as possible to avoid the rush of tide in and out of **Le Kerpont**. This outer anchorage is somewhat exposed to the west and the north-west, but is said to be better sheltered than it appears. Riding light is necessary as the entrance fairway is sometimes used by crabbers at night. Land at jetty on the north side or on beaches on the south, as tide permits. Pleasant walk to Le Bourg. Fishermen use La Corderie as a temporary anchorage, taking the ground at low water if necessary.

2. **La Chambre** (Chart No 12b inset). A small drying harbour, between Ile Bréhat and Ile Logodec, in some ways preferable to Port Clos. At neaps there is about 2·1 m of water half-way between the first two Lateral port beacons, with excellent shelter, but some of the best positions are occupied by moorings. Small craft with legs will find perfect anchorage in the inner part of the harbour at all tides. As there are moorings in the vicinity, it is best to buoy the anchor. There is also anchorage at neap tides in winds from WNW through north to ENE to the west of the islet on the west side of the approach to La Chambre. It is possible to avoid the tide here, by going as far into the bay as soundings permit.

3. **Port Clos** (Chart 12b inset). A small drying harbour on the S side of the island. It is reported that there is seaweed on the bottom in parts of the harbour, and that an ordinary fisherman anchor holds best. At MLWN there should be about 2·4 m of water with **Men Joliquet** bearing 145° True distant 130 m. Small craft can take the ground alongside the jetty on the west side of the harbour, which dries about 3·3 m or, with legs, anywhere in the inner part of the harbour in perfect shelter. Port Clos is the harbour to which *vedettes* ply, taking excursions to the island.

The pyramid on Quistillic, an important landmark on the eastern approach to Le Ferlas channel. It is situated off Ile Bréhat about 0·5 mile east of La Chambre.

Entering La Chambre.

La Chambre. At neap tides there is about 2 m half-way between the first two beacons, but it shoals towards the island shown above. By calculating the tide of the day it is sometimes possible to find water further into the anchorage. The yacht in the foreground is probably about 1·5 m draft.

Facilities

Bréhat is a pleasant little island with a fair-sized population and many day excursionists in summer. In its mild climate there is much cultivation and sub-tropical vegetation grows in the open air. The village of Le Bourg, half-way between La Chambre and La Corderie, has several shops and restaurants of which La Vieille Auberge is well spoken. There is a small but thriving yacht club near the south-east corner of the island.

There is a small restaurant on the west side of the entrance to La Chambre and a very reasonable meal is reported at the Hotel des Roes at Port Clos.

La Corderie. On the left is Kervarec rock and the outlying rock beyond it. The entrance to La Corderie lies between the outlier and the land beyond. The north entrance to Le Kerpont channel is on the right of the picture.

The entrance to La Corderie, leaving to port the offlier of Kervarec rock (on which the first of the ebb from Le Kerpont sets strongly) and passing between the Lateral port and starboard beacons. The second Lateral port beacon can also be seen.

Part Two
Tréguier to Ile de Bas

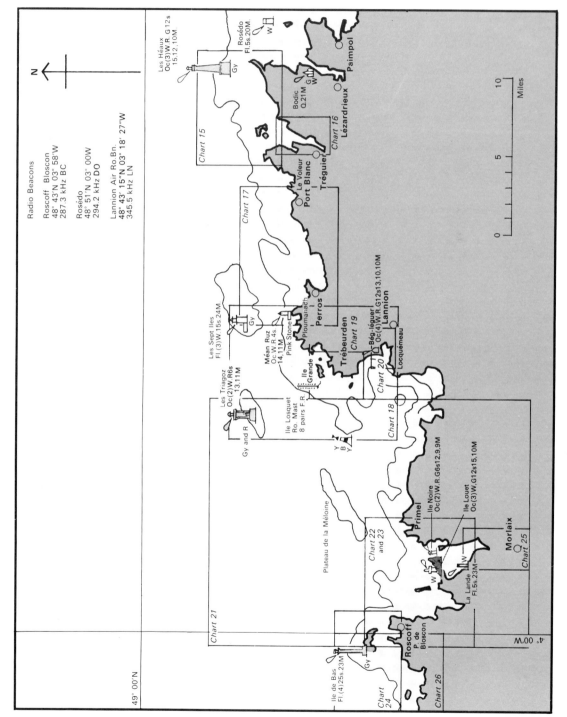

49° 00'N

N

Radio Beacons

Roscoff Bloscon
48° 43'N 03° 58'W
287.3 kHz BC

Rosédo
48° 51'N 03° 00W
294.2 kHz DO

Lannion Air Ro.Bn.
48° 43' 15"N 03° 18' 27"W
345.5 kHz LN

Les Héaux
Oc(3)W.R G12s
15.12.10M

Rosédo
Fl.5s.20M.

Paimpol

Bodic
Q.21M

Lézardrieux

Chart 15

Chart 16

Le Voleur
Port Blanc

Tréguier

Chart 17

Les Sept Iles
Fl.(3)W.15s.24M

Méan Ruz
Oc.W.R 4s.
14.11M

Pink Stone

Perros

Ploumanäch

Les Triagoz
Oc(2)W.R6s
13.11M

Ile Losquet
Ro. Mast
8 pairs F.R.

Gy and R

Ile
Grande

Bég-léguer
Oc(4)W.R.G12s13,10M

Lannion

Trébeurden

Chart 19

Chart 20

Locquémeau

Chart 18

Plateau de la Méloine

Chart 22
and 23

Primel

Ile Noire
Oc(2)W.R.G6s12.9.9M

Ile Louet
Oc(3)W.G12s15,10M

Morlaix

Chart 25

La Lande
Fl.5s.23M

Chart 21

Ile de Bas
Fl.(4)25s 23M

Gy

Roscoff
P. de
Bloscon

Chart 24

Chart 26

4° 00'W

0   5   10
Miles

Chart 14. Tréguier to the Ile de Bas (or Batz). *Based on Admiralty Chart No 2675.*

Part Two Tréguier to Ile de Bas

The whole of this length of coast is encumbered with off-lying rocks and shoals. In places the coastal dangers extend three miles offshore, and outside them lie the **Sept Iles, Plateau de Triagoz**, and **Plateau de la Méloine**, with off-lying shoals of their own.

The shore consists mostly of low cliffs and sandy bays, backed by rolling hilly country, without many distinctive natural features.

LIGHTS AND FOG SIGNALS

Details of the main coastal lights are given below, reading from east to west. Bearings of sectors and leading lines are True *looking towards the light*. To convert to magnetic, *add* the variation, which during the early 1980s is about 7° west for the area covered in Part Two of this book.

The heights of the light structures are measured from the centre of the lantern to the base of the structure. Elevation is measured between the centre of the lantern and MHWS.

Les Héaux Oc (3) WRG 12s, vis W 15M, R 12M, G 10M. R from 227° to 247°, W thence to 270°, G thence to 302°, and W thence to 227°. Grey granite tower 57m high; elevation 48m.

Tréguier River, Synchronised leading lights 137°.

(1) **Port de la Chaine** (*front*) Oc 4s, vis 12M. White house 5m high; elevation 12m.

(2) **St Antoine** (*rear*) Oc R 4s, vis 15M. Intensified 134° – 140°. White house with red roof 6m high; elevation 34m. 0·7M from (1).

La Corne Oc (2) WRG 6s, vis W 9M, R 6M, G 6M. G from 173° to 213°, W thence to 220°, R thence to 052°, W thence to 059°, and R thence to 173°. White tower red base, 23m high; elevation 14m.

Port Blanc-Le Voleur Dir Fl WRG 4s, vis W 11M, R 10M, G 10M. White tower 12m high; elevation 17m.

Perros Harbour leading lights for Passe de l'Est: 224·5°.

Le Colombier (*front*) Oc (4) 12s, vis 18M. Intensified 219·5° to 229·5°. White house 7m high; elevation 28m.

Kerprigent (*rear*) Q vis 20M, intensified 221° to 228°. White tower 14m high; elevation 79m. (Only top visible).

Perros Harbour Passe de l'Ouest: 143·5°.

Kerjean Dir Oc (3) WRG 12s, vis W 12M, R 11M, G 11M. G from 133·7° to 143·2°, W thence to 144° (0·8°), R thence to 154·3°. White tower upper part grey 16m high; elevation 78m.

Ploumanac'h-Méan-Ruz. Oc WR 4s, vis W 14M, R 11M. W from 226° to 242°, R elsewhere. Square pink tower 15m high; elevation 26m.

Les Sept Iles Fl (3) 15s vis 24M, but obscured by islands from 237° to 241°. Gy tower and dwelling 20m high; elevation 59m.

Les Triagoz Oc (2) WR 6s, vis W 13M, R 11M. R from 339° to 010°, white elsewhere. Obscured in places 258°–268° by the Sept Iles. Square grey tower with red top 30m high; elevation 31m.

Ile Losquet Radio mast. Eight pairs of FR.

Beg-Léguer Oc (4) WRG 12s, vis W 13M, R 10M, G 10M. G from 007° to 084°, thence W to 098°, thence R to 129°. House painted white towards the west, with red lantern, 8m high; elevation 60m.

Locquemeau harbour leading lights, 122° True:
> *Front* FR vis 6M 068° – 228°. R and W pylon 19m high; elevation 21m.
> *Rear* Oc (1+2) R 12s, vis 7M. White house with gable 6m high; elevation 39m. 484m from *Front*.

Primel harbour leading lights, 151° True:
> *Front* FR vis 6M. 7m high; elevation 35m.
> *Rear* FR vis 6M. 4m high; elevation 56m. Both white with red stripes.

Primel (jetty) Fl G 4s. W column G top on hut. 5m high; elevation 6m.

Ile Noire Oc (2) WRG 6s, vis W 12M, R 9M, G 9M. W from 019·5° to 051°, G thence to 135°, R thence to 211°, W thence to 289·5° and W unintensified to 019·5° (*Obscured* in places). W square tower R top. 13m high; elevation 15m.

La Lande Fl 5s, vis 23M. W square tower B top 19m high; elevation 85m. This light forms two transits: 190° with **Ile Noire** and 176° with **Ile Louet**.

Ile Louet Oc (3) WG 12s, vis W 15M, G 10M. G from 244° to 305°, W thence to 244°. W square tower B top, 12m high; elevation 17m.

Men Guen Bras Cardinal north Q WRG, vis W 9M, R 6M, and G 6M. W from 068° to 073°, R thence to 197°, W thence to 257°, G thence to 068°. 20m high; elevation 14m.

Port de Bloscon (on jetty head) Fl WG 4s, vis W 10M, G 7M. W from 210° to 220°, G elsewhere. Ro Bn: BC 287·3kHz, range 10M.

Ar Chaden Cardinal south Q (6) + LFlWR 15s, vis W 9M, R 6M. R from 262° to 288°, W thence to 294°, R thence to 326°, W thence to 110°. (*Obscured* elsewhere). 22m high; elevation 14m.

Roscoff Harbour Synchronised leading lights 210°.
> *Front* Oc (1+2) G 12s, vis 6M from 078° through E to 318°. W and G tower on a W block with black stripe. 7m high; elevation 7m.
> *Rear* Oc (1+2) 12s, vis 13M from 062° through E to 242° Square Gy tower, W on NE side, 24m high; elevation 24m.

Roscoff-Ile de Bas ferry pier. Fixed Violet, vis 1M. White and purple column 13m high, elevation 5m.

Ile de Bas Fl (4) 25s, vis 23M. Gy circular tower 40m high elevation 69m. Auxiliary light Fixed R elevation 66m. Visible 024° to 059°.

OFF-LYING BUOYS AND MARKS

Radio Mast. The principal feature on the coast between Trégastel and Primel is the very tall radio mast on **Ile Losquet** 48° 47′ 50″ N, 03° 36′ 30″ W. It is painted in red-and-white stripes and can be seen for miles in good visibility. There is a gleaming white spherical 'Radome' on the mainland to the south.

In addition to the light houses listed above, the following off-lying buoys and marks, some of which are unlit, may be useful when navigating along this coast. Reading from east to west:

La Jument (2 miles WNW of Les Heaux) Cardinal N pillar *light* and *bell* buoy.

Basse Crublent (3·75 miles W of Les Heaux) Lateral port pillar *light and whistle* buoy Fl (2) R 6 s, Radar Reflector.

Les Dervinis (1·5 miles E by S of Sept Iles LH). Cardinal south spar buoy.

Bar ar Gall Cardinal west pillar buoy, 3 M SE of Les Triagoz lighthouse.

Basse Blanche (les Crapauds) 5·75 miles S by W of Les Triagoz LH). Cardinal west spar buoy.

Plateau de la Méloine A conspicuous rock (Grande Roche, alias Le Neveu) 19 m high, stands in the centre of the plateau, in which there are many rocks.

Les Trépieds (3 miles N by W of Primel) Cardinal west spar *whistle* buoy. This is moored to the NW of Les Trépieds shoals and rocks.

Stolvezen (2 miles N of Ile Louet). Lateral port spindle buoy.

Le pot de Fer (3·5 miles N of Ile Louet). Cardinal East Spar *bell* buoy.

Roches Duon (2·5 miles E by N of Roscoff). White or stone-coloured tower standing on rocks and containing a small room for shipwrecked sailors.

Basse Astan (2·5 miles E of Ile de Bas LH). Cardinal east *light and whistle* pillar buoy.

Basse de Bloscon (0·3 mile S by E of Men Guen Bras). Cardinal north pillar light buoy.

AERO RADIO BEACON

Lannion/Servel 48° 84′ 15″ N, 3° 18′ 27″ W. LN 1345·5kHz, range 50 miles.

Basse Crublent Lateral port buoy. The line of the Grande Passe is about 0·3 mile west of this buoy.

18 Tréguier River

Tidal Data

Tidal Heights
High Water: approx −0055 St Helier, −0550 Dover, +0120 Brest.
Heights of Tide above Datum: approx MHWS 9·7 m, MLWS 0·9 m, MHWN 7·3 m, MlWN 3·3 m.
Mean Tide Level. 5·3 m. Index 10 A.

Tidal Streams

1. Outside the river at **La Jument** and **Basse Crublent** buoys the E-going stream begins at −0435 Brest (+0035 Dover) and the W-going at +0135 Brest (+0540 Dover). Both streams reach 3·8 knots at springs.
2. In the **Passe de la Gaine** the ENE-going stream begins at −0450 Brest (+0020 Dover) and the WSW-going at −0025 Brest (+0445 Dover). Both streams reach 2·8 knots.
3. Northward of **La Corne** light tower the SW-going stream begins at −0435 Brest (+0035 Dover) and the NE-going stream at +0135 Brest (−0540 Dover). Both streams reach 2·8 knots at springs.
4. In the river the in-going stream begins at −0425 Brest (+0045 Dover) and the outgoing at +0130 Brest (−0545 Dover). Both streams reach 2·4 knots at springs.

General

Although described by one French writer as *un cul-de-sac scabreux*, this river in fact provides a safe and charming anchorage for small craft. Some yachtsmen think it the best on the north coast of France.

The **Grande Passe** offers a fairly easy approach through the off-lying dangers at any state of tide, and can be taken by day or night, in reasonable visibility.

The river winds through wooded, hilly country for four miles to the old cathedral town of **Tréguier**, which is the normal limit of navigation. Since the upper part of the river has been buoyed by twelve light buoys, six to port and six to starboard, the channel is reasonably clear at any state of the tide.

Approaches

Grande Passe. By Day

Navigate so as to pass through a position 0·3 mile to the SW of **Basse Crublent** Lateral port pillar light and whistle buoy. From here, the light structures of **Port de la Chaine** (*front*), and **St Antoine** (*rear*) come into line bearing 137° True. **Port de la Chaine** is a white

111

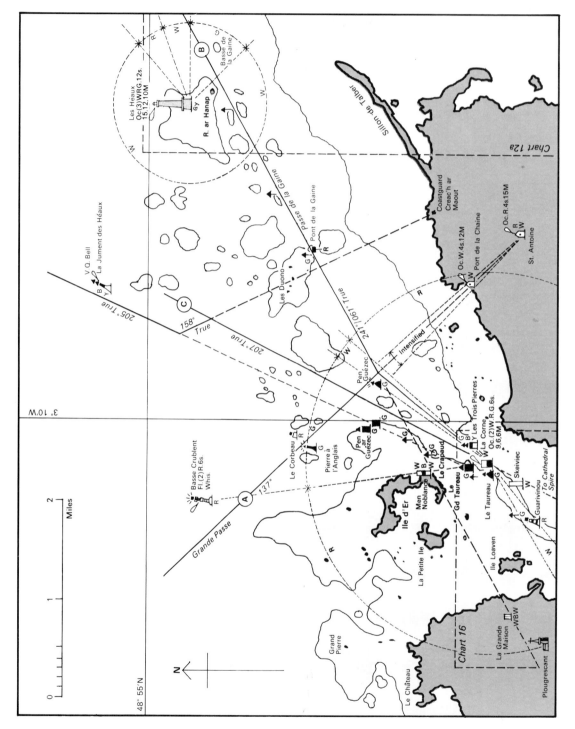

Chart 15. Approaches to Tréguier River. Based on French Chart No 972.

112

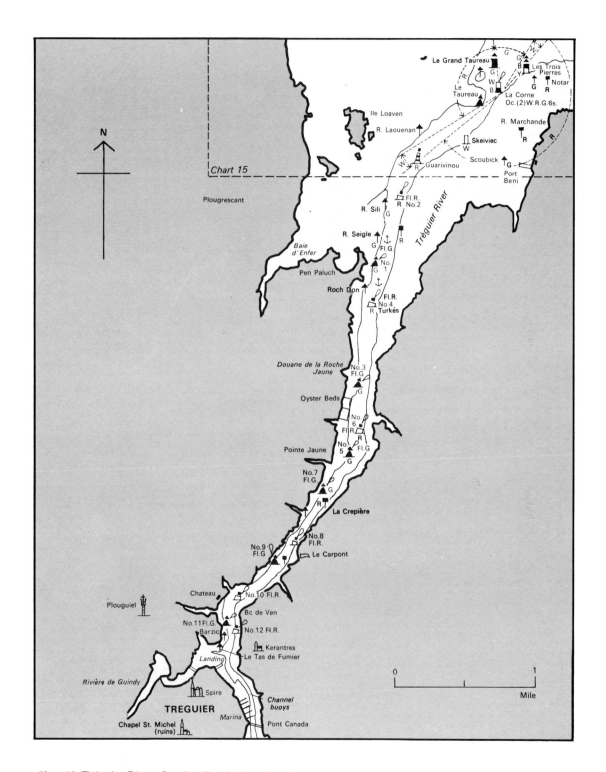

Le Grand Taureau
Les Trois Pierres
Notar
Le Taureau
La Corne
Oc.(2)W.R.G.6s.
R. Marchande
Ile Loaven
R. Laouenan
Skeiviec
Scoubick
Chart 15
Guarivinou
Port Beni
Plougrescant
R. Sili
Tréguier River
Fl.R. No.2
R. Seigle
Fl.G
Baie d'Enfer
No. 1
Pen Paluch
Roch Don
Fl.R. No.4
R. Turkés
Douane de la Roche Jaune
No.3 Fl.G
Oyster Beds
No. 6
Fl.R
Pointe Jaune
No. 5 Fl.G
No.7 Fl.G
La Crepière
No.8 Fl.R.
No.9 Fl.G
Le Carpont
Chateau
No.10 Fl.R.
Plouguiel
Bc de Ven
No.11 Fl.G.
Barzic
No.12 Fl.R.
Kerantres
Le Tas de Fumier
Landing
Rivière de Guindy
Spire
TREGUIER
Channel buoys
Marina
Chapel St. Michel (ruins)
Pont Canada

0   1
Mile

Chart 16. Tréguier River. *Based on French Chart No 973.*

113

Men Noblance beacon is left about 0·45 mile on the starboard hand when entering. The beacon is the front leading mark for Passe de la Gaine.

house, 5 m high, elevation 12 m, and **St Antoine** is a red and white house 6 m high, elevation 34 m. These marks are difficult to pick up in daylight, and it is better to make good a compass course, leaving the following marks on the sides shown:

Le Corbeau Lateral port buoy, 0·1 mile to port. Beware of the shoal southward of this buoy (previously marked by a beacon tower) and to the SE. Here a yacht must be nothing to the east of the leading line.

Pen Ar Guézec Twin beacon towers 0·35 mile to starboard (in 1982 the southernmost tower had no top and was only visible near low water).

Pen Guézec Lateral starboard buoy, 150 m to starboard. As soon as this buoy is abaft the beam, quit the leading line and alter course to 217° True, keeping the western edge of **La Corne** white lighthouse in line with **Skeiviec** white beacon tower. This line leaves the following marks on the sides shown:

Two Lateral starboard beacons on the east side of **Ile d'Er**, 0·3 mile to starboard.

Men Noblance black-and-white pyramid 0·45 mile to starboard.

Les Trois Pierres Cardinal north beacon tower with two green painted cones 110 m to port. (If entering at very low water, note the 1·1 m rock (2·1 m at MLWS) which lies 0·2 mile north of this tower and about 60 m NW of the leading line.)

When **Les Trois Pierres** tower is abeam, quit the leading line and steer as if to leave **La Corne** lighthouse 150 m to port, leaving **Le Grand Taureau** Lateral starboard beacon tower 170 m to starboard; but when **La Corne** lighthouse bears about 180° True, alter course to leave **La Corne** lighthouse 100 m to port and **Le Taureau** Lateral starboard buoy 35 m to starboard.

La Corne. When entering the river, La Corne is left about 150 m to port and Le Taureau Lateral starboard buoy about 35 m to starboard. Skeiviec white beacon tower is in the centre and Le Taureau to its right.

When this buoy is abeam, alter course to make good 232° True, keeping **Les Trois Pierres** beacon tower touching the west side of **La Corne** lighthouse as a stern transit.

This line leaves:

Skeiviec small white beacon tower on a rocky shoal which at LW looks like a small island 0·1 mile to port.

Laouenan beacon 0·15 mile to starboard, and leads straight to **Guarivinou** Lateral port light pillar buoy; leave this to port.

From this buoy the position of the deep channel can best be seen from Chart No 16. This is marked by twelve Lateral light buoys, six to starboard and six to port, as well as the old Lateral beacons, which are on drying rocks. For the first mile and a quarter the channel lies towards the west side of the river; note in particular the drying rock just upstream of No 4 Lateral port light buoy, off **Turkés** rock. Thereafter it is roughly in midstream all the way to **Tréguier** except at the **Banc de Ven**, where it hugs the west bank. The corner of the **Banc de Ven** is marked by No 10 Lateral port light buoy, which should be left to port and given a wide berth near low water. Note the shoal water (1·0 m LAT) as shown on the chart SE of the entrance of the creek **Rivière du Guindy** and the drying banks on each side.

Grand Passe. By Night

Keeping well to seaward of the off-lying dangers, come on to the leading line formed by the synchronised lights of **Port de la Chaine** (*front*) Oc 4 s, vis 12 miles and **St Antoine** (*rear*) Oc R 4 s vis

115

15 miles and steer to follow this line bearing 137° True. The rear light is intensified 134° to 140° True (line **A**).

For vessels equipped with radar, the **Basse Crublent, Pierre à l'Anglais** and **Pen Guézec** buoys are fitted with radar reflectors.

The vessel will pass through the red and green sectors of **La Corne** light Oc (2) WRG 6 s (Chart No 15, page 112) and enter the white sector bearing 213° True close to the unlit **Pen Guézec** buoy. Alter course to leave this buoy to starboard and steer to keep in the white sector of **La Corne** between 213° and 220° True and keep in this sector until **Les Trois Pierres** beacon tower (unlit) is abeam to port, and about 0·2 mile from the lighthouse, then alter course about 10° to starboard, so as to pass round the west side of the lighthouse in a shallow curve, leaving it about 100 m to port. When it bears 059° True the white sector, between this bearing and 052° True will open up (the sectors may be difficult to see when close to the light, owing to the beams passing overhead), and course should be altered to starboard to keep in this sector, taking particular care to leave the unlit **Taureau** Lateral starboard buoy, which is well inside this sector, to starboard. The southern edge of this sector, on a course made good of 232° True leads to **Guarivinou** Lateral port *light* buoy, which should be left to port. From this buoy the position of the deep channel can best be seen from Chart No 16 as in *Approach By Day*, above. The Lateral light buoys are on alternate sides of the channel and, to be sure of avoiding the danger upstream of No 4 and the **Banc de Ven** to the east of No 10, it would be as well to record each buoy as it is passed.

Passe de la Gaine. By day only

This pass can be taken only in daylight and clear visibility. If the leading line is followed exactly, the least depth is 0·3 m (1·2 m at MLWS=3·6 m at MLWN); but a divergence of 36 m from the line will give 2·1 m less water in two places and a divergence of 100 m to the west will give 3·6 m less water when passing through the south-east outliers of **Les Duono**. At half tide there should be a least depth of 3·3 m for 36 m either side of the line and of 2·1 m for 100 m each side.

To enter the pass from the eastward, approach **Les Héaux** and identify the **Roch ar Hanap**, which lies 0·25 mile SSE of the lighthouse and never covers. It is the outermost of several rocks on this side, and is steep-to to the south-eastward. Avoiding, if need be, the **Basse de la Gaine** (a rock drying 0·3 m about 0·4 mile east of **Roch ar Hanap** and about 100 m south-east of the leading line). Make a position from which **Roch ar Hanap** bears 360° True,

The leading marks for the Passage de la Gaine are difficult to distinguish from a distance. The front one is Men Noblance tower (see close-up picture on p. 114) and the rear is a white wall mark with a vertical line in centre situated 500 to 600 m west of the prominent church spire, just on the left of a wood. They should be in transit at 241° True.

Les Heaux lighthouse bearing about west. Roch ar Hanap is the extreme SE above-water rock in the group.

distant 0·2 mile. From here the leading marks will be in line (line **B**): **Men Noblance** white beacon tower with horizontal black stripe, in line with the white wall beacon with vertical black stripe, bearing 241° True. The rear wall beacon stands below the skyline in a field just below the first clump of trees and about 500 to 600 m west of the prominent **Plougrescant** church. Follow this line through leaving the first Lateral starboard beacon 200 m to starboard, the second Lateral starboard beacon 150 m to starboard, passing between the Lateral port and starboard beacons at **Pont de la Gaine**, leaving the former 80 m to port and the latter 50 m to starboard and finally **Pen Guézec** Lateral starboard buoy about 100 m to starboard. Then proceed as for the Grande Passe.

The difficulty about the **Passe de la Gaine** is that the wall beacon is over 6 miles and **Men Noblance** over 4 miles from the entrance and, in poor visibility or in the haze of a summer's day, particularly in late afternoon, one or both marks cannot be seen.

117

The tidal streams are strong and the set must be allowed for. In the outer part of the Passe the east-going stream is deflected to the north-east, so that when entering, the tide is foul, although the flood is fair up the Tréguier river. There are also, incidentally, quite heavy overfalls at certain states of the tide on the shoals, seaward of **Les Héaux**.

Passe du NE. By day only

This pass can only be taken in daylight and clear visibility but, if the leading marks can be seen, it provides a useful alternative to the Passe de la Gaine, for vessels approaching from the Channel Islands, particularly in the late afternoon, when it is not possible to distinguish the marks for the latter, or at LWS when it has a least depth of 2·3 m, as compared with 1·2 m.

Navigate so as to pass 100 m north-west of **La Jument** (otherwise

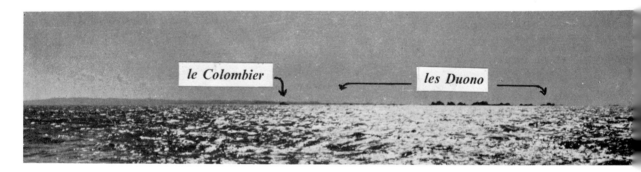

Le Colombier is the 'key' rock when sailing through the passe de la Gaine. It is the most easterly of the above-water rocks in Les Duono group, but viewed from a distance it appears almost as an isolated rock. The picture is taken from southward of Les Heaux.

A nearer view of Le Colombier rock and Les Duono. The rock is left about 0·1 mile to starboard when sailing on the leading marks. At high water most of the lower rocks are covered. The picture is taken from about ENE.

Jument des Heaux). From here **Tréguier** cathedral spire (which is the right hand of two spires visible between the river banks) will be between the two beacon towers on **Pen ar Guézec** (the southernmost one had temporarily lost its top half in 1979. If not visible, the spire should be kept open to the S of the one that can be seen) bg 205° True. Steer to follow this line for about 0·75 mile. When the summit of the middle rock in the **Duono** group is in line with the Coastguard building on the **Creac'h ar Maout**, bearing 158° True, steer to follow this line for about 0·3 mile until **Skeiviec** white beacon comes in line with the Cathedral spire bearing 207° True (line **C**). Steer to follow this line, leaving **Pen Guézec** Lateral starboard buoy 0·2 mile to port, **Pen ar Guézec** beacon towers 0·2 and 0·15 mile to starboard, **Roche Dourouenès** Lateral starboard beacon 0·1 mile to starboard, **Le Crapaud** Lateral starboard beacon 0·15 mile to starboard, **Les Trois Pierres** Cardinal north beacon tower with green cones 0·15 mile to port and **La Corne** lighthouse 100 m to port, then proceed as for Le Grand Passe.

Owing to the presence of many fishing markers in the area, it might be preferable to quit this line when on the leading marks for Le Grand Passe, and to continue as for that channel.

Anchorages

It is possible to anchor in good holding ground almost anywhere in the channel (which is used by coasters), but the following positions are recommended.

(a) In mid-channel near the **Guarivinou** buoy in 5–6 m LAT sandy mud.
(b) Towards the west side of the channel between **Pen Paluch** and **Roch-Don** beacons in 5 m LAT, mud.

Approaching Tréguier. The Lateral port buoy on the right of the picture is left to port, as here the deep water is off the west bank of the river. The Lateral beacons in the background are left on the appropriate sides.

(c) Towards the west side of the channel near the **Douane de la Roche Jaune** 7·8 m LAT, sandy mud. There are oyster-beds inshore which dry and are steep-to. Care must be taken to allow swinging room clear of these. There is a village half a mile inshore from the quay, where there are shops, a self-service store and telephone. Oysters are for sale near the jetty.

(d) In mid-channel near the **Gorrejo** buoy No 6 in 7·5 m LAT, mud. This reach of the river is called the **Mouillage de Palamos**.

(e) In mid-channel north of the **Banc de Ven**, in 6·8 m LAT, mud.

(f) Under the **château**, close inshore opposite **Banc de Ven** in 5·2 m, mud.

(g) Anchoring is now forbidden between anchorage (f) and the bridge, and there are no mooring buoys in this reach. A marina has been built below the bridge, having 5 pontoons extending from the W bank. These have fingers on each side for berthing boats up to 12 m. There is one berth only for a boat up to 16 m at the end of the first pontoon. A notice directs visitors to berth head-on to the current on the second pontoon. The tide runs very strongly under the pontoons and, whilst the tide is running, if berthed stern-to the tide, one cannot safely vacate a berth, without taking lines to the next pontoon.

(h) With permission from the Harbour Master for the commercial quay, it might still be possible to take the ground alongside the quay when not required for commercial shipping.

(i) When the tide serves, small craft which can pass under the bridge may go a farther 3·5 miles up the river to **La Roche-Derrien**, where there is said to be a quay that dries 5·7 m LAT. The channel dries 5·1 m.

Tréguier River. Roche Jaune anchorage at LWS, showing drying oyster beds, drying rocks and, just above the bow of the yacht, the Lateral starboard buoy.

Facilities

The marina has berths for 330 boats. Water is laid on to the pontoons. There is a Yacht Club with lounge, bar, showers and WCs. There is also a sailing school. For boats anchored downstream, there are three main dinghy landings on the town side of the river:

(a) At the steps just north of the old custom house. These dry about 2 m at MLWS, soft mud.

(b) At the slipway and steps at the little promontory at the entrance of Rivière de Guindy, this is rather rough and weedy.

(c) At the slipway farther up the Rivière de Guindy, beyond the two bridges. This only dries at extreme LWS.

There are two yacht chandlers, one at the south end of the quay and the other at the north. At HW it is possible to go alongside outside the latter, where stores may be loaded and water is available. Butagaz is available here also.

Water is also available from a tap at the new public conveniences in the middle of the quay. Fuel is available opposite the Yacht Club. The post office is up the main road to the town. There is a good restaurant on the quay and good shops in the town. There is a self-service supermarket in the road from the north end of the quay up to the town. Travellers' cheques can usually be cashed at the Banque de Bretagne, 200 m from the quay.

Historical

Tréguier is a pleasant, quiet old town which traces its history back to the monastery of Trécon, founded by St Tugdal in the sixth century. The fine church, formerly a cathedral, was founded in the ninth century but mostly rebuilt in the fourteenth; there is an eleventh-century tower on its northern side. The strange granite spire, a sort of honeycomb of irregular openings, was finished in 1787.

St Yves, the Friend of the Poor, lived at Tréguier in the thirteenth century. A procession from Tréguier Cathedral to his birthplace in the nearby village of Minihy takes place each year on May 19th, and is known as the Pardon of the Poor. Tréguier is the birthplace of Renan.

19 Port Blanc

Tidal Data

Tidal Heights
High Water: approx −0100 St Helier, −0555 Dover, +0120 Brest.
Heights of Tide above Datum: approx MHWS 9·4 m, MLWS 0·9 m, MHWN 7·0 m, MLWN 3·3 m.
Mean Tide Level: 4·9 m. Index 9 A.

Tidal Streams

Off the entrance the east-going stream begins at −0450 Brest (+0020 Dover) and the west-going at −0120 Brest (−0555 Dover). Both streams reach 2·4 knots at springs.

General

This small natural harbour, half-way between the Tréguier river and Perros, is well sheltered except from winds between NW and NNE which make the anchorage uncomfortable and which, if strong, make the entrance rough (especially on the ebb) and the anchorage untenable. In easterly weather it is more sheltered than the Anse de Perros, but at high water there is always liable to be a certain amount of swell in the anchorage.

The entrance is straightforward but rather difficult to identify, and can be taken by day or night at any state of the tide.

The village has few resources, but the rocky island scenery is attractive in fine weather.

Approaches

By Day Owing to the lack of distinctive landmarks, it is not easy to identify the entrance from seaward, but bearings of **Plougrescant** church, **Ile Tomé** and of **Ile Rouzic**, the most easterly of the **Sept Iles**, will give reasonable fixes for the approach. Navigate so as to reach a point from which **Basse Guazer** Lateral port whistle buoy bears 218° True distant 0·7 mile. This point is at the intersection of the leading line for Perros (line **D**), and the leading line for the entrance (line **C**), formed by **Port Blanc** in line with **Moulin de la Comtesse**, bearing 150° True. The lighthouse, a white tower, with a square window at its half height, is visible when the observer is almost on the leading line, when it appears amongst the trees, half-way up the hillside – see photograph – and the **Moulin** is only the remains

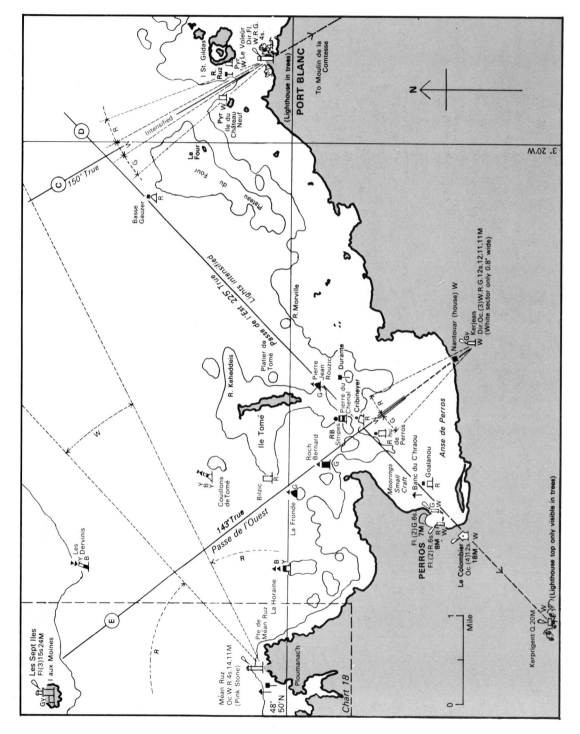

Les Sept Iles
Fl(3)15s24M
I aux Moines
Gy

Méan Ruz
Oc.W.R 4s.14,11M
(Pink Stone)

48°
50'N

Ploumanac'h

Chart 18

Pte de Méan Ruz
La Horaine

R

La Fronde

R

Bilzic

Couillons
de Tomé
Y
B

Ile Tomé

Platier de Tomé

R.Keheddeis

Roch
Bernard

RB
Stripes

Pierre du
Chenal
G

Cribineyer
R

Pierre
Jean
Rouzic

Durante

R.Morville

Passe de l'Est 225° True

Lights intensified

143 True
Passe de l'Ouest

Moorings
Small
Craft

Banc du C'hraou

Goalanou
R

R hu
de
Perros

Anse de Perros

Nantouar (house) W
Gy

W Kerjean
W Dir.Oc.(3)W.R.G.12s.12,11,11M
(White sector only 0.8° wide)

PERROS

Fl (2)G.6s
7M

Fl(2)R.6s
8M R

G

W

Le Colombier
Oc.(4)12s.
18M W

Kerprigent Q.20M
W

(Lighthouse top only visible in trees)

0   1
         Mile

Basse
Gauzer
R

C   150° True

D

Intensified

R

W

G

Le
Four

Plateau   du   Four

Pyr W
Ile du Château
Neuf

I St. Gildas

R
Ruz

Pyr
W Le Voleur
Dir.Fl.
W.R.G.
4s.

(Lighthouse in trees)

PORT BLANC

To Moulin de la
Comtesse

N

3° 20'W

E

Les
Dervinis
Y
B
W

R

Chart 17. Approaches to Port Blanc and Perros. *Based on French Chart No 974.*

124

Left Port Blanc lighthouse in the trees and *right* Ile du Château Neuf with white beacon, which is the only means of identifying the entrance except in very clear weather.

A close-up view of the lighthouse hiding shyly in the trees. It is difficult to see except when exactly on the leading line.

thereof and is not conspicuous and not visible at all west of the leading line.

The best means of identifying the entrance is by the **Ile du Château Neuf**, an islet of bare rock and grass, which is situated on the west side. It has a slender white pyramid on its summit and is conspicuous, but rather narrower than shown on the photograph. The island, being rather steep-to, can be treated, with caution, as a starboard hand mark. Although the lighthouse is not easy to see, there is a reasonably conspicuous white cottage with slate roof (see photograph) about 100 m to the NE. **Ile Saint Gildas** is a bigger island on the east side of the entrance. It is wooded and also has a white pyramid, which is not nearly as conspicuous as that on the **Ile du Château Neuf**.

Once these features have been recognised, there is no difficulty in the approach, holding the white cottage at 148° True until the lighthouse is identified, then steer to make good 150° True towards the lighthouse.

Line **C** leads straight into the anchorage, and leaves the following marks on the sides shown:

Basse Guazer Lateral port conical whistle buoy 0·7 mile to stbd.
Le Four white painted rock 0·5 mile to starboard.
Ile du Château Neuf white pyramid, 0·125 mile to starboard.
Ile Saint Gildas white pyramid, 0·25 mile to port.
Roc'h Ruz Lateral port beacon 100 m to port.

By Night   From any direction, navigate so as to reach the line of the leading lights for the east pass into Perros: **Le Colombier** (*front*) Oc (4) ev 12 sec, in line with **Kerprigent** (*rear*) Q bearing 225° True. This line (**D** on Chart 17), passes close to seaward of the unlit **Basse Guazer** whistle buoy, and clears all dangers on each side of the entrance to Port Blanc. Sail along line **D** in the required direction until the W sector of **Port Blanc** Dir Fl WRG 4 s opens up, intensified between 148° and 152° True. Steer to keep within this intensified sector which clears all dangers as far as the anchorage.

Anchorages

Twenty-three white visitors' mooring buoys have been laid in the pool, these are well spaced but there should nevertheless be room to anchor clear of these, the bottom being generally sand and shells. The berths at the southern end are the most sheltered. Small craft will be able to lie afloat to the eastward of the leading line and south of the **Ile Saint Gildas** pyramid on most tides; for example at MLWN there should be 1·8 m of water in a position midway between **Ile Saint Gildas** pyramid and **Port Blanc** lighthouse.

The best dinghy landing is at the small slip east of Port Blanc, but this dries 1·5 m LAT. The alternative is to land anywhere round the anchorage on sand and rock. There is also a good landing slip 0·4 mile west of the lighthouse. Although it dries 3 m it is convenient for some shops farther to the west.

Surroundings

Port Blanc is a small fishing village and seaside holiday resort, with two or three hotels and restaurants. Simple provisions can be purchased, and there is a post-box on the side wall of the Grand Hôtel, which is described as modest and good. A taxi can be hired at the café to fetch petrol from a neighbouring village. There are shops, including a butcher and a baker beyond the western landing mentioned above.

The harbour shelters a few small fishing boats and day boats, all of which lie on drying moorings clear of the pool.

The sixteenth-century chapel of Notre Dame de Port Blanc stands above the village, and is the scene of a *pardon* held on September 8th and attended mainly by fishermen and sailors.

Anatole le Braz, the author of several classics on Breton traditions and legends, lived at Port Blanc.

One of the local legends tells of a long procession of drowned seamen, led by a woman, which can sometimes be seen landing on the beach of the Ile Saint Gildas in search of fresh water, while the shape of their vessel is dimly visible in the offing.

20 Perros

Tidal Data

Tidal Heights
High Water: approx −0100 St Helier, −0555 Dover, +0120 Brest.
Heights of Tide above Datum: approx MHWS 9·1 m, MLWS 0·9 m, MHWN 6·3 m, MLWN 3·0 m.
Mean Tide Level: 4·9 m. Index 9 A.

Tidal Streams

1. At the **Couillons de Tomé** buoy, the east-going stream begins at −0435 Brest (+0035 Dover) reaching 3·8 knots at springs and the west-going at +0250 Brest (−0425 Dover) reaching 2·8 knots.
2. In the **Passe de l'Ouest** the south-east-going stream begins at −0435 Brest (+0035 Dover) and the north-west-going at +0250 Brest (0425 Dover). Both streams reach 2·8 knots at springs.
3. In the **Passe de l'Est** the north-east-going stream begins at −0435 Brest (+0035 Dover) reaching 4·7 knots at springs and the south-west-going stream begins at +0250 Brest (−0425 Dover) reaching 4·2 knots.

General

The Anse de Perros is a large shallow bay, most of which dries at MLWS leaving a tongue of deeper water in which a small vessel can lie afloat about 0·4 mile from the western shore. It provides good shelter in westerly weather, but the anchorage is far from a convenient landing.

The port of Perros was formerly a drying harbour and is in the SW corner of the bay, it is protected by two stone jetties. The inner part has been made into a wet basin by the construction of a submersible dyke and a dock gate holding a least depth of 7 m above datum.

There are two approach channels, one east of Ile Tomé and the other west of it. The eastern channel has leading lights and the western channel a directional sectored light, and both can be taken at night, but towards springs it is necessary to consider the depth of water near the southern ends of the leading lines.

Approaches

Passe de l'Est

By Day   The leading line (**D** on Chart 17) carries a least depth of 0·3 m if followed exactly, but this can be increased to 2·1 m by observing the

Roc'h Bernard beacon and Castell Perros. Roch Bernard Lateral starboard beacon tower is left to starboard when entering Anse de Perros. In the background is the Castell Perros headland.

le Colombier

Le Colombier front leading light is situated in the gable of the white house which is lettered 'Le Colombier', 0·15 mile south of the harbour which is out of the picture to the right.

following instructions. The line is formed by **Le Colombier**, a white house light structure on which the name is shown, 5 m high elevation 28 m and **Kerprigent** lighthouse a white tower 14 m high elevation 79 m, among the trees on the skyline, bearing 225° True. The marks are difficult for a stranger to pick out at a distance and it may be easier to navigate by the buoys and beacons alone.

The leading line leaves the following marks on the sides shown:

Basse Guazer Lateral port whistle buoy 0·1 mile to port.

Roc'h Morville (dries 1·5 m), the seaward end of a dangerous unmarked shoal, 0·15 mile to port. **Pierre Jean Rouzic** Lateral starboard buoy 50 m to starboard. **Durante** Lateral port beacon 0·25 mile to port. **Pierre du Chenal** beacon tower, formerly red-and-white surmounted by a globe and cross, 150 m to starboard. **Cribineyer** Lateral port buoy 100 m to port.

0·1 mile beyond this buoy, the line passes over a 0·4 m patch. To avoid this, as soon as **Cribineyer** buoy is abeam, alter course to 270°

129

True and hold it until **Roc'h hu de Perros** Lateral port beacon tower bears 180° True then rejoin the line.

Continuing along it, if the tide serves, we leave: **R. hu de Perros** Lateral port beacon tower 0·125 mile to port, **Banc du C'hraou** Lateral starboard beacon 50 m to starboard, **Goalenou** Lateral port beacon tower 0·1 mile to port, after which course may be altered as necessary to enter the port.

By Night   Navigate so as to reach the leading line formed by **Le Colombier** (*front*) Oc (4) 12 s (intensified 219·5° to 229·5° True) and **Kerprigent** (*rear*) Q (intensified 221° to 228° True) (line **D**), bearing 225° True. Follow this line as for *By Day* above, except that if **Cribineyer** buoy and **Roc'h hu de Perros** cannot be seen, as soon as **Kerjean** light to port Dir Oc (3) WRG, changes from red to white, alter course sharply to starboard to bring this astern and steer so as to keep in the narrow white sector for 150 m and then rejoin the line on a converging course of about 215° True.

Small fixed lights are exhibited at the entrance to the port; green at the end of the eastern jetty and red on the western jetty.

Passe de l'Ouest

By Day   Keep well clear of the off-lying dangers on the south side of the **Sept Iles** and on the north side of **Ile Tomé**. Note **Les Dervinis** Cardinal south spar buoy; **Couillons de Tomé** Cardinal west Pillar buoy and **La Horaine** Cardinal north beacon tower. Navigate so as to pass through a point from which **Bilzic** Lateral port beacon tower bears 090° True distant 0·2 mile, from here **Nantouar**, a white house with a former light tower on its roof, standing near the foreshore, will be in line with **Kerjean**, a white light tower 16 m high, elevation 78 m with a conical grey roof, amongst the trees on the skyline, bearing 143° True (line **E**). This line carries a least depth of 0·9 m, but is rather difficult for a stranger to pick out at a distance, and it may be easier to navigate by the buoys and beacons alone. Line **E** leaves the following marks on the sides shown:

La Fronde Lateral starboard buoy just 0·125 mile to starboard; **Roc'h Bernard** Lateral starboard beacon tower 0·125 mile to starboard; and **Pierre du Chenal** isolated danger beacon tower, 0·2 mile to port.

As soon as **Pierre du Chenal** beacon tower is abeam, quit the leading line and steer 190° True to pick up the **Passe de l'Est** (line **D**).

By Night   Note that the white sector of **Méan Ruz** light near **Ploumanac'h** clears all dangers between **Les Sept Iles** and the mainland.

Navigate to pick up the narrow white sector of **Kerjean** light which is only between 143·2° and 144° True and is flanked by a green sector to the west and a red sector to the east. Follow this line and proceed as for *By Day*, above, taking care to quit the leading line and alter course to starboard just before **Le Colombier** (*front*) Oc (4) 12 s comes in line with **Kerprigent** (*rear*) Q.

Anchorages

1. The **Anse de Perros** offers good holding ground and is sheltered from south-east through south to north-west. Recommended positions are:
   (a) With **Roc'h hu de Perros** tower bearing 120° True distant 0·15 mile. Least depth 2·4 m (= 3·3 m at MLWS), sand.
   (b) With **Roc'h hu de Perros** tower bearing 100°, and with **Bilzic** Lateral port beacon tower, without top mark, just open west of **Roc'h Bernard** tower. Least depth 1·2 m (=2·1 m at MLWS), sand. With the aid of soundings it may be possible to anchor further to the south-west.
   (c) At neap tides, small vessels will be able to stay afloat about 0·2 mile north-east of **C'hraou** beacon in 1·8 m at low water. There is said to be a slightly deeper runnel near line **D**, the position of which is variable, but may be found by sounding.

The disadvantage of all these positions is the long and rather exposed dinghy journey to reach the facilities of the port. Landing may be made on rocks on the shore over 0·25 mile away, but the nearest reasonable landing place, which also carries more water than the outer harbour itself, is at the lifeboat slip, just south of the **Banc du C'hraou**.

The gate to the wet basin and marina. The lock is only 6 m wide.

2. The **Port de Perros** has a large wet basin in which there is a yacht marina. The basin is enclosed by a wall which maintains within a level of 7 m above datum and is marked by five red and white poles. The gate is on the east side and it is opened when the level of the tide is at or above 7 m. The wall is well covered at HW springs but it may not be possible for the gate to be worked at weak neap tides for 2 or 3 days. There are no visitors' berths as such but yachts are directed to one of the pontoons and left to find a vacant berth. The quays outside the basin are used by the fishermen, and dry 3 to 4·8 m.

3. In westerly weather there is a good temporary anchorage on the south-east side of **Ile Tomé**, 0·15 mile offshore in about 3·6 m, sand and shells. The island is precipitous and uninhabited.

Facilities

Water and electricity are laid on to the pontoons in the marina. A hose is needed otherwise by can. There are moorings laid in the northern part of the harbour and a fuelling pontoon is moored just north of the lock, which can supply petrol, diesel and Butagaz. There are reasonable shopping facilities, several hotels and restaurants, a launderette and a sub-post office at the port.

It is about a mile uphill to **Perros Guirec** town itself, which has all the facilities of a holiday resort. There is an interesting twelfth-century church.

21 Ploumanac'h

Tidal Data

Tidal Heights
High Water: approx −0105 St Helier, −0600 Dover, +0120 Brest.
Heights of Tide above Datum: approx MHWS 8·8 m, MLWS 0·9 m, MHWN 6·7 m, MLWN 3·0 m.
Mean Tide Level: 4·9 m. Index 9 A.

Tidal Streams

Between **Ile Rennat** and **Méan Ruz** the east-going stream begins −0435 Brest (+0035 Dover) and the west-going stream begins +0100 Brest (+0610 Dover). Both streams attain 2·8 knots at springs, but are much stronger to seaward towards **Les Sept Iles**.

General

The entrance to Ploumanac'h lies between dramatic looking rocks about 0·25 mile west of **Méan Ruz** lighthouse and leads to a beautiful almost land-locked bay, most of which dries out at low water springs. At neap tides anchorage can be found with about 1·8 m of water in the pool and 2 m south-east of the islet on which the château stands, with ample room to swing. There is a dredged pool off the lifeboat. This harbour is used principally by fishing boats, but is so remarkable in its rock formations that it is well worth visiting under suitable conditions.

Approaches

Make a position about 0·3 mile west of **Méan Ruz** lighthouse and the entrance will be seen clearly. It lies east of the little island of **Costaerès** on which stands a prominent château. The entrance is now clearly marked by conspicuous beacons, four Lateral port and two Lateral starboard. The beacons sometimes become broken.

The channel lies, first in a south-western direction and is deep, though narrow, until east of the château. It then begins to shoal and turn southwards and continues to be well marked, but soon dries and finally bends south-eastwards to the entrance of the inner harbour.

Anchorages

Calculation or estimate of the tide of the day is the first requirement in the choice of anchorages. Ploumanac'h is obviously unsuitable at spring tides, other than for craft

133

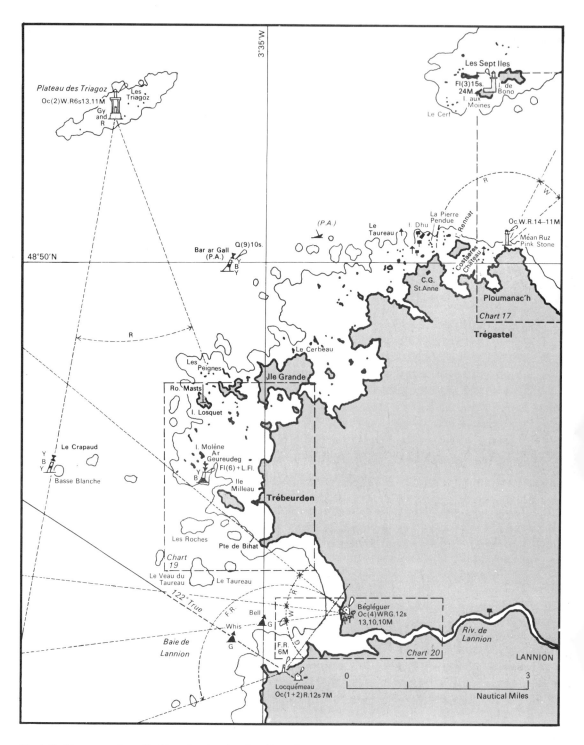

Chart 18. Ploumanac'h to Ile Grande, showing Les Sept Iles. *Based on French Chart No 967.*

Méan Ruz lighthouse and to the right of it the entrance to Ploumanac'h. The château to the right of the lighthouse is conspicuous and is situated on the small island of Costaerès which is on the starboard hand when entering.

The island and conspicuous château of Costaerès, with entrance of Ploumanac'h on left.

The entrance is clearly marked by beacons.

The entrance to the inner harbour.

135

which can take the bottom with legs, twin keels etc, or lie in the busy narrow channel at the entrance. At MLWN there is 3·0 m above datum giving depths of from 1·8 to 1·2 m in the channel about 0·1 mile SSE of **Costaerès**. There are many moorings for local craft hereabouts and soundings must be taken to find a berth on sand, allowing swinging room clear of rocky bottom. Other positions may be found nearer the inner entrance where there is a possible anchorage, which is recommended by the original author of this chapter, as suitable for a draft of 1·5 to 1·8 m on a 7·9 m tide at **St Helier**. Soundings must be taken all round to ensure swinging room. On such a tide there is 1·2 m just inside the inner entrance but too many moorings, although there is room for drying out on legs or twin keels.

Facilities

In the harbour there are the usual facilities for a small port (including marine engineers) and holiday resort. Since the channel has been marked there has been increased activity by speed craft. Good landing, shops, hotels and restaurants.

22 Les Sept Iles

Tidal Data

Tidal Heights
High Water: approx −0105 St Helier, −0600 Dover, +0120 Brest.
Heights of Tide above Datum: approx MHWS 8·8 m, MLWS 0·9 m, MHWN 6·7 m, MLWN 3·0 m.
Mean Tide Level: 4·9 m. Index 9 A.

Tidal Streams

1. 1 mile south-west of **Ile aux Moines** the SE-going stream begins at −0435 Brest (+0035 Dover) and the NW-going at +0130 Brest (−0545 Dover). Both streams reach 4·7 knots at springs.
2. Between the **Sept Iles** and **Plateau des Triagoz** the ENE-going stream begins at −0320 Brest (+0150 Dover) and the WSW-going at +0250 Brest (−0425 Dover). Both streams reach 3·8 knots at springs.
3. 1 mile southward of **Ile Rouzic** (the easternmost of **Les Sept Iles**) the SE-going stream begins at −0435 Brest (−0035 Dover) and the NW-going at +0130 Brest (−0545 Dover). Both streams reach 2·8 knots at springs.

General

The group consists of four principal islands (uninhabited except for the lighthouse keepers on **Ile aux Moines**), and many islets. There are many dangers and strong tidal streams within the group but there is no difficulty in entering the anchorage between **Ile de Bono** and **Ile aux Moines** under suitable conditions.

Approach

By Day   If approaching from the east, first make a position close southward of **Les Dervinis** Cardinal south buoy, which lies 115° True from **Ile aux Moines** lighthouse, distant 1·4 miles. Leaving this buoy close to starboard, with the lighthouse bearing 285° True, steer to make good 285° True. If approaching from the west, make an easterly course, passing about 0·5 mile to the south of **Le Cerf** and **Ile aux Moines**. When the gap between **Ile aux Moines** and **Ile de Bono** has opened, and the western end of **Ile de Bono** bears 350° True, alter course to make good 350° True. These directions clear the dangers shown on the chart but, as these are marked by reference to LAT

Les Sept Iles from the southward. On the left is Ile aux Moines with the old fort at the western end and the lighthouse near the eastern. To the right is Ile de Bono which is a bird sanctuary and uninhabited. The anchorage lies in the bay formed by the two islands.

they may in practice be ignored at most states of tide, e.g. at MLWN there will be a least depth of 3 m over them.

By Night   The narrow white sector of **Kerjean** light, bearing between 143·2° and 144° True and flanked by a red sector to the east and a green sector to the west, leads on a reciprocal course of between 323·2° and 324° True into the anchorage very close to the outer rock marked as drying zero metres and over the 0·3 m rock, but clear of the dangers to the east. With adequate tide, as in *By Day* above there should be no difficulty in approaching the anchorage, or in leaving it. The light on **Ile aux Moines** Fl (3) 15 s, also helps to pinpoint the anchorage.

Anchorage

The anchorage lies south-east of the gap between **Ile aux Moines** and **Ile de Bono** with **Ile aux Moines** lighthouse bearing about 270° True and the west end of **Ile de Bono** bearing about 360° True. There is a mooring buoy in the anchorage which is used by vedettes from the mainland and, in any case is not suitable for yachts. Anchor between the buoy and the landing slip, which has a beacon at its end. Do not go far directly northward of the buoy towards the strand between the two islands as there are two rocks which cover towards high water.

The anchorage is protected from the NNE and NE by **Ile de Bono** and from the W by **Ile aux Moines**. The strand of sand, stones and rocks which dry out between the two islands, break the seas from that direction, but the anchorage must be regarded as a fair weather one, as it is open to all southerly winds. The anchorage is frequently rather full of yachts in the daytime, particularly at week-ends. Land at the slip from which a road leads up to the lighthouse.

Facing NE from Ile aux Moines towards Ile de Bono near low water. The mooring is in the best position, but there is room to anchor between it and the landing slip.

Historical and Amenities

The only inhabitants of the islands are the lighthouse keepers on Ile aux Moines, although at one time the islands were a resort of corsairs. The old fort on the western side of Ile aux Moines was occupied until 1875, and is worth seeing. There are striking views from the fort over the islets, rocks and inlets of the sea. In the season many *vedettes* carry tourists to the island, when a *buvette* is opened on the terrace overlooking the anchorage. The neighbouring Ile de Bono is a bird sanctuary where landing is forbidden.

23 Trégastel

Tidal Data. See under Ploumanac'h.

General

This anchorage should not be confused with the seaside village of the same name near **Primel**. It is situated on the rocky coast about a mile west of **Ploumanac'h** and less than 3 miles south-west of the **Sept Iles**. **Trégastel** is worth visiting when cruising in these waters. Chart 18 does not show the entry or the harbour in any detail.

Approach

By Day only   Make a position 1·5 miles west of **Méan Ruz** lighthouse (see photograph page 135). Observe the prominent overhanging rock **la Pierre Pendue** (see photograph below) locally known as the '*dice*' rock. About 0·2 mile west of this rock is the low rocky **Ile Dhu** and **Le Taureau** a dangerous rock which dries 4·5 m LAT about 0·2 mile farther west. This is normally marked by a Cardinal north beacon but only the stump was standing in 1979. Its existence should not therefore be taken for granted.

    Le Taureau beacon, or its stump, should be identified by a stranger before attempting to enter, and approach for the first time is therefore easier at half-tide or below. Make a position about half-way between **Ile Dhu** and **Le Taureau** and note the prominent house

La Pierre Pendue (locally known as Dice Rock) is the most conspicuous feature near Trégastel. Picture taken from the entrance with remains of Ile Dhu Lateral port beacon to its left.

Trégastel. This is the prominent house which should be steered for between 165° and 170° True. Anchor on this line, with more water to the west and quickly shoaling water to the eastward.

ashore, which is shown in the photograph (not to be confused with the rather similar house near **Méan Ruz** lighthouse). Bring this house to bear between 165° and 170° True. Steer to make good this course allowing for any cross current. Then leave:

> **Le Taureau** Cardinal north beacon (if existing) 0·125 mile to starboard.
> **Ile Dhu** Lateral port beacon 0·125 mile to port.
> **Second** Lateral port beacon 100 m to port.
> **First** Lateral starboard beacon 50 m to starboard.
> **Third** Lateral port beacon 50 m to port.

Anchorage

Many white mooring buoys have been laid and space for anchoring may be difficult to find. Many moorings are occupied by local boats. There is a greater depth to the north-west and less to the eastwards, and soundings should be taken. The anchorage is better sheltered than appears on the chart, from east through south to south-west. As at Port Blanc and Primel there is often a swell if the wind is from a northerly quarter and the anchorage would be dangerous in strong onshore winds. There are no leading lights to facilitate departure at night.

Facilities

Land by dinghy on the sands. There are hotels and restaurants on the front but no shops. Baths can be had (not cheaply) at the Grand Hôtel de la Mer, which has an obliging management who serve excellent meals at a reasonable price. The town of St Anne is nearly half a mile inland, where there are a post office, garage and shops. Trégastel itself is about a mile farther inland. The bay is a very pretty little seaside resort, with bathing huts facing wide sands and is almost landlocked at low water. This could be a good place for the family cruising man, provided he is ready to clear out if there is a threat of inclement weather.

24 Trébeurden and Ile Grande

Tidal Data

Tidal Heights
High Water: approx +0110 Brest, +0620 Dover.
Heights of Tide above Datum: approx MHWS 8·8 m, MLWS 1·2 m, MHWN 7·0 m, MLWN 5·7 m.
Mean Tide Level: 5·1 m. Index 9 B.

Tidal Streams

1. North-east of **Ile Losquet** the ENE-going stream begins at −0335 Brest (+0135 Dover) and the WSW-going stream at +0230 Brest (−0445 Dover). Both streams attaining 3·8 knots at springs.
2. 0·5 mile south-west of **Ile Losquet** the north-going stream begins at −0355 Brest (+0115 Dover) and the south-going begins +0200 Brest (−0515 Dover). Spring rate about 2 knots.
3. At **Basse Blanche** (**Le Crapaud**) buoy the south-east to east-going stream begins at −0405 Brest (+0105 Dover) and the south-west to west-going stream at +0220 Brest (−0455 Dover). Both streams reach 2 knots at springs.

General

Trébeurden and Ile Grande are rarely visited by British yachts, but they deserve more attention as Trébeurden has one of the few deep-water and readily accessible anchorages on this part of the coast and leads to a delightful neap tide anchorage off Ile Grande. French Chart 6056 is desirable.

Trébeurden is situated to the east of the prominent Ile Milliau on the northern entrance of the bay of Lannion and is 1·5 miles south of the tall radio mast on Ile Losquet, which is the most conspicuous feature for miles on this coast and is illuminated at night with eight pairs of red lights.

Approaches: *By Day Only*

Southern Approach: Chenal de Toull ar Men Melen

This is a deep water channel but there are two rocks awash at chart Datum less than 0·5 mile northward of the approach, and rocks to the southward as shown on the chart.

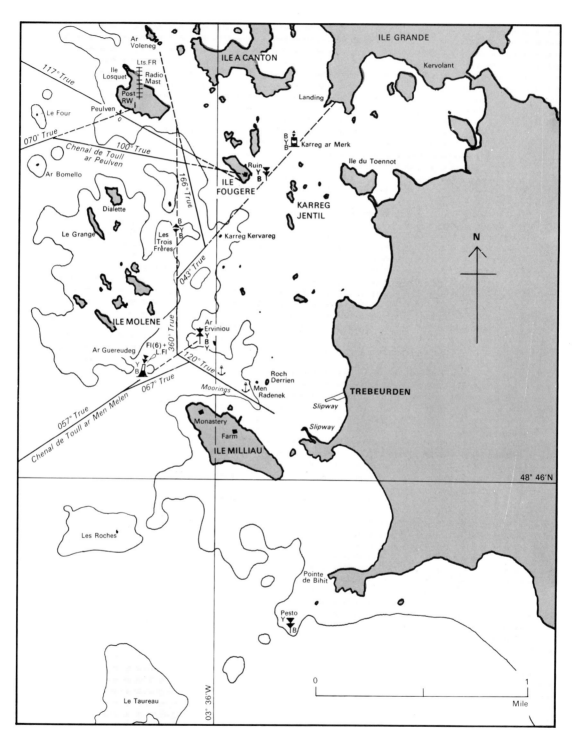

117° True

Ar Voleneg

ILE A CANTON

ILE GRANDE

Kervolant

Ile Losquet

Lts.FR

Radio Mast

070° True

Le Four

Peulven

Post RW

Landing

100° True

B
Y
B

Karreg ar Merk

Chenal de Toull ar Peulven

166° True

Ar Bomello

Ruin
Y
B

ILE FOUGERE

Ile du Toennot

Dialette

KARREG JENTIL

Le Grange

B
Y
B

Les Trois Frères

Karreg Kervareg

043° True

360° True

ILE MOLENE

Ar Erviniou
Y
B
Y

Ar Guereudeg

Fl(6)
L.Fl

Y
B

120° True

Moorings

Roch Derrien

067° True

Men Radenek

TREBEURDEN

057° True

Slipway

Chenal de Toull ar Men Melen

Monastery

Slipway

Farm

ILE MILLIAU

48° 46′N

N

Les Roches

Pointe de Bihit

03° 36′W

Pesto
Y
B

Le Taureau

0   1

Mile

Chart 19. Trébeurden and Ile Grande. *Based on French Chart No 6065.*

Make a position 1·25 miles south of **Basse Blanche** Cardinal west spar buoy, marking the end of **Le Crapaud** shoals. Identify the conspicuous **Ile Milliau** some 3 miles away, bearing about 075° True. Make good a course of 070° True. When about a mile off the island the **Ar Geureudeg** Cardinal south buoy will clearly be seen about 0·3 mile north-west of the island. Bring this in line with the Cardinal west beacon on **Ar Erviniou** bearing 057° True. If bound for **Trébeurden** anchorage steer for the point north of Trébeurden bearing 067° True, and when 0·1 mile from **Erviniou** beacon, alter course to make good 120° True into the anchorage. If bound north, alter course so as to leave **Ar Erviniou** beacon 0·1 mile to starboard when **Les Trois Frères** Cardinal east beacon, north-east of **Ile Molène** will be in line with the eastern edge of **Ile Losquet** bearing 360° True. Follow this line for about 0·3 mile until **Karreg Jentil** Cardinal south beacon and **Karreg ar Merk** Cardinal east beacon tower are in line bearing 043° True. If the tide serves this line can be followed to the **Ile Grande** anchorage, but it passes 20 m to the north-west of **Karreg Kervareg** a rock which dries 2·4 m LAT.

If bound for the northern entrance, follow this transit for 0·2 mile when **Ar Voleneg** island will just be appearing beyond the eastern edge of **Ile Losquet** bearing 346° True then alter course to follow this transit, to join the lines· directed for *Northern approach* below.

Northern approach: (1) Chenal de Toull ar Peulven (2) By Day Only

The outer approach may be made with **Les Triagoz** lighthouse bearing 360° True. When Ile Losquet (with radio mast) bears 125°

Ar Peulven, the conspicuous rock which must be left very close to port when using the northern Ile Losquet approach to Ile Grande.

Ile Milliau is yellow and has two humps. It looks like a headland. Steer between it and Ar Geureudeg Cardinal south buoy which is left to port.

True, identify the following marks: **Ar Peulven** a very conspicuous rock 8·8 m above datum (situated to the south-west of the radio mast) and **Ile Fougère** (see position on chart).

(1) Chenal de Toull ar Peulven

Steer with the southern tip of **Ile Fougère** just open of **Ar Peulven** at 117° True, leaving **Le Four** (dries 3·6 m LAT) about 300 m to starboard. This approach is deep but, when off **Ar Peulven** keep close to this rock as there is a drying shoal 2·4 m LAT only about 50 m SSE of it which must be left to starboard. When **Ar Voleneg** appears beyond the eastern edge of **Ile Losquet** bearing 347° True alter course to make good the reciprocal 167° True and proceed as for *Southern approach* above in reverse.

Alternatively, if the tide serves and if bound for the **Ile Grande** anchorage alter to leave **Ile Fougère** 150 m to port and join the leading line for **Ile Grande**.

(2) By Day Only

Using French Chart 6056, one can leave this channel near LW when **Le Four** and **Ar Bomello** are showing, by bringing the summit of **Ile Fougère** on a stern bearing of 100° True and steering 280° True for the gap between them, then when **Ar Peulven** (which is painted white towards the south-west) bears 070° True in line with the highest part of the cliff, and a red and white post to the right of the mast, follow this line until clear of the dangers.

Ile Grande. Inner Approach

The inner approach to **Ile Grande** is not difficult, when there is sufficient height of tide and provides an interesting and reasonably sheltered anchorage at neap tides.

The line of approach is the stone pier landing at **Ile Grande** on with **Karreg ar Merk** Cardinal east beacon tower at 038° True. The landing is difficult to pick up but there are two cottages with painted gable ends, which coincide with the line. The line leaves **Karreg Jentil** Cardinal south beacon about 50 m to port. On close approach alter course to leave **Karreg ar Merk** Cardinal east beacon tower about 50 m to starboard.

Anchorages

(a) *Trébeurden.* Anchor with the north-west edge of Ile Milliau bearing about 250° True and **Ar Erviniou** beacon about 330° True or between the north of the island and **Roch Derrien**, which is a conspicuous above-water rock, in over 2·2 m LAT or between the landing slip on the island and **Roch Derrien** in 1·4 m LAT. The farther south-eastwards the better the shelter and, at neaps, it is possible to anchor east of the slip with the aid of soundings. Several white mooring buoys have been laid in this area, which appear to be available to visitors, and which may restrict the room to anchor. This anchorage is very uncomfortable at HW springs with winds W-SW for about two hours either side. There is a heavy swell from the NW.

(b) *Ile Grande.* On a neap tide when the height of HW Brest is 6·1 m there is 1·5 m at MLWN between **Karreg Jentil** beacon and **Karreg ar Merk** beacon tower and 1·8 m close south of **Karreg Jentil** beacon. These positions are sheltered except when the wind is from the SW between **Ile Molène** and **Ile Milliau**, or if there is a swell from that direction. Usually the anchorage is very sheltered as in this area, in a south-westerly weather system, the wind seems to blow from the W or WNW. As swell is most commonly experienced from the NW, the anchorage is comparatively free from swell, being sheltered by islands from this direction. At

The anchorage between Ile Milliau and Trébeurden foreshore.

Ile Moléne (not to be confused with the island of the same name near Ushant) is to the north of Ile Milliau and affords one of the many anchorages near sandy shores in the neighbourhood of Trébeurden and Ile Grande. In the background is the radio mast on Ile Losquet which is the most conspicuous feature on the coast between Les Sept Iles and Lannion.

HW, anchorage is good right up to the pier and boats which can take the ground may do so almost anywhere.

Facilities

There is a landing slip on Ile Milliau (presumably private) and landing by dinghy for Trébeurden is at a slip on the waterfront, which dries near low water. There are many hotels and restaurants ashore and good shopping facilities. It is a centre for small yachts and dinghies and has a sailing school. There are good beaches, in particular at Ile Molène and in settled weather is an ideal harbour for the cruising man with a young family. If the large-scale French Chart No 6056 is carried there are opportunities to explore the neighbouring islands, as well as the HW anchorage at Ile Grande.

At Kervolant, the village on Ile Grande, there are good shops and restaurants. Petrol can be obtained at a garage at Kervolant. Water may be had at the camping site to the north of a cemetery near the landing, or from a tap at the head of the slip.

25 Lannion

Tidal Data

Tidal Heights
High Water: approx +0110 Brest, +0620 Dover.
Heights of Tide above Datum: approx MHWS 8·8 m, MLWS 1·2 m, MHWN 6·7 m, MLWN 3·3 m.
Mean Tide Level: 5·1 m. Index 9 B.

Tidal Streams

1. For approaches see under Trébeurden and Primel.
2. Within the Baie de Lannion the streams are weak, attaining only one knot at spring tides and are variable in direction.

General

The Port of a large town 4 miles from the open sea on the Rivière de Lannion, alias Le Guer, which is narrow and twisting and dries for almost its entire length. With a strong wind between NW and WNW, the sea is liable to break across the entrance, which is then impassable, even at high water. No doubt a large westerly swell makes the bar equally dangerous, especially on the ebb, but the entrance is partly or wholly protected from winds from other directions. The reason why the river is so little used by deep-keeled yachts is that, although there are now deep pools in which to anchor, access to them is tidal and it is off the beaten track from Roscoff to Perros, also the navigation is described as difficult and requiring local knowledge. It is, however, not

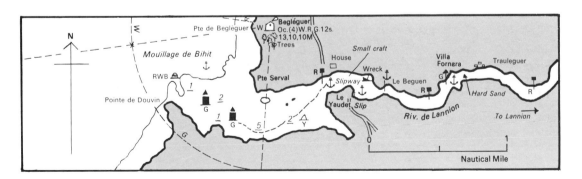

Chart 20. Lannion River. *Based on French Chart No 5950.*

149

Bégléguer lighthouse at the entrance of Lannion River is shown here on the left of the highest clump of trees, but is easy to confuse with other white buildings.

as difficult as reputed, and the river is exceptionally pretty. Lannion itself is a pleasant country town. The channel of the river is marked by beacons and dries 4·8 m at Lannion. As a result of dredging for sand, there are now an increasing number of deep pools in which yachts can anchor, even at spring tides.

Approach

By Day Make a position from which **La Basse Blanche (le Crapaud)** Cardinal west pillar buoy bears 360° True distant 2 miles. From here steer so as to being **Bégléguer** lighthouse (a conspicuous white house, see photograph) on a bearing of 095° True, and then make this good as the course. This leaves:

Le Taureau rocks about 0·3 mile to port.

Baie de Lannion Lateral starboard whistle buoy 0·5 mile to starboard.

Kinierbel Lateral starboard bell buoy 0·25 mile to starboard

The entrance of Lannion River and the two Lateral starboard beacon towers to be left on the starboard hand.

The first Lateral port beacon and the riverside house on which side the channel lies in the bend in the river.

There was formerly a beacon on **Kinierbel** rocks but this has not been replaced. When the second Lateral starboard beacon tower in the estuary has opened from the first, course can be altered for the river entrance passing, on either side, the (in 1979) spherical red white and black buoy marking the river entrance. The bar, which dries 0·2 m LAT lies north of **Pointe de Dourvin**, and in the absence of swell, is protected from NE through E to S.

Leave the first beacon tower 150 m to starboard and the second close to starboard, then keeping the beacons in line astern, sail to within 100 m of the south bank. Then take a curving gradual sweep to port, and heading for the Lateral port beacon shown on the chart on the north bank opposite the headland. What appears like an islet (but according to the French chart is a rock which covers) is left about a cable to port. After the beacon is passed, the channel leads close to the house on the north shore and then gradually back to the south shore off **Le Yaudet** where small local boats dry out. Here the river is extremely pretty and the best water farther upstream is found in the bights on the opposite side of the river to the headlands. In the reach 0·5 mile beyond **Le Yaudet** there is a Lateral starboard beacon at the bend (see Chart) where the channel lies on the north

151

Sand dredger at work off Le Yaudet where there is an excellent and unspoilt anchorage.
Beware of steel mooring wires of the dredgers which stretch far.

side. There are occasional beacons farther upstream. The approximate positions, especially of the Lateral port beacons, is shown on Chart No 20. The river is spanned by overhead cables in a reach west of **Loguivy**, these are stretched between pylons high on each side of the river, but sag in the middle. The **ligne d'Aval**, which carries electricity to the **Radome** is stated to be 36·6 m above highest water and the **Ligne d'Amont**, near **Loguivy**, is 34·7 m above.

In the upper reaches the river is narrow and partially canalised. There are a few Lateral starboard beacons. The first quays to be reached are used by barges and a new bridge has been constructed near the quay which was formerly most convenient for visiting yachts, making it now necessary to berth at the quays farther downstream. A yacht of 1·8 m draught will take the bottom about 2 hours after HW.

The river bottom is said to be mud and rocks and thus, in places, it would be dangerous to dry out, if a yacht is accidentally grounded on the ebb.

By Night   Approach from the north or north-west by keeping to the west of the red sector of **Les Triagoz** Oc (2) WR 6s bearing between 010° and 020° True. Then pick up the leading lights for **Locquémeau**: *rear light* Oc (1+2) R 12 s vis 7 miles and *front light* Fixed R vis 6 miles bearing 122° True. Steer to follow this line which leaves **Le Crapaud** and associated dangers about 0·5 mile on the port hand. When **Bégléguer** light, Oc (4) WRG 12 s, changes from red to white alter course and steer towards it in the white sector, which leads into the outer anchorage.

Anchorages

1. Outside, with the wind from N through E to SSW, there is sheltered anchorage in the bay immediately north of the river mouth, known as the **mouillage de Bihit**.
2. A yacht can take the ground at **Le Yaudet** against the outer part of the quay, where it dries about 2·1 m LAT.
3. For several years now the bed of the river has been dredged for sand, leaving deep pools suitable for anchorage. The approximate positions of some are marked on the accompanying chart, viz: (a) near the riverside house off the north shore beyond the first Lateral port beacon in 2·7 m least water; (b) in a pool east of **Le Yaudet** in 1·2 m least water; (c) in a large pool 200 m by 100 m situated 0·25 mile east of **Le Yaudet** just beyond the headland on the north bank near **Le Beguen** in the middle of the river in 2·7 m least water; (d) a small pool with 1·8 m to 4·8 m on the north of the river, just beyond the Lateral starboard beacon before reaching **villa Fornara**. There is a bank of hard sand and a slip on the south of the river, as indicated on the chart, where yachts with legs or twin keels can dry out. Do not dry out alongside the slip as the bottom is rock and mud. The positions of the anchorages can be found by soundings but, as they are in the nature of pools, it is better to obtain local advice from the skippers of the sand dredgers, who know where the bottom has been dredged as, in some parts, the bed of the river is rocky and the streams are strong. The anchorages near **Le Yaudet** are now excellent as they are not far from the entrance and the river is beautiful.

Facilities

Lannion is a large town with banks, good shops, restaurants and other facilities. The restaurant **Relais de Bretagne** is well spoken of. Petrol and oil from garage near the quay, and water at a hydrant. Customs office. Yacht Club. Branch line station. Airport and buses.

    Le Yaudet. Land at the slip and walk up the steep hill to small shops (open in mornings) and two good restaurants. Picturesque little church with a curious statue of the Virgin Mary in bed with the infant Jesus.

TOULL AN HERY AND LOCQUIREC

Toull an Héry is a small drying harbour on the east bank of the Douron river, a mile from the open sea. The channel leading to it is encumbered with shifting sandbanks and the berths alongside the jetty dry 4·8 m.

Locquirec is a small drying harbour on the west side of the entrance to the same river. The berths alongside the jetty dry from 4·5 m to 6·1 m LAT, and there is considerable surf in the harbour with the wind in the exposed quarter.

The **Anse de Locquirec** lies about 0·5 mile east of Locquirec, and affords anchorage in 2·7 m and upwards, sand, sheltered from west through south to south-east.

26 Primel

Tidal Data

Tidal Heights
High Water: approx +0105 Brest, +0620 Dover.
Heights of Tide above Datum: approx MHWS 8·5 m, MLWS 1·2 m, MHWN 6·7 m, MLWN 3·0 m.
Mean Tide Level: 4·9 m. Index 8 B.

Tidal Streams

1. About 6 miles north of **Primel** the east-going stream begins at −0300 Brest (+0210 Dover), and the west-going at +0315 Brest (−0400 Dover). The greatest rate of the east-going is attained at about HW Brest and of the west-going at LW Brest, both reaching 2·25 knots at springs; about 1·0 knot at neaps.
2. For streams to the westward off **Plateau des Duons**, see under *Morlaix*.
3. A local eddy runs inshore between **Pointe de Primel** and **Roches Jaunes** (1·5 miles to the westward) during the greater part of the east-going stream in the offing. The eddy north-east-going (2 knots at springs) begins at −0450 Brest (+0020 Dover) and south-west-going (2·5 knots at springs) begins at −0220 Brest (+0250 Dover).

General

The **Anse de Primel** is a small natural harbour, which has been improved by the construction of a breakwater and quay.

The entrance itself is easily identified and is fairly simple to enter by day or night. In the offing however there are dangers:

Les Trépieds: drying rocks about 2·5 miles to the north, about 0·75 mile to the

The Pointe de Primel is easily identified by its shape. Here it is seen when approaching from the eastward.

east of the leading line, and extending – as the Plateau de la Meloine – 4·5 miles to the north-east.

Les Chaises de Primel: drying rocks which extend for about 2·5 miles from Pointe de Primel to the north-east.

Les Roches Jaunes: which extend for about 2 miles to the south-west.

At high water it is exposed to winds from NW to N by E, and might be dangerous in heavy weather from this quarter, when the sea is said to break right across the entrance, and no attempt should be made to enter. Conversely, any yacht using the anchorage should be prepared to leave on the approach of bad weather from the northward. It is uncomfortable if there is any north-west or northerly swell, except possibly under the lee of the new breakwater.

Approaches

By Day   First identify the prominent **Pointe de Primel**, and then make a position from which this point bears 120° True, distant 0·5 mile.

The picture is taken from the land on the SW side of the entrance facing NE towards Pointe de Primel. The yacht entering is leaving Le Zamègues on her starboard hand.

pointe de Primel

Primel. The leading marks for Primel at 151° True. They are the three white beacons, two with red centre lines, above the white gable and chimney of Repredou farm house. The

From here bring the leading marks in line at 151° True. These are:
1. The lowest is the white chimney of **Réprédou Farm**.
2. The white support of the front leading light, elevation 35 m.
3. White wall mark with red vertical line.
4. White wall mark with red vertical line and rear light, elevation 56 m.

Follow this line very closely, noting that the submerged dangers lie to port, and leave the following marks on the sides shown:

    Les Zamègues, a prominent rock with a green and white patch, 30 m to starboard.

    Cam Lateral port beacon 30 m to port.

    Raoul Lateral starboard beacon 15 m to starboard.

By Night   Approaching from the east or west, keep on the line of the edge of the green and white sectors of **Men-Guen Bras** Q WRG at 257° True, until the **Primel** leading lights, both fixed red, are in line bearing 151° True. This point is slightly east of the intersection of this edge-line and the leading line for the **Chenal de Tréguier**, **Morlaix**. The front **Primel** light has an arc of 34° from 134° to 168° True. See Chart No 23.

Approaching from the north, keep between the two **Morlaix** leading lines (*Grand Chenal* and *Chenal de Tréguier*), until the **Primel** lights are picked up or, failing this, until **Men Guen Bras** Q changes from white to green, showing that course may be altered to the eastward along this line to pick up the **Primel** lights.

When the Primel lights are in line, bearing 151° True, alter course to follow this line right through the entrance, leaving to starboard the light Fl G 4 s at the end of the breakwater.

picture is taken about half flood. Le Zamègues is left close on the starboard hand and the channel narrows between beacons marking extensive below-water rocks on either hand.

Anchorages

Inside the harbour, the S-shaped pool trends, first slightly to the west of the leading line, then well to the east of it, round **Roch-an-Trez-Bras** Lateral starboard beacon. When the depth of water permits a yacht may proceed farther up the harbour, following the line given by the stern transit **Roch-an-Tres-Bras** beacon in line with the western edge of **Pointe de Primel**. The following positions are available:

1. Moored with two anchors in the dredged area about 50 m wide between the elbow in the breakwater and the outer end, in depths of between 0 and +1 m LAT (about 1·2 to 2·1 m MLWS and 3·0 to 3·9 m MLWN).
2. Secure alongside the breakwater at the outermost of the two projections on the inner face near the light. The innermost elbow is used by fishing boats. Do not attempt to go alongside between the projections as this part dries and there are rocks and boulders on the bottom.
3. On the leading line off the breakwater in about 9 m MLWS.
4. 100 m SE of the **Roch-an-Tres-Bras** beacon in about 1·5 m MLWS.
5. 120 m NE of the **Roch-an-Tres-Bras** beacon in about 3·0 m MLWS but this is not recommended locally.

The last three positions are all exposed to northerly winds. Swinging room is rather restricted and it is advisable to moor if conditions call for a full scope of chain.

Facilities

Landing at the slip on the breakwater, at the small slip by the *plage de Primel*, on the rocks to the west of the leading line, and at the landing slip at Le Diben on the west side of the harbour. There are a few shops and hotels at Primel and Le Diben.

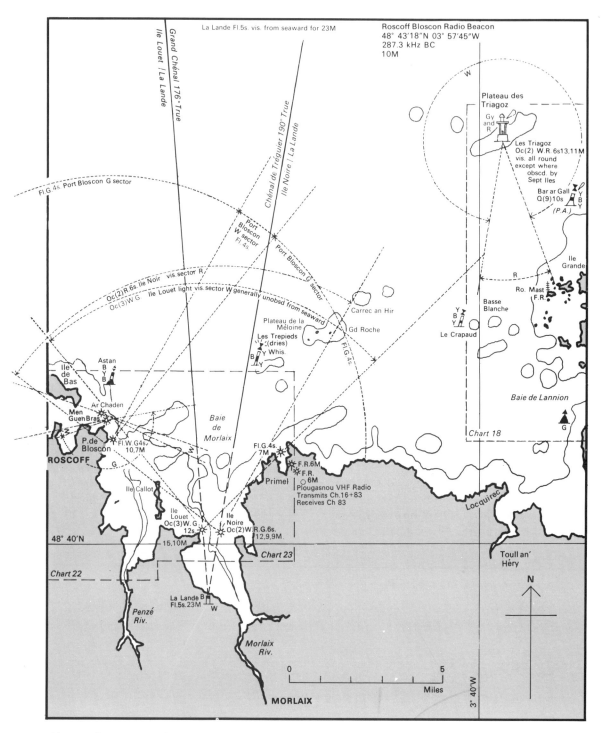

La Lande Fl.5s. vis. from seaward for 23M

Roscoff Bloscon Radio Beacon
48° 43′18″N 03° 57′45″W
287.3 kHz BC
10M

Grand Chénal 176° True

Ile Louet / La Lande

Chénal de Tréguier 190° True

Ile Noire / La Lande

W

Plateau des
Triagoz

Gy
and
R

Les Triagoz
Oc(2) W.R. 6s13,11M
vis. all round
except where
obscd. by
Sept Iles

Bar ar Gall
Q(9)10s
(P.A.)

Y
B
Y

Fl.G.4s. Port Bloscon G sector

Port
Bloscon
W
sector
Fl. 4s.

Port Bloscon G sector

Ile
Grande

R

Ro. Mast
F.R.

Oc(2) R.6s. Ile Noir vis. sector R

Oc(3) W.G. Ile Louet light vis. sector W generally unobsd from seaward

Carrec an Hir

Gd Roche

Le Crapaud

Y
B
Y

Basse
Blanche

Plateau de la
Méloine

Les Trepieds
(dries)

B
Y

Y Whis.

Fl.G.4s.

Astan
B
Y
B

Ile
de
Bas

Ar Chaden

Baie
de
Morlaix

Baie de Lannion

Men
GuenBras

Chart 18

P.de
Bloscon

Fl.W.G4s.
10,7M

Fl.G.4s.
7M

G

F.R.6M
F.R.
6M

ROSCOFF

Plougasnou VHF Radio
Transmits Ch.16+83
Receives Ch 83

G

Ile Callot

Primel

Locquirec

48° 40′N

Ile
Louet
Oc(3)W.G.
12s
15,10M

Ile
Noire
Oc(2)W.R.G.6s.
12,9,9M.

Toull an′
Héry

Chart 23

N

Chart 22

Penzé
Riv.

La Lande B
Fl.5s.23M
W

Morlaix
Riv.

0   5

Miles

3° 40′W

MORLAIX

Chart 21. Outer approaches to Morlaix. *Based on Admiralty Chart No 2644.*

27 Bay of Morlaix, Morlaix and Penzé Rivers

Tidal Data

Tidal Heights
High Water (Baie de Morlaix): approx +0105 Brest, +0610 Dover.
Heights of Tide above Datum: approx MHWS 8·8 m, MLWS 1·2 m, MHWN 6·7 m, MLWN 3·3 m.
Mean Tide Level: 5 m. Index 8 B.

Tidal Streams

1. North of **Roches Duon** the east-going stream begin −0505 Brest (+0005 Dover) gradually changing clockwise to end +0050 Brest (+0600 Dover) when running SSE. The SSW-going stream begins at +0140 Brest (−0535 Dover) changing clockwise through west and ending NNW at −0535 Brest (−0025 Dover). The SE-going and NW-going streams attain 2·75 knots at springs.

2. In the **Grand Chenal** and **Chenal de Tréguier** the in-going stream begins about −0450 Brest (+0020 Dover) and the outgoing stream about +0105 Brest (−0610 Dover). The spring rates in the **Grand Chenal** are about 2·5 knots and in the **Chenal de Tréguier** about 2 knots.

3. In the **rade de Morlaix** the streams are weak and variable attaining about 1 knot at springs. The ingoing stream begins about −0430 Brest (+0040 Dover) and the outgoing +0200 Brest (−0515 Dover).

4. In the **Rivière de Morlaix** to 0·5 mile above **Locquénolé** the rate of the ingoing stream does not exceed 2 knots and in the canalised part of the river the stream nearly always runs northward.

5. In the **Penzé River** the ingoing stream begins about −0450 Brest (+0020 Dover) and the outgoing stream about +0105 Brest (−0610 Dover). In the river the spring rate does not exceed 2·5 knots.

6. For **Chenal de l'Ile de Bas** see under **Roscoff**.

General

The Morlaix and Penzé rivers flow into the Baie de Morlaix which is about 6 miles wide, between (on the east) Pointe de Primel and (on the west) Roscoff and the eastern entrance to the Ile de Bas channel. A vessel approaching from the north has to pass through a 2·5 mile wide gap between **Les Trépieds** Cardinal west spar whistle buoy, marking the western end of the **Plateau de la Meloine** and **Le Pot de Fer** Cardinal east spar bell buoy, marking the eastern end of the **Plateau des Duons**. Both the outer lit channels pass through this gap, as does also the leading line for Primel already mentioned. Approach on a clear night presents no difficulty

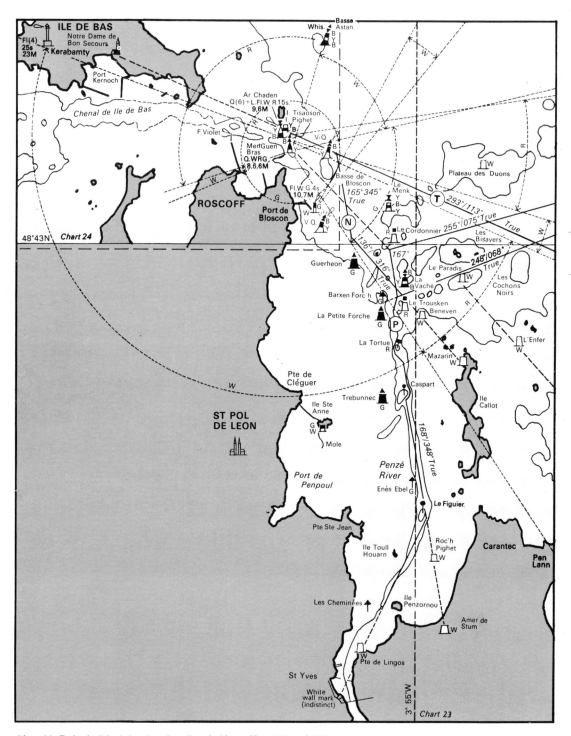

ILE DE BAS

Fl(4)
25s
23M
Kerabamty

Notre Dame de
Bon Secours

Port
Kernoch

Chenal de Ile de Bas

F. Violet

Ar Chaden
Q(6) + L.Fl.W R15s
9,6M

I. Tisabson
Pighet

V.Q

MerfGuen
Bras
Q.WRG
8,6,6M

Whis.
Basse
Astan
B
Y
B

Plateau des Duons
W

ROSCOFF

Port de
Bloscon

Fl.W G.4s
10,7M

W
G

V.Q
B
Y

Basse de
Bloscon
165°345°
True

Le
Menk
B
Y
Y

ⓉＴ
293°/113°
True

Le Cordonnier *255°/075°True*

136°

Ⓝ

167°

Les
Bisayers

248°/068°
True

48°43N   *Chart 24*

Guerheon
G

316°
True

Le Paradis
W

Les
Cochons
Noirs

Barxen Forc'h
G

La
B.Vache

Le Trousken
Beneven
R

La Petite Forche
G

ⓅＰ

W

L'Enfer
W

La Tortue
R

Mazarin
W

Ile Callot

Pte de
Cléguer

ST POL
DE LEON

Ile Ste
Anne
G
W

Mole

Trebunnec
G

Caspart

168°/348°True

Port de
Penpoul

Penzé
River

Enès Ebel G

Le Figuier

Pte Ste Jean

Ile Toull
Houarn

Roc'h
Pighet
W

Carantec

Pen
Lann

Les Cheminées

Ile
Penzornou

Amer de
Stum
W

St Yves

White
wall mark
(indistinct)

W
Pte de Lingos

3° 55'W   *Chart 23*

Chart 22. Baie de Morlaix. *Based on French Charts Nos 5950 and 5827.*

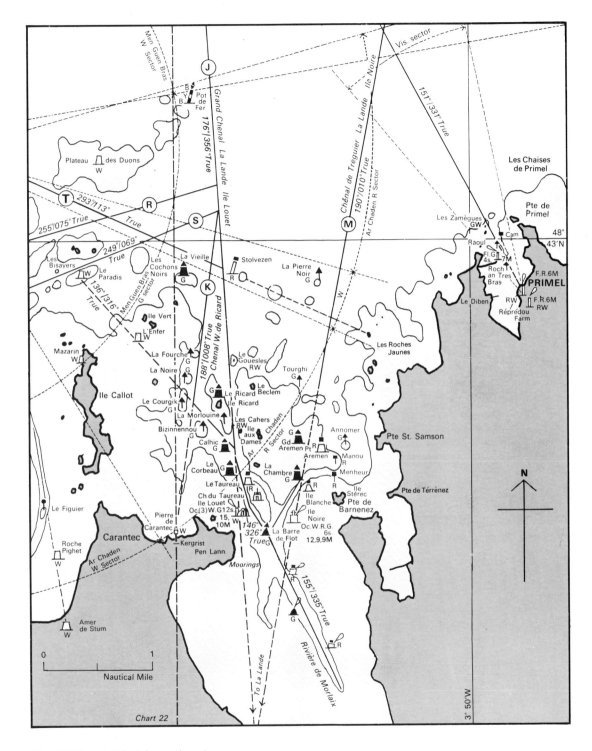

J

Men Guen Bras W Sector

Pot de Fer
B

Plateau des Duons
W

T 293°/113° True
R
255°/075° True
S
249°/069° True
Les Bisayers
Le Paradis W
136°/316° True
Men Guen Bras G sector
Les Cochons Noirs
La Vieille
G
Stolvezen R
La Pierre Noir G

Grand Chenal La Lande Ile Louet
176°/356° True

Chénal de Treguier La Lande Ile Noire
190°/010° True
Ar Chaden R Sector
Vis. sector
151°/331° True

Les Chaises de Primel

Pte de Primel

Les Zamègues GW
Raoul
Cam
48° 43'N

Fl.G. 4s 7M
Roch an Tres Bras
F.R.6M
PRIMEL
Le Diben RW
F.R.6M RW
Réprédou Farm

Ile Vert
L'Enfer W
Mazarin W
La Fourche G
La Noire G
Le Courgik G
La Morlouine G
Bizinnennou G
Calhic G
Le Corbeau G

Chenal W.de Ricard
188°/008° True

Le Gouesles RW
Le Beclem
Le Ricard Ile Ricard

Les Cahers RW
Ile aux Dames
Ar Chaden R Sector

Tourghi G

Les Roches Jaunes

Pte St. Samson

Ile Callot

Le Figuier

Roche Pighet W

Carantec

Pierre de Carantec W

Kergrist Pen Lann

Amer de Stum W

Ar Chaden W Sector

Le Taureau
Ch du Taureau
Ile Louet
Oc.(3) W.G12s. 15, 10M

146° 326° True G

La Chambre G

Annomer G

Gd Aremen G
Pt Aremen R
Manou R
Menheur R
Ile Stérec
Pte de Térrénez

Ile Blanche R
Ile Noire
Oc.W.R.G. 6s. 12,9,9M

Pte de Barnenez

La Barre de Flot G

Moorings

155°/335° True

To La Lande

Rivière de Morlaix

G

R

N

0   1
Nautical Mile

Chart 22

3° 50'W

Chart 23. Baie de Morlaix continued.

163

Château du Taureau
Les Cahers

Corbeau Black Beacon

Ile Louet Lighthouse

The beacons marked as Black have now been changed to Green.

Grand Chenal. After approaching on the leading marks of Ile Louet lighthouse and Tour de la Lande at 177° True, quit the leading line when Calhic Lateral starboard beacon bears WNW. Steer to leave Taureau Lateral port beacon tower and Château du Taureau (on left of picture) to port and Corbeau Lateral starboard beacon Tower and Ile Louet (in the centre of picture) to starboard.

but in poor visibility, a vessel with DF facilities, would be better advised to home on **Port Bloscon** Radiobeacon – BC 287.3 kHz, on a course of about 230° True. This is clear of the tanker track to and from Roscoff, one mile wide, running 202°–022° True from the breakwater light. This is about ten miles long, which is the nominal range of the beacon, and is marked on the French Chart *Navigation Reglémentée*. Approach can then be made as if coming from the Chenal de l'Ile de Bas.

Approaches

Grand Chenal: To Morlaix River

By Day The principal entrance to the Baie de Morlaix is the Grand Chenal due north of Pen Lann. This provides two alternative routes to La Rivière de Morlaix and access to the Penzé river. Navigate so as to

Ricard Black Beacon

Calhic Black Beacon

Photo Robinson

pass 0·2 mile east of the **Pot de Fer** Cardinal east spar bell buoy.
This buoy lies about a mile NE of the **Roches Duon** white beacon
tower, 9·7 m high. From here follow the leading line: **Ile Louet**
lighthouse in line with **Tour de la Lande** (see view) (line **J**). This
line leaves the following marks on the sides shown:

    Stolvezen Lateral port spindle buoy 0·1 mile to port.

    La Vieille Lateral starboard beacon tower 0·4 mile to starboard.

    La Fourche Lateral starboard beacon 0·3 mile to starboard.

    Le Gousles a rock painted white and red 0·1 mile to port.

    Le Ricard Lateral starboard beacon tower 55 m to starboard.

    La Morlouine Lateral starboard beacon 45 m to starboard.

    Les Cahers a rock painted white and red 0·1 mile to port.

    Calhic Lateral starboard beacon tower 0·15 mile to starboard.
When **Calhic** tower bears about 290° True, quit the leading line
and steer so as to leave:

    Le Corbeau Lateral starboard beacon tower 100 m to starboard
and

    Le Taureau Lateral port beacon tower 100 m to port.
Then midway between **Ile Louet** and the **Château du Taureau**

165

and from here proceed into the river. Towards LWS it will be necessary to avoid **La Barre de Flot**, a rocky shoal 0·3 mile SE of **Ile Louet**. The NE corner of this shoal is awash at datum, and is marked on its NE side by the Rade de Morlaix No 1 Lateral starboard buoy, which should be left to starboard when proceeding up the river, or well to port if proceeding to **Pen Lann** anchorage. See page 180.

Grand Chenal and Chenal Ouest de Ricard: To Morlaix River

By Day Proceed as for **Grand Chenal**, passing 0·2 mile east of **Pot de Fer** Cardinal east spar bell buoy and following the leading line **Ile Louet-Tour de la Lande** (line **J**) for a farther mile, when in the bay to the west of **Pen Lann**, **Pierre de Carentec**, which appears like two small white painted rocks, will be in line with a white wall mark (not always very clear) (line **K**) bearing 188° True. Alter course to starboard to follow this line which leaves the following marks on the sides shown:

> **Stolvezen** Lateral port spindle buoy 0·2 mile to port.
> **La Vieille** Lateral starboard beacon tower 0·2 mile to starboard.
> **La Fourche** Lateral starboard beacon 135 m to starboard.
> **La Noire** Lateral starboard beacon 135 m to starboard.
> **Le Courgik** Lateral starboard beacon 135 m to starboard.

Just before reaching **Le Courgik** alter course to make good 139° True to follow the stern transit: **Trépied Jaune** (alias **L'Enfer**) white beacon tower in line with **Le Paradis** white beacon tower bearing 319° True. At low water **Le Paradis** is almost hidden by rock. This line leaves:

> **Bizinnennou** Lateral starboard beacon 135 m to starboard and
> **Calhic** Lateral starboard beacon tower 0·125 mile to starboard.

As soon as **Ile Louet** is brought on with **La Lande** again, alter course to make good 160° True and proceed as for the Grand Chenal.

Grand Chenal and Channels to the Penzé River: From the North

By Day Only 1. Proceed as for Grand Chenal, passing 0·2 mile east of **Pot de Fer** Cardinal east spar bell buoy and following the leading line **Ile Louet – Tour de la Lande** (line **J**). When **Roches Duon** white tower is in line with **Ile Pighet** W pyramid bearing 280° True alter course to make good 255° True heading for a position midway between **Le**

166

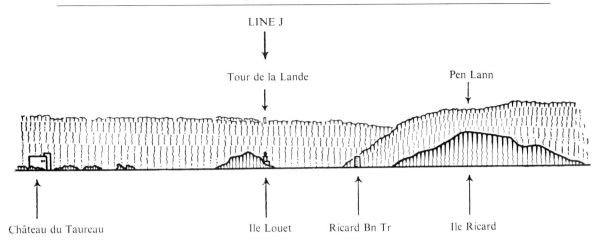

Grand Chenal, Morlaix, looking southwards at LWN from a position midway between Stolvezen and Pot de Fer buoys.

Cordonnier Lateral port beacon tower and **Guerheon** Lateral starboard beacon tower so as to leave **Le Cordonnier** 160 m to starboard (line **R**).

When the latter is abeam alter course to make good 167° True and heading directly for **Trousken** Lateral port beacon tower, and leaving **La Vache** Cardinal east beacon tower 0·125 mile to port.

When **La petite Forche** Lateral starboard beacon tower is in line with the green and white beacon on the end of the slip on **Ile St Anne** (not very easy to see) bearing 205° True, follow this line until the leading line for the river is reached: **Roc'h Pighet** white pyramid and **Amer de Stum** black and white daymark (line **P**), bearing 168° True. Follow directions for Penzé River, below.

2. Proceed as for *Grand Chenal* as above but continue for a farther 0·25 mile until the white pyramid on **Le Paradis** bears 245° True then steer to make good 248° True heading directly for **Barxen en Forc'h** Lateral starboard beacon (line **S**). There are two isolated rocks in the channel, one drying 0·3 m LAT south-east of **Les Bisayers** 80 m north of the line and the other drying 2·6 m south-west of **Les Bisayers** 120 m north of the line. **Les Cochons Noirs**, **Le Paradis** and **Les Grandes Fourches** are all steep-to on their northern sides and, apart from a 5·9 m patch over a rock at the east end, there is a least depth of 12 m LAT.

When the leading line for the river is reached: **Roc'h Pighet** white pyramid and **Amer de Stum** black and white daymark (line **P**) bearing 168° True follow directions for *Penzé River*, below.

167

Grand Chenal and Channels to Penzé River: From the South

By Day Only To proceed from the Morlaix river to the Penzé river proceed northwards either by the Grand Chenal or the Chenal Ouest de Ricard until just north of **La Vieille** and **Stolvezen** buoys, when the **Ile Pighet** W pyramid (just north of **Ar Chaden**) comes in line with **Notre Dame de Bon Secours** bearing 293° True (line **T**), then turn to follow this line until it meets one or other of the lines mentioned above and continue as appropriate.

Grand Chenal: To Morlaix River

By Night By reference to the following lights:
Les Sept Iles Fl (3) 15 s, vis 24 M.
Les Triagoz Oc (2) 6 s, vis (W) 13 M.
Men Guen Bras Q, vis (W) 9 M.
Ile de Bas Fl (4) 25 s, vis 23 M.
La Lande Fl 5 s, vis 23 M.
Ile Louet Oc (3) 12 s, vis (W) 15 M.
Ile Noire Oc (2) 6 s, vis (R) 9 M.

Navigate to keep well clear of the **Roches Duon** and the **Plateau de la Méloine**, both unlit, and to bring **Ile Louet** into line with **La Lande** bearing 176° True (line **J**). Follow this line very closely until just past **Calhic** beacon tower, when the **Ile Noire** light will change from red to green. Then alter to make good 160° True and proceed as for daylight entry, leaving **Chateau de Taureau** beacon and fort to port.

Chenal de Tréguier: To Morlaix River

By Day If approaching from the northward, navigate so as to pass 0·25 mile west of **Les Trépieds** buoy, on the western edge of the **Plateau de la Méloine** (Cardinal west whistle with radar reflector). From here a course made good of 190° True leads straight along the leading line (**M**) formed by **Ile Noire** lighthouse (front) white square tower 13 m high, elevation 15 m, and **Tour de la Lande** lighthouse (rear) white square tower black top 17 m high, elevation 85 m (see view).

If approaching from the north-east, to the south of the **Plateau de la Méloine**, proceed as for *Primel, Approaches By Day* above, then navigate to make a position 0·2 mile east of **La Pierre Noire** Lateral starboard beacon. From here make good a course of 190° True along the leading line (**M**) mentioned above.

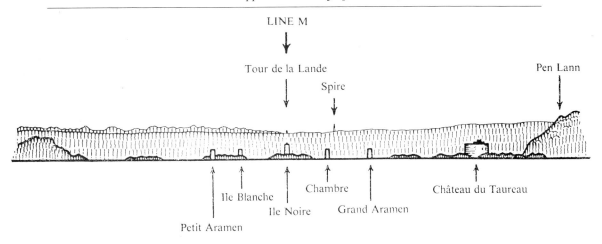

Chenal de Tréguier, Morlaix, from a position on line **M** and 0·3 mile NE of Pierre Noire Lateral starboard beacon at LW neaps.

Chenal de Tréguier. The leading marks are Ile Noire lighthouse in line with Tour de la Lande lighthouse on the skyline at 191° True. Here the yacht is about the pass between Petit Aramen Lateral port (off the picture to the left) and Grand Aramen Lateral starboard beacon towers.

This line leaves the following marks on the sides shown:

Pierre Noire Lateral starboard beacon 0·2 mile to starboard.

Tourghi Lateral starboard beacon 0·2 mile to starboard.

Petit Arémen Lateral port beacon tower 0·1 mile to port.

Grand Arémen Lateral starboard beacon tower 0·1 mile to starboard.

La Chambre Lateral starboard beacon tower 100 m to starboard.

Ile Blanche Lateral port beacon tower 100 m to port.

When **Ile Blanche** is abeam to port, quit the leading line and steer about 240° True for 0·15 mile until **La Chambre** beacon tower and **Petit Arémen** beacon tower are in line, then alter course to make

169

Nautical Mile

1 0

N

ILE DE BAS

Pte Bilvidic

Notre Dame de Bon Secours

Ile aux Moutons

Portz Kernoch

Malvoch

Ferry slip

Kerabamty Fl(4)25s.23M Gy + F R 7M

Pte Occidentale

Lavandières

Basse Plate B

106° True

074° True

065° True

48° 44'N

Kerabamty R aux sector

Mean Eren

La Croix L'Oignon

Tehi Bihan

Pen ar Cleguer Per Roch

Ar Poloss Treas

An Oan

Anchorage Prohibited

R. Le Loup W

Pte des Jacobins

Pte Perharidic

4° 02'.W

Duslen

Ar Chaden Q(6)+L.Fl.W.R15s9.6M Y Ile Pighet

Moorings

Basse Astan Whis. B Y B

I. Verte Violet

Ferry Slip

Belfry

Roche Zhu

Rannic

Benven Bras Oc(1+2) 12s. 6M WBW

Men Guen Bras B Q.W.R.G 9.6M

Pte de Bloscon Basse Bloscon

Fl.W.G.10.7M

St. Barbe

Port de Bloscon

W of NE Oc(1+2)12s 13M

ROSCOFF

V W U X

good 211° True, keeping on this line as a stern transit; this leads to the **Rade de Morlaix No 1**. Lateral starboard buoy (formerly **La Barre de Flot**).

Chenal de Tréguier: To the Morlaix River

By Night By reference to the lights listed under *Grand Chenal By Night* above, navigate to keep well clear of the **Plateau de la Méloine** and the **Roches Duon**, both unlit, and to bring **Ile Noire** Oc (2) 6 s, vis (R) 9 miles, and **La Lande** Fl 5 s in line bearing 190° True (line **M**), then make good a course to follow this line.

When almost midway between **La Chambre** beacon tower and **Ile Blanche** beacon tower, the **Ile Louet** light (Oc (3) 12s) will change from white to green. At this point quit the leading line and alter course to make good 215° True for the **Rade de Morlaix No 1** buoy.

Chenal de l'Ile de Bas: From the West

By Day Only The **Chenal de l'Ile de Bas** (otherwise **Batz**) provides a short cut to the **Baie de Morlaix** for vessels coming from the west and vice versa, as well as giving access to **Roscoff** and **Portz Kernoch**. The central part of the channel carries a least depth of 0·3 m (1·5 m at MLWS), but owing to the strong tides and lack of satisfactory leading lines it would be unwise for a stranger to rely on being able to keep exactly to the recommended track, even under power. At half tide there is plenty of water, and enough for a yacht of twenty tons to work through under sail. In fresh or strong westerly winds against a west-going spring tide, the water is rough west of **Per Roch** beacon tower. Approaching from the north, keep over 0·8 mile west of **Pointe Occidentale** until **Basse Plate** Cardinal north beacon tower, bears about 110° True then steer so as to leave it 100 m to starboard. When passing west of the **Ile de Bas** with a flood tide take care not to be set on to the dangers west of the island, shown on Chart No 24. Approaching from the west, keep **Ile de Bas** lighthouse, a grey tower 40 m high elevation 69 m bearing 074° True (line **W**) until **Basse Plate** beacon tower bears about 110° True then steer so as to leave it 100 m to starboard as above.

From here steer to make good 106° True along line **V** which is formed by:

Le Loup, a small steep rock with a white patch painted on its northern end in transit with **St Barbe**, a white pyramid.

Note: All captions to photographs of marks in the Chenal de L'Ile de Bas refer to passage from the east.

Proceeding east to west. Men Guen Bras lighthouse is left about 0·125 mile to port when entering Canal de l'île de Bas from east to west. (Pre IALA.)

Ar Chaden lighthouse is left about 30 m to starboard. To the right is the Ile Pighet wh[i] pyramid beacon which is an important leading mark when approaching from the Gra[n] Chenal from Morlaix. The white pyramid in line with the steeple of Notre Dame de Secours church at 294° True leads between Plateau des Duon and Le Menk. The chur[ch] steeple is difficult to locate as only the top appears above a wood and it cannot be seen [at] all on near approach (a mile or so) off Ile de Bas.

Roch Zu Cardinal north beacon is left 100 m to port. The picture is taken at low water.

View from moorings off Roscoff, showing yacht (left) following passage between ferry pier light and Duslen Cardinal S beacon. *Waterwise.*

Leave the beacon at the end of Roscoff ferry pier close to port before bearing to starboard.

172

An Oan Cardinal south beacon is left about 65 m to starboard. Here it is seen near low water.

Course is then altered to port to bring An Oan beacon in line with Pighet white pyramid (with arrow) on a stern bearing. The picture is taken near low water.

The course leaves Per Roch Cardinal north beacon tower about 100 m to port.

173

Malvoch Cardinal south beacon tower is left 0·1 mile to starboard. The picture is taken at low water. Malvoch jetty is seen above the rocks to the right of the beacon tower and farther to the right is Portz Kernoch all dried out. Mooring buoys are laid SE of the beacon. (Pre IALA.)

Portz Kernoch. The whole of this bay dries out at LAT. On the right is the landing place at Ile aux Moutons, at the far end of which is a restaurant. The shops and post office are about half a mile from the landing place beyond the church (Notre Dame de Bon Secours). The picture is taken at about half tide. The slip covers at HW.

Ile de Bas lighthouse bearing about north when former radio beacon functioning.

174

Finally, Basse Plate Cardinal north beacon tower is left about 100 m to port. At low water many rocks are exposed 0·25 mile to the ESE of the beacon tower. (Pre IALA.)

(These marks are difficult for a stranger to identify from a distance, but it is possible to navigate by the fairway marks alone.)

Continue along line **V** until **L'Oignon** Cardinal north beacon is abeam to starboard, 100 m distant and **La Croix** Cardinal south beacon is abeam to port distant 0·125 mile.

At this point alter course to port and steer for **Pen ar Chleguer**, the most southerly point of the **Ile de Bas**, leaving:

Tehi Bihan Cardinal north beacon 0·1 mile to starboard.

Malvoch Cardinal south beacon tower and **Ile aux Moutons** Cardinal south beacon about 0·1 mile to port.

But when **An Oan** Cardinal south beacon comes into line with **Ile Pighet** Cardinal south pyramid, alter course to follow this line (**U**) leaving:

Per Roch Cardinal north beacon 100 m to starboard.

When about equidistant from **Per Roch** and **An Oan**, alter course to leave:

An Oan 65 m to port.

Then head for the Roscoff ferry violet beacon leaving:

Roscoff ferry beacon 50 m to starboard.

Then steer so as to leave:

Duslen Cardinal south beacon about 50 m and **Duslen** white tower 110 m to port.

When **Duslen** Cardinal south beacon is abeam, steer towards **Ar Chaden** (Cardinal south marking) lighthouse, leaving:

Roch Zu Cardinal north beacon 100 m to starboard and finally,

Ar Chaden lighthouse 30 m to port.

Steer from here so as to leave **Basse de Bloscon** Cardinal north buoy 150 m to starboard then

If bound for Morlaix or the east bring the south Cardinal light beacon on the centre of **Ile Pighet** in line with **Notre Dame de Bon Secours** spire on **Ile de Bas** on a stern bearing of 293° True and

175

make good 113° True to follow this line (**T**) and then pick up the leading lines, either for the Chenal Ouest de Ricard or the Grand Chenal as desired, and follow these (lines **J** or **K**). If bound for the Penzé River then steer to make good 165° True with **Guerheon** Lateral starboard beacon tower fine on the starboard bow. When the white beacon towers **Beneven** and **Maxarin** on **Ile de Callot** come into line (line **N**) bearing 136° True follow this line until reaching the leading line for the Penzé river **Roc'h Pighet** and **Amer de Stum** black-and-white daymark (line **P**).

Caution: This passes over or near to rocks awash or drying 0·3 m LAT, i.e. covered 0·9 m MLWS, 3·0 m MLWN.

Chenal de l'Ile de Bas: From the East

By Day Only   The approach to the eastern entrance may be:
  (a) From the NE between the **Roches Duon** and **Astan** (Chart No 23).
  (b) From the ESE and the **Grand Chenal** between the **Roches Duon** and the dangers to the south of them by following the line **Ile Pighet** pyramid in line with **Notre Dame de Bon Secours** bearing 293° True. (Line **T** on Chart No 23.)
  (c) From the SSE and the **Penzé** river from a position in which **Guerheon** beacon tower (formerly black-and-white diagonal with cone point-up topmark) bears about 270° True distant 0·15 mile make good 316° True following the stern transit of the white beacon towers **Beneven** and **Maxarin** on **Ile de Callot** until **Guerheon** beacon tower bears 180° True then steer to leave **Basse de Bloscon** Cardinal north pillar buoy 150 m to port then proceed along line **T** as (b) above.

In all the above cases, having reached a position about 150 m east of the **Basse de Bloscon** buoy identify **Ar Chaden** lighthouse (Cardinal south marking) and approach it on a bearing of about 295° True. (See Chart 24.) This line leaves **Men Guen Bras** lighthouse (Cardinal north marking) about 0·125 mile to port. Steer a course to pass 50 m south of **Duslen** Cardinal south beacon and 120 m south of the non-IALA beacon tower, leaving:
  Ar Chaden lighthouse about 30 m to starboard.
  Roch Zu Cardinal north beacon 100 m to port.
When **Duslen** Cardinal south beacon is abeam, alter course for the trumpet-shaped violet and white beacon (light fixed violet) at the end of the long ferry pier, which looks like a bridge and a slipway. Pass close to the beacon and alter course again so as to leave **An Oan** Cardinal south beacon 65 m to starboard. Then bring this beacon

176

into line astern with the centre of **Ile Pighet** and follow this line (**U**) leaving:

    Per Roch Cardinal north beacon tower 100 m to port.

When **Ar Poloss Tréas** Cardinal north beacon bears 145° True alter course to port so as to leave:

    Ile aux Moutons long ferry slipway Cardinal south beacon and **Malvoch** Cardinal south beacon tower 0·1 mile to starboard.

    Tehi Bihan Cardinal north beacon 0·1 mile to port.

    La Croix Cardinal south beacon 0·125 mile to starboard.

    L'Oignon Cardinal north beacon 100 m to port.

Just before **L'Oignon** is abeam pick up the stern transit of **Le Loup**, a small steep rock with a white patch painted on its northern end, in line with **St Barbe** white pyramid, just south of the conspicuous chapel, bearing 106° True. Make good a course of 287° True to follow this line (**V**). This leaves: **Basse Plate** Cardinal north beacon tower 100 m to port.

If bound north, follow this line for a farther mile in order to clear the dangers on the west side of the **Ile de Bas**.

If bound westward down the coast, follow this line until the **Ile de Bas** lighthouse, a grey tower 40 m high elevation 69 m bears 074° True. Then alter course to make good 254° True so as to keep it on that bearing astern. This line (**W**) clears all dangers for the next 10 miles.

Anchorages

Bay of Morlaix

The favourite anchorage for yachts is between La Barre de Flot and Pen Lann, with Ile Louet bearing about 340° True. This position has a depth of about 9 m and is well sheltered from westerlies but somewhat exposed from other quarters at high water, so that a yacht sometimes rolls in the anchorage, particularly on the ebb. There is a good dinghy landing at all states of tide at, or near the north-east corner of Pen Lann. From here a footpath climbs the hill and joins the road to Carentec, which lies a mile farther west. Three mooring buoys in deep water are reserved for visitors.

In settled weather and neap tides, yachts sometimes anchor near the Pierre de Carantec.

In easterly weather and neap tides, small yachts may anchor close south of the Pointe de Terrénèz about 1 mile to the eastward of Ile Noire, where there is said to be 2·1 m at LW neaps.

Inside the estuary it is possible to anchor in good holding ground on either side of the fairway, but there is no reasonable landing for dinghies at low water.

Chenal de l'Ile de Bas

It is possible to anchor almost anywhere in the channel where there is enough water, but all such anchorages are exposed to winds from certain quarters, are subject to a strong tidal stream and thus are uncomfortable with a weather-going tide. Anchorage is prohibited owing to cables, in an area bounded by a line almost due south from Pen ar Chleguer and on the east by a line running about NNW from the Roscoff ferry beacon. The following positions are frequently used:

1. Between Ar Chaden lighthouse and Duslen beacon tower. If it is desired to anchor at spring tides it may be necessary to anchor in deep water in the strong stream, but at neaps it is possible to find a more sheltered position northward with the aid of soundings and clear of the rocks indicated on the chart. In northerly weather this is uncomfortable at HW. About six moorings have been laid here.
2. There is an anchorage to the south-west of Malvoch beacon tower (avoiding the 0·1 m rock shown on the chart) and at neaps south of Ile aux Moutons, but these can be uncomfortable in fresh westerly winds.
3. About 100 m east of Rannic beacon tower in about 1·7 m LAT.

Penzé River

These will be dealt with under *Penzé River Estuary*, below.

Morlaix. Before the château among the trees comes abeam to starboard, it is time to bear to port towards the stony promontory on the east side of the river.

28 Morlaix: Estuary and River

Approaches

From Pen Lann to the river entrance off Locquénolé, the fairway is deep and is marked by six numbered Lateral port and starboard buoys. Buoy No 1, which was formerly **La Barre de Flot**, is unlit, but has a large radar reflector beneath its cone. The next four on alternate sides of the channel are lit. The mean course is about 155° True.

When approaching **Le Dourdu** it will be seen from Chart 25 that the best water lies on the east side. A yacht should steer for a point off the stony promontory on that side and then sweep round in a curve to leave buoy No 7 to starboard and the first unlit Lateral port buoy to port.

The channel is then well marked by Lateral port and starboard buoys leading close to Locquénolé off which local shallow draft craft are moored on each side of the fairway. Care must be taken not to miss a buoy, obscured by a moored boat. Occasionally one or other of the buoys south of Locquénolé may be absent.

At the bend in the river half a mile above this village the channel lies in the bight on the west side and is marked by Lateral port buoys and then by a Lateral port beacon. Do not steer from the last Lateral port buoy direct to the beacon as the shallows bulge out close to the fairway on the port side.

Off Dourdu River a wide turn is made to starboard, to leave buoy No 7 to starboard and to enter fairly between this and the first unmarked Lateral port buoy.

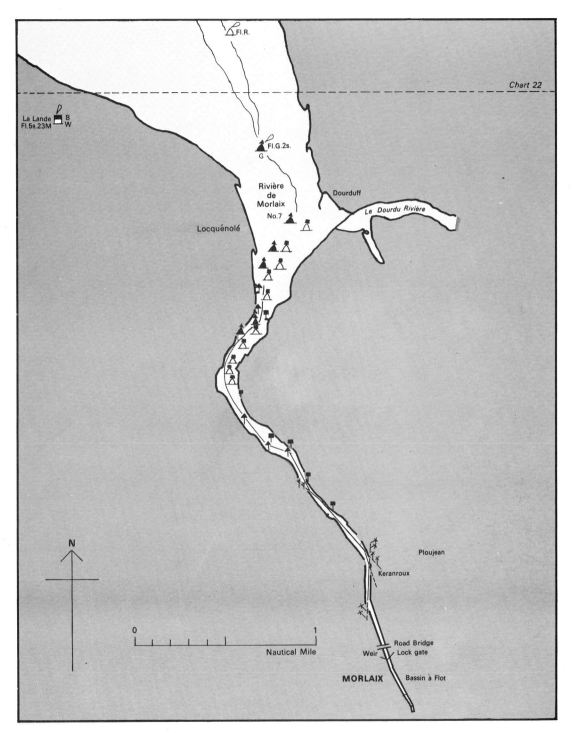

Chart 22

La Lande
Fl.5s.23M B
W

Fl.R.

Fl.G.2s.
G

Rivière
de
Morlaix
No.7

Dourduff

Le Dourdu Rivière

Locquénolé

Ploujean

Keranroux

N

0   1
                    Nautical Mile

Road Bridge
Weir   Lock gate

MORLAIX   Bassin à Flot

Chart 25. Morlaix River. *Based on French Chart No 5827.*

The sand barge, after passing Loquénolé and a Lateral port beacon, is turning to starboard between two channel buoys towards the bight on the west side of the river.

In the bight on the west side, where the river bends from a SE to a SW direction, the channel lies on the west side and is marked on the port hand by Lateral buoys and a Lateral beacon. Do not cut it too fine when steering from the last Lateral buoy to the beacon, because the mud on the east side bulges close to the fairway between the two.

In the upper reaches of the river there are clear leading marks on the bank, which gives transits which should be carefully steered on. In this picture the transit marks are on the east bank of the river.

The canal narrows as Morlaix is approached. Note the rear transit mark on the east bank.

The channel is then marked by Lateral port and starboard beacons for the next half mile but for the last mile up to the lock it is very narrow and the best water is indicated by the clear pairs of transit marks on the shore.

The lock leading to the basin is 63 m long, 16 m wide, the lower sill is 2 m and the upper 3·1 m above datum giving approximately 3·0 m at MHWN. The gates open 3 times each tide: $1\frac{1}{2}$ hrs before, at HW and 1 hr after. The bridge below the lock has a clearance of 33·5 m at top of spring tides. Whilst waiting for the gates to open, go alongside the quay on the west side, about 150 m from the outer gate. Yachts may safely dry out in this position but not nearer to the lock gate, where there are rocks which dry.

183

The alternative position in which to dry out (which is perhaps better) is below the weir alongside the middle arm of the lock quay on its east side where there are steps and soft mud bottom. Depths in the basin, which is over half a mile long, vary from 2·4 m to 5·4 m alongside the quays. The southern end of the basin is now a marina with pontoons on the east side. Visitors may also lie alongside the quays in certain places at slightly less charge. The original pontoon at the south wall is now reserved for local yacht club members.

Facilities

The basin is situated near the centre of Morlaix with small shops nearby on the west bank, and the principal shops about a quarter of a mile beyond towards the high railway viaduct, which dominates the town. Fresh water points near roots of pontoons (supply your own hose), also rubbish bins. Diesel, petrol and oil at nearby garages.

Yachts are absolutely secure at Morlaix, so far as weather is concerned, and arrangements can be made with the Harbour Master to leave them there if one has to return to the UK for any reason. The water in the basin appears to be fresh.

Morlaix is one of the biggest towns in Brittany, and has all services and facilities which may not be available in smaller ports such as doctors, dentists, banks, opticians (quick repairs), photographic dealers (quick developing) and first-rate shops of all kinds. There are many restaurants of which Hotel Europe is the largest and probably the best. The Auberge des Gourmets serves a good meal at a reasonable price, but it is situated up the hill about a hundred yards below the station.

There is a good train service to Brest and Paris and also connections with St Malo or Dinard, though the latter are slow as one or two changes may be involved.

Historical

Morlaix is an historical town. At the time of the Roman occupation there was a fortress and the town was called Mons Relaxus. In the Middle Ages it had many warlike connections with England. The Fontaine des Anglais on the east bank of the river marks the place where, in 1522, 600 English who had disembarked to attack the town were surprised while asleep and killed. Ten years later it was actually captured by the English, but in 1542 the merchants of the town built the Château du Taureau, to discourage any further raids.

184

29 Carentec – Penzé River

Approaches

By Day Only   Having arrived on the leading line: **Roc'h Pighet** bottle-shaped W pyramid in line with **Amer de Stum** black-and-white daymark bearing 168° True (line **P** on Chart No 22), from the Rade de Morlaix or the **Chenal de l'Ile de Bas**, follow this line. These marks may not be easily identified from the distance but deviations are necessary at beacons and the following marks should be left on the sides shown.

La Vache Cardinal east beacon tower 200 m to port.

Barzenen Lateral starboard beacon 200 m to starboard.

Trousken Lateral port beacon tower 140 m to port.

La Petite Forche Lateral starboard beacon 150 m to starboard.

La Tortue Lateral port beacon 20 m to port (but note that, if beating in, there is an alternative course with a wider channel, leaving the beacon well to starboard, avoiding, if necessary, the small rock 30 m to the east of it 0·9 m LAT and the rock south of it drying 3·0 m.

Caspart, formerly black-and-red beacon surmounted by a sphere (lying about 0·25 mile ENE of Trébunnec Lateral starboard beacon tower) 50 m to starboard or 150 m to port, making the necessary alteration in good time to avoid the small rock 0·5 m about 100 m north of this beacon and two drying about 0·3 m about 50 m south-west of it.

Trébunnec Lateral starboard beacon tower about 0·2 mile to starboard.

From here continue on the leading line, but if this is still not identified the deep channel is shown on each side by large numbers of withies marking oyster beds. These withies cover round about half tide, but they are not heavy enough to cause any damage if accidentally touched. Continuing leave:

Enès Ebel Lateral starboard beacon (east of Penpoull) 140 m to starboard.

Figuicr, formerly black and red beacon surmounted by a disc, 50 m to starboard.

When this beacon is abeam alter course to about 200° True for 0·3 mile then about 210° True to follow the leading line (**Q**) given by **L'Ingoz** small bottle shaped white pyramid and a white rectangular

The last leading line. The white beacon on l'Ingoz and a white rectangular mark on a wall at St Yvres (almost invisible). Oyster stakes help to locate the channel, but there are no marks for the river beyond l'Ingoz.

mark on a wall at **St Yvres**, overgrown and almost invisible. This line, leading on the south-east side of the channel leaves:

Les Cheminées Lateral starboard beacon 120 m to starboard. When it is abeam quit the leading line and steer about 230° True. Thereafter the river is not marked and the course of the channel has to be judged from the chart and the oyster withies; it is easiest at HW when the shallows are covered or at LW when the direction of the channel can be seen.

There is a least depth of about 0·9 m (2·1 m at MLWS) up as far as the old ferry. Towards high water small vessels can continue up the river for a farther mile above the bridge to the village of **Penzé**, where there is said to be a quay which dries 4·8 m.

Anchorages

There are now numerous moorings between Les Cheminées and L'Ingoz beacon but room is left to anchor clear of them. There is better shelter farther up the river

Penzé river beyond l'Ingoz. The arrow indicates the wall mark which is difficult to locate.

186

south-west of L'Ingoz pyramid in 3·6 m MLWS, or just south of the old ferry in about 1·8 m MLWS, mud. There is a landing hard each side of the river at the old ferry, available at all states of the tide. There is a big new bridge and the noise of traffic may be troublesome. The holding ground in the lower reaches has been reported poor.

Facilities

There are no facilities at St Yvres.

Carentec. There is a landing stage which dries about 4·6 m and two yacht yards which face the estuary. The town is about a quarter of an hour walk from the landing where there are good shopping facilities, a night club and a number of hotels and restaurants. The sandy beaches north of Kergrist Farm are popular with local holiday-makers. Milk, eggs and poultry can sometimes be had from farms between Carentec and Pen Lann. Between half ebb and half flood the Ile de Callot is accessible on foot from Carentec across the Passe aux Moutons.

Historical

On the Ile de Callot stands the pilgrimage chapel of Notre Dame des Victoires, founded in the sixth century to commemorate a victory over Norse pirates. On August 15th every year seamen from the surrounding districts come to pay their devotions.

The anchorage off the old ferry.

St Pol de Léon is an ancient cathedral town which lies about one mile west of the landing at Pen Poull. It has played a leading part in the history of Brittany. Its name is a corruption of St Paul Aurelian, its first missionary, who came from Wales in AD 530. The cathedral is entirely medieval, partly twelfth century, and its twin spires form one of the most distinctive landmarks in the district.

30 Roscoff

Tidal Data

Tidal Heights
High Water: approx +0055 Brest, +0605 Dover.
Heights of Tide above Datum: approx MHWS 8·5 m, MLWS 1·2 m, MHWN 6·4 m, MLWN 3·3 m.
Mean Tide Level: 4·7 m. Index 8 B.

Tidal Streams

HW Slack water at the entrance to Roscoff occurs −0005 Brest (+0505 Dover). One mile NE of the Ile de Bas, and in the channel itself, the E-going stream begins at −0435 Brest (+0035 Dover) and the W-going stream begins at −0110 Brest (−0605 Dover). Both streams reach 3·75 knots at spring. NE of the Ile de Bas, the directions of the streams are SE and NW. For other streams see under *Bay of Morlaix*, above.

General

Although Roscoff has the disadvantage of a harbour which dries out it is nevertheless an interesting and convenient port for the visiting yachtsman.

Approach

There are two alternative inner approaches which can be used with sufficient rise of tide from the Chenal de l'Ile de Bas:

By Day or Night

(a) **Passe à L'Est de Benven**
Having reached a position 0·75 mile west of **Ar Chaden** as already described, turn to bring the front and rear leading lights and structures, in line bearing 210° True. The front light is Oc (1 + 2) G 12s, on a white column 6 m high, elevation 7 m, on New Mole.
The rear light is Oc (1+2) 12 s. The two lights are synchronised.
Follow this line closely until the end of the eastern jetty is abeam to port, then steer as necessary to enter the port.

By Day

(b) **Passe de Rannic**
From a position 100 m north of **Basse de Bloscon** buoy, steer along the line formed by **Rannic** Cardinal north beacon tower and **Roscoff Belfry** bearing 261° True. (This is line **X** in Chart No 24.) This line leaves **Men Guen Bras** lighthouse (Cardinal north) 100 m to

189

Approach to Roscoff should be made with sufficient rise of tide. Leave to starboard Roch Zu
Cardinal north beacon and enter on the line of the low white lighthouse above the white
patch at the end of the mole in line with the tall white lighthouse in the rear, bearing 210°
True. There is often a strong cross stream in the approach.

starboard, after which course should be altered slightly to starboard
so as to leave **Rannic** tower about 30 m to port, avoiding the rocks
which lie 0·9 mile WSW of **Men Guen Bras**, and which dry
approximately 5·4 m. Then bring **Rannic** tower into line astern
with **Men Guen Bras** lighthouse and follow this transit until past
the end of the eastern jetty, when course may be altered to enter the
port.

Anchorage and Harbour

While waiting for sufficient rise of tide to enter Roscoff the choice of anchorage must
depend on the direction and strength of the wind and, in particular, on whether it is
springs or neaps when in the latter case there is more choice.

(a) Between **Ar Chaden** and **Duslen** beacon tower, described on page 175. About 6
white mooring buoys have been laid in this reach. These are very exposed and do not
always watch at HW, but would be convenient while waiting for the tide to enter
Roscoff.

(b) In about 0·1 m LAT just east of the **Roscoff** leading line and approximately
ESE of **Roch Zu** beacon; but note the existence of a rock which dries 3·3 m only
100 m west of this position.

(c) East of **Rannic** beacon tower, having approached by directions for **Passe de
Rannic** above.

The outer harbour, **Le Port Neuf**, has good berths alongside its N and W sides,
drying from 2·4 – 3 m LAT on hard bottom. The steps are in constant use by vedettes
and other local craft. It is preferable to lie alongside the second or third ladder where

a yacht of 1·8 m draft takes the bottom just after half tide. If these are occupied, one may have to berth against the quay without a ladder, which is awkward at low water. It provides excellent HW berths for shopping.

The inner harbour dries from 3·6 m to 5·1 m LAT. The old jetty is rather rough, but there are excellent berths for yachts alongside it which may be unoccupied, even if the outer harbour is full. The jetty on the eastern part of the harbour cannot be used for berthing.

It is said that there is liable to be a heavy surge in the harbour if there is any swell in the offing; presumably this occurs in strong NE winds or northerly winds at high water springs. The inner harbour may then provide better shelter.

Facilities

The facilities for yachtsmen at Roscoff are good. Water in bulk can be obtained from the hydrants on the quays on application to the Harbour Master, or from a tap on the

The picture is taken from the mole facing west across the town end of the outer harbour (Le Port Neuf). If possible berth alongside a ladder, as the wall is high when the yacht dries out at LW. The entrance to the town is just to the left of the white sail. Turn left for restaurant, post office, customs and old harbour. Turn right for hotels, church square, garage and aquarium.

wall of a café at the shore end of the old jetty. On landing leave the big sheds housing the sailing school (who will give local advice) to the right and enter the main road. Turning left down the Rue Gambetta one will pass the modest Restaurant du Centre (a *pension* supplying well cooked meals at a modest price), a photographer, a baker and several small shops. The Inscription Maritime is on the right and on turning to the left is Monsieur Larher's shop where bonded stores can be obtained by arrangement with the Customs. There is a capable marine engineer and a sailmaker on the south side of the old harbour. Repairs to wooden vessels can be undertaken.

The road turning right from the quay leads to the church. On this road will be found shops of all kinds and hotels including the Talabardon which has a good restaurant. The aquarium on the northern front has specimens of marine life found in the Chenal de l'île de Bas; it is quite worth seeing. Diesel oil from Monsieur Gillet who has a tanker lorry and hose, he is contacted through the sailing club. There is a railway station. There are frequent ferry services to and from Plymouth and weekly sailings to Cork from nearby Port Bloscon.

Historical

Mary Queen of Scots landed at Roscoff in 1548, when she was five years old, to be married to the Dauphin in Paris. Here also came Prince Charles Edward Stuart in a French privateer, after the battle of Culloden and after narrowly missing capture by English ships in the channel.

The church has a remarkable Renaissance tower and spire (1550) decorated with carvings of ships and pieces of ordnance. The *pardon* of Sainte Barbe takes place on the third Monday in July and on August 15th.

Some yachtsmen prefer to dry out in the inner harbour (Vieux Port) which is seen here. The picture is taken from the inner quay at high water facing to the SE.

31 Port de Bloscon

Tidal Data: See under Roscoff.

General

An unattractive artificial harbour half a mile south of Basse de Bloscon Cardinal north buoy, and about twenty minutes walk to Roscoff. Considerable reclamation work has been carried out to provide parking space for vehicles. The port is intended for commercial shipping and the car ferries mentioned under Roscoff. With permission from the Harbour Master, it might be possible for yachts to berth or to anchor south of the harbour, clear of the ferry's swinging ground and local moorings.

Approach

By Day   Make a position 0·25 mile east of **Basse de Bloscon** buoy; in poor visibility this can be assisted by homing on **Port Bloscon** Radio beacon – BC 287·3 kHz. From here steer to give the end of the jetty a fair berth, to allow for ferries leaving and, when the way is clear turn to starboard and enter harbour.

By Night   Visually or with the assistance of the Radio beacon, bring the breakwater light to bear 215° True which is in the centre of its white sector from 210° to 220° True; elsewhere it is green. Make good 215° True until **Basse de Bloscon** Cardinal north light buoy is abeam to starboard, then proceed as for *By Day* above.

Anchorage

As mentioned above.

Facilities

None. When tide serves land at ladder on the quay but at springs this is too short to reach a dinghy and the only other way ashore is by landing on the rocky foreshore.

Part Three
Ile de Siec to Ushant

VHF Radio
Ushant Transmits Ch. 16,24,26,+82
Receives Ch. 24,26+28

Brest Le Conquet Transmits Ch. 16,26+28
Receives Ch. 26+28

Ushant Traffic Control
Broadcasts on Ch.11 in
English ev. H+20,
H+50 general bulletins
and ev 3 hours from 0150 GMT–
Weather Forecasts

Radio Beacons
Pte St Mathieu
48° 19'50"N 4° 46'17" W
289.6kHz SM
(Grouped with Penmarc'h Group)

Roscoff Bloscon
48° 43'18"N 3° 57'45"W
287.3kHz BC

Ushant Créac'h
48° 27'37"N 5° 07'43"W
308kHz CA
(Grouped with Barra Head Group)

Ile Vierge
48° 38'23"N 4° 34'06"W
298.8 kHz VG
(Grouped with Penlee Point Group)

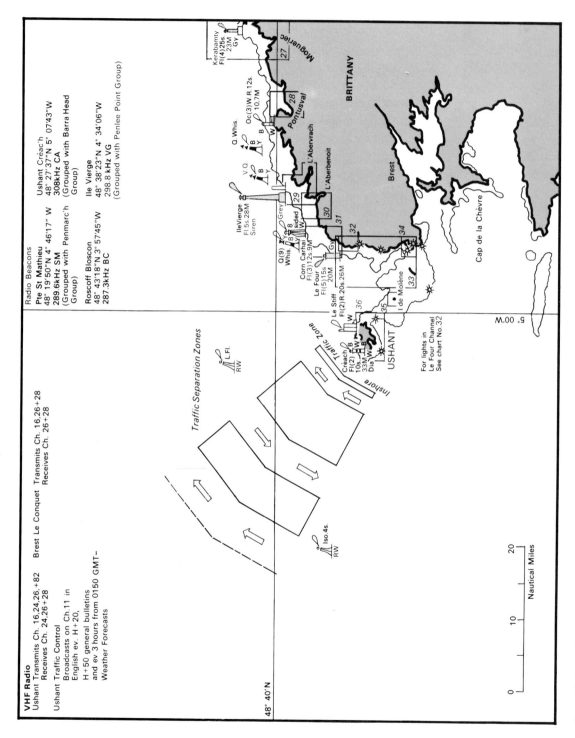

Chart 26. Ile de Bas to Ushant. Based on Admiralty Chart No 2675.

The coast of the mainland, from Ile de Siec to Pointe de St Mathieu, is heavily encumbered with off-lying rocks and shoals, in places, reaching nearly 3 miles offshore. Farther offshore there are no dangers except for the island of Ushant and the maze of rocks and small islands lying to the south-east of it. Ushant itself has a coastal belt of off-lying dangers extending to a maximum of 1·5 miles at its south-west corner.

The shore consists of mostly low cliffs and rocky bays backed by hilly country without many distinctive natural features. The only reliable marks for daylight identification are radio masts, water towers and lighthouses, particularly the Ile Vierge tower, which is said to be the tallest light structure in the world and can be positively identified by the presence of the disused 30 m high tower alongside it.

The western part of the area has a reputation for bad visibility, due partly to the smoke produced by the local industry of kelp-burning. Nevertheless it provides some of the most interesting harbours in the whole of Brittany, which can be visited when conditions are suitable.

Caution. The western part of this area is often subject to a heavy swell from the Atlantic. Under certain conditions the sea will occasionally break over isolated shoals with as much as 38 m of water over them. Such shoals occur in many places outside the tinted areas on the charts in this book, but can be located from the official charts.

LIGHTS AND FOG SIGNALS

Details of the main coast lights are given below, reading from east to west. Bearings of the sectors and leading lines are from the ship looking towards the light, and are expressed in degrees True. To convert to magnetic, *add* variation, which during the early 1980s is about 8 degrees west in the area covered by Part Three of this book. The heights of the light structures are measured from the lantern to the base of the structure. Elevation is measured between the centre of the lantern and MHWS.

Ile de Bas Fl (4) 25s, vis 23M. Grey circular tower 43m high; elevation 69m. Auxiliary light FR vis 7M 024°–059°.

Moguériec.
Leading lights 162°.
{ Jetty light (*front*): Iso WG 4s, vis W 11M, G 6M. W 158°–166°, G elsewhere. G and W tower 10m high; elevation 9m. (*Rear*): G vis 7M 142°–182°. W support G top 11m high; elevation 22m.

Pontusval Oc (3) WR 12s, vis W 10M, R 7M. W from the land to 056°, R thence through E to 096°, W thence to the land. W square tower with black top and white house; 15m high; elevation 16m.

Ile Vierge Fl 5s, vis 28 M. Fog siren, one blast ev minute. Ro Bn: VG 298·8 kHz, grouped with Penlee Point, Seq No 5. Grey circular tower 83m high; elevation 77m, with old lighthouse square tower about 30m high (painted W to seaward) close NW of it.

L'Abervrac'h. Leading lights for Grand Chenal 100°. Rear intensified about 090°–110°.

> **Ile Vrac'h** (*Front*): Q R, vis 7M. W square tower with red top on dwelling 11m high; elevation 19m.
> **Lanvaon** (*Rear*) Q, vis 10M over an arc of about 18° either side of the leading line, intensified about 10° either side. Rectangular Gy tower 27m high; elevation 55m.

L'Abervrac'h harbour Dir Oc (2) WRG 6s, vis W 8M, R 6M, G 6M. G 125·7° to 127·2°, W thence to 128·7° and R thence to 130·2°. Thin white concrete tower on N side of N breakwater.

Corn Carhai Fl (3) 12s, vis 9M. W octagonal tower, B top, 20m high; elevation 19m.

Portsall Oc (3+1) WRG 12s, vis W 10M, R 7M, G 6M. G from 058° to 084°, W thence to 088°, and R thence to 058°. W column R top to N of village 7m high; elevation 9m.

Le Four Fl (5) 15s, vis 20M. Fog siren (3+2) 75s. Gy circular masonry tower 28m high; elevation 28m.

L'Aberildut Dir Oc (2) WR 6s, vis W 19M, R 15M. W from 081° to 085°, R thence to 087°. Small rectangular white building 5m high; elevation 12m.

Les Platresses Fl RG 4s, vis (both sectors) 6M. R 343° to 153°, G thence to 333°. White tower 23m high; elevation 17m.

Le Faix VQ Cardinal north beacon tower, 21m high; elevation 16m.

Les Trois Pierres Iso WRG 4s, vis W 10M, R 7M, G 7M. G 070° to 147°, W thence to 185°, R thence to 191°, G thence to 197°, W thence to 213°, and R thence to 070°. W column 15m high; elevation 15m.

Chenal du Four. Leading lights for N part of channel 158·5° intensified.

> **Kermorvan** (*Front*) Fl 5s, vis 23M. W square tower 20m high; elevation 23m. Reed 60s.
> **St Mathieu** (*Rear*) Dir FW, intensified 157·5°–159·5°. W square tower red top 37m high; elevation 54m. Ro Bn: SM 289·6 kHz range 20M.

La Grande Vinotière Oc R 6s, R octagonal Lateral port beacon tower 24m high; elevation 5m.

Directional light for centre part of channel.

> **Corsen** Dir Q WRG, vis W 12M, R 8M, G 8M. R from 008° to 012°, thence W to 015°, thence G to 021°. W hut 3m high; elevation 33m.

Leading lights for **Chenal de la Helle** 138°. Rear intensified 2° each side of transit.
{ **Kermorvan** (*Front*) (As above)
Lochrist (*Rear*) Dir Oc (2+1) 12s, W tower R top 15m high; elevation 49m.

St Mathieu (same tower as above) Fl 15s, vis 29M. Elevation 56m.
Plougonvelin Radio Masts. 3 FR situated 0·7M SE of Kermorvan.

Ushant

Le Stiff Fl (2) R 20s, vis 25M. Two adjoining white towers 32m high; elevation 85m.

Créac'h Fl (2) 10s, vis 33M from 255° to 247° (352°). Circular tower painted in black and white bands, 55m high; elevation 70m. Diaphone 2 blasts ev 120s. Radiobeacon CA (grouped with Barra Head Seq No 6) 308 kHz range 100M.

Nividic VQ (9) 10s, vis 9M from 290° to 225° (295°). Octagonal Cardinal W tower with helicopter platform, 36m high; elevation 28m.

La Jument Fl (3) 15s, vis 18M from 241° to 199° (318°). Octagonal grey tower with red top, 48m high; elevation 36m. Reed, 3 blasts ev minute.

Men Corn VQ (3) WR 5s, vis W 8M, R 8M. W from 145° to 040° (255°), R elsewhere. *Obscured* 058°–119°. Cardinal E beacon tower 29m high; elevation 21m.

Kéréon Oc (2+1) WR 24s, vis W 18M, R 15M. W from 019° to 248° (229°), R elsewhere. Gy circular tower 41m high; elevation 38m. Fog siren (2+1) ev 120s.

Ile de Molène
Directional light for northern entrance
{ **Breakwater** Dir Fl (3) WRG 12s, vis W 9M, R 7M, G 7M. G from 183° to 190°, thence W to 192°, thence R to 203°. Column on breakwater 5m high; elevation 6m.

Directional light for eastern entrance
{ **Breakwater** Dir Fl (2) WRG 6s, vis W 9M, R 7M, G 7M. G from 252·5° to 259·5°, thence W to 262·5°, thence R to 269·5°. Column on breakwater 5m high; elevation 9m.

OFF-LYING BUOYS AND MARKS

In addition to the lighthouses listed above, the following off-lying buoys and marks may be useful when making passages along this coast:

Basse Plate Cardinal north beacon tower (1 mile SW of Ile de Bas lighthouse, unlit).

Port de Pontusval isolated danger spar buoy (unlit).

Aman ar Ross (4 miles WNW of Pontusval lighthouse). Tall Cardinal north pillar light-and-whistle buoy, Q.

Lizen Ven W Cardinal north pillar buoy, VQ. E Cardinal north spar bell buoy (unlit).

Libenter (3 miles NNE of Ile Vierge lighthouse). Cardinal west pillar whistle light buoy, Q (9) 15 s.

Petite Fourche (3·25 miles WSW of Ile Vierge lighthouse). Cardinal west spar buoy (unlit).

Grande Basse de Portsall (2 miles NW of Corn-Carhai lighthouse). Cardinal west pillar whistle light buoy, VQ (9) 10 s.

Basse Paupian Cardinal west spar buoy (unlit).

Le Lieu (0·7 mile W of Laberildut lighthouse). Lateral port beacon tower (unlit).

Pierre de Laber (1·0 mile W by S of Laberildut lighthouse). Lateral starboard beacon (unlit).

INSHORE MARKS

The following recent conspicuous marks should be noted:

Radio Mast (48° 38′ 20″N–4° 21′ 10″W) (Occasional fixed orange light)
Water Tower (48° 37′ 10″–4° 11′ 50″W)

32 Ile de Siec and Moguériec

Tidal Data

Tidal Heights
High Water: approx +0050 Brest, +0600 Dover.
Heights of Tide above Datum: approx MHWS 8·2 m, MLWS 1·2 m, MHWN 6·7 m, MLWN 3·3 m.
Mean Tide Level: 5·2 m. Index 8 B.

Tidal Streams

1. In the northern approach from the direction of the Ile de Bas the streams are rotary and vary in different positions both in direction and strength. It may be broadly stated that the north-east-going stream, which runs for some 8 hours, begins at −0505 Brest (+0005 Dover) soon attaining the spring rate of 2·4 knots, weakening and turning ENE to east in the last 2 hours. The SSW-going stream begins at +0255 Brest (−0420 Dover) and runs for 4 hours through south-west to north-west. The spring rate is 1·4 knots except in its second hour, when the rate is doubled.
2. In the western approach between **Ile de Siec** and **Roch Haro** some 2 miles to the westward, the ESE-going stream begins −0450 Brest (+0020 Dover) and the WNW-going stream begins +0110 Brest (−0605 Dover), the former reaching nearly 2 knots and the latter 1 knot at springs.

General

The Ile de Siec and Moguériec may be coupled as they are close together and have the same approaches.

Approaches

By Day   First make a position from which **Ile de Bas** lighthouse bears 065° True distant 2·8 miles (Point X.) Here the leading marks for **Moguériec** harbour are in line bearing 162° True. These are a green and white beacon tower on the jetty and a white tower with green top having elevations of 9 and 22 m respectively. In some lights it might be difficult to see the front mark but an additional mark on the line is **Sibiril** church spire which can be seen against the skyline. It is in wooded country and is the first spire to the left of the conspicuous water tower south of Moguériec. Turn to make good 162° True and

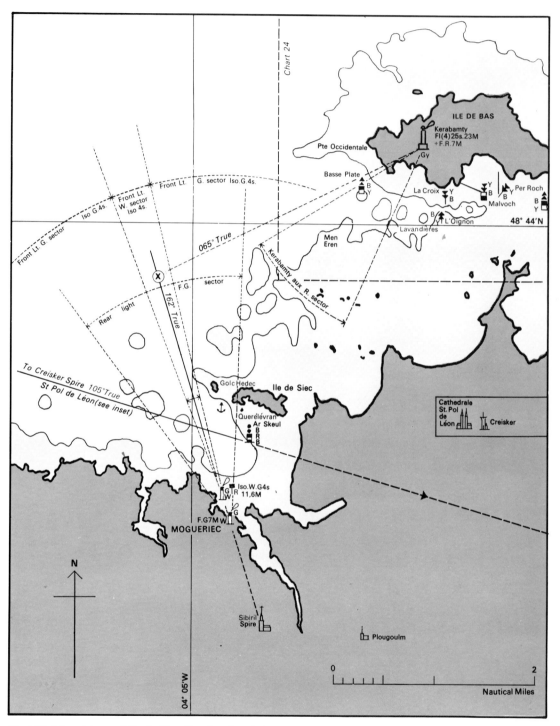

Chart 27. Moguériec and Ile de Siec. *Based on French Chart No 966.*

202

follow this line leaving **Golc Hedec** (just west of and, at low water, connected to **Ile de Siec**) 0·2 mile to port, and various dangerous drying rocks 0·3 mile to starboard.

As an alternative, a vessel coming from the west can pick up the line **Ar Skeul – Creisker** spire (to the right of **St Pol de Leon** Cathedral) bearing 105° True and follow this until **Mogueriec** lights come into line, then proceed as above. This clears a patch drying 0·6 m but crosses a 1·5 m patch.

If proceeding to the **Siec** anchorage, after passing **Golc Hedec** bear eastwards, head midway between the south shore of **Ile de Siec** and the little pile of rocks known as **Querélvran**.

If proceeding to **Moguériec** (with sufficient rise of tide) hold on the transit until 0·5 mile off the breakwater lighthouse when bear to port to bring it bearing 170° True then steer to pass between the end of the breakwater and the Lateral port beacon.

By Night Steering on a safe course towards or away from **Ile de Bas** light (Fl (4) 25 s) pick up the rear light (fixed G) which has a range of 7 miles and is visible over an arc from 142° to 182° True and the front light which is fixed G except for a white sector between 158° and 166° True, that is 4° True either side of the alignment. Turn to follow the line. Close approach to the anchorage or the harbour might be difficult for a stranger, it should not however be difficult to make departure by night by steering a compass course from the anchorage into the white sector of the front light and then following the transit.

Anchorage

The anchorage at Ile de Siec is south of the western end of the island and the exact position depends on the state of the tide. At springs there is 7·3 m sand and shells with the end of the island jetty bearing ENE 0·25 mile, but with the aid of soundings a yacht

Ile de Siec and Moguériec. The yacht is anchored at neap tides in the narrow channel with sand bottom between Querelvran on the south and Ile de Siec on the north. At spring tides it is necessary to anchor farther to the westward.

Facing west across Moguériec harbour.

can find a position nearer to the jetty where it is more sheltered. On a neap tide (6 m at Brest) there is 2·1 to 2·4 m midway between the island and the **Querélévran**, the rock bearing about 160° True. This rock is clearly identifiable at high water but, there are blocks of rocks which dry out close north of it, so that care must be taken to find the narrow strip of sand bottom between these rocks and those off the island, which gives limited swinging room. The water is generally transparent, but strangers may prefer to anchor farther westward in water which rapidly deepens. The harbour itself consists merely of a rough jetty, the end of which dries over 2·4 m LAT. The harbour seems quite well protected and small fishing boats lie there, but the rough jetty is stated to be unsuitable for lying alongside.

Facilities

The island has no resources and appears to be deserted at night, but it is joined to the mainland by a causeway (which is probably dry at half-tide).

Moguériec is described as a most attractive and friendly fishing village. There is an *alimentation* 200 m from the harbour and a restaurant 'Coz Canol', by the quay. There is a water tap behind the public convenience on the quay. There are excellent beaches.

Historical

During the Second World War, two British airmen parachuted into the sea nearby and, as a reprisal for help given to them by the inhabitants, all the buildings on the island were blown up by the occupying forces.

33 Pontusval

Tidal Data

Tidal Heights
High Water: approx +0050 Brest, +0600 Dover.
Heights of Tide above Datum: approx MHWS 8·2 m, MLWS 1·2 m, MHWN 6·4 m, MLWN 3·3 m.
Mean Tide Level: 4·7 m. Index 7 B.

Tidal Streams

1. 5 miles seaward of **Pontusval** the east-going stream begins at −0250 Brest (+0220 Dover) and the west-going stream at +0315 Brest (−0400 Dover). Both streams reach 2·8 knots at springs.
2. Inshore the streams turn earlier. Off **Aman ar Ross**, 4 miles westward, the east-going stream begins at −0405 Brest (+0105 Dover) and the west-going at +0215 Brest (−0500 Dover). Both streams reach 2·8 knots at springs.

General

Many cruising men will have passed Pontusval on their passages between Roscoff and l'Abervrac'h, without attempting entry, as the approach looks forbidding if there is any swell or sea running. However in southerly winds there is a deep water anchorage in the entrance and small yachts which can take the ground, find shelter, except from northerly winds, drying out in the pretty and almost land-locked harbour.

Approaches

By Day Only   Dangerous rocks and shoals extend for up to 1 mile north of this coast and it should not be approached more closely, until one is sure of one's position. The most conspicuous landmarks from offshore are the water tower and radio mast mentioned on page 200. The next mark to identify is **Pontusval** lighthouse, square tower and white house 13 m high, elevation 16 m. This, in line with the radio mast, bears 185° True. Then identify **Pontusval** isolated danger buoy which lies 057° True from this lighthouse, distant 1·1 miles. Approach this buoy from the northward and leave it 0·1 mile to starboard. At this point the leading marks will be in line, viz: **Plounéour-Trez** spire in line with the white beacon on the east side

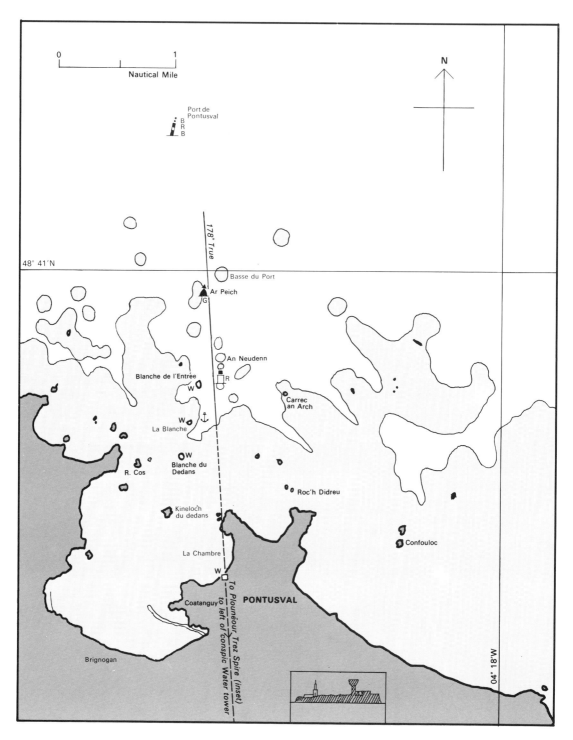

Port de
Pontusval

B
R
B

N

0   1
Nautical Mile

178° True

48° 41'N

Basse du Port

Ar Peich
G

An Neudenn

Blanche de l'Entrée
W   R

Carrec
an Arch

W
La Blanche

W
Blanche du
Dedans

R. Cos

Roc'h Didreu

Kineloch
du dedans

Confouloc

La Chambre

W

To Plounéour Trez Spire (inset)
to left of conspic Water tower

Coatanguy   **PONTUSVAL**

Brignogan

04° 18'W

Chart 28. Pontusval. *Based on French Chart No 966.*

of the harbour. **Ar Peich** Lateral starboard buoy will then be fine on the starboard bow and **An Neudenn** Lateral port beacon tower fine on the port bow. Follow this line 178° leaving:

> **Ar Peich** Lateral starboard buoy close to starboard.
>
> **An Neudenn** Lateral port beacon tower 50 m to port.

First white painted rock 50 m to starboard. There is deep water exactly on the transit as far as a cable beyond the beacon tower, but there are rocks close on each side which are awash or dry 0·3 m at low water.

When entering there is the first white painted rock (**Blanche de l'Entrée**) and two others to be left to starboard farther in (**La Blanche** and **Blanche du Dedans**). South of **La Blanche** the entrance shallows rapidly and a yacht can only proceed farther with adequate rise of tide.

Anchorage and Harbour

The usual anchorage is on the approach transit with **An Neudenn** beacon tower bearing about NE in 4·5 m LAT with rather restricted swinging room, or with **La Blanche** bearing NW with even less room. At neaps a yacht can sound her way and anchor farther in, finding about 2·7 m at low water. The anchorage is indifferent except in offshore winds with no prospect of a shift of wind to or swell from a northerly direction, when it can become dangerous. The harbour itself can be entered near high water but no precise instructions can be given as there is an unmarked rock in the centre named **Kineloch du Dedans** which dries 4·3 m LAT. The striking line for the rock is with **Blanche de l'Entrée** in line with **La Blanche**. The approximate way in is to bring **An Neudenn** on a NNE bearing and to steer SSW, borrowing to starboard as necessary to avoid the fringes of the rock on the east side. Then when the houses on the headland to port bear east, alter course to west (leaving the underwater rock to starboard) steer into the anchorage on the west side and anchor (buoy the anchor) on sand bottom near the small craft moorings. This anchorage is well protected from west but dries over 3 m LAT, **La Chambre** drying 4·2 m LAT situated on the east side also provides an anchorage for small craft, but there are occasional outcrops of rocks on the bottom. There is a slip farther south on the east side of the harbour with rocks on its north side and sand on its south side, but it dries 4·2 m LAT and approach would be difficult in a deep-keeled yacht.

Facilities

There are good shops, a number of holiday hotels, banks and post office at **Brignogan**, a quarter of a mile walk from the beach at the south side of the harbour.

34 Le Correjou

Tidal Data

Tidal Heights
High Water: approx +0030 Brest, +0540 Dover.
Heights of Tide above Datum: approx MHWS 7·9 m, MLWS 1·2 m, MHWN 6·4 m, MLWN 3·0 m.

Mean Tide Level: 4·7 m. Index 7 B.

Tidal Streams

No local information available but see under Pontusval and L'Abervrac'h.

General

Like **Pontusval** this harbour provides anchorage for deep-keeled yachts in settled southerly weather and better shelter for yachts capable of drying out. This harbour should only be approached in good visibility and settled weather.

Approaches

From the North

By Day Only   From a position about 1·3 miles west of **Aman ar Ross** Cardinal north pillar whistle buoy, identify **Plouguerneau** belfry, which is about 0·25 mile west of a prominent water tower. Bring this to bear 189° True, then identify **Mean Yan**, a small above-water rock, on this bearing and lying about 0·25 mile to the east of a much larger above-water rock, **Lizen Du**. Turn on to this transit and follow it until about 0·3 mile north of **Mean Yan** and when **Penven** rock is abeam to starboard, distant 0·2 mile. Then quit the leading line and steer to make good 178° True, heading for a point midway between the two pinnacles of **Carrec Crom**. This line passes between two 1 m LAT patches and must be regarded as having such minimum depth. When 100 m north of the north-east pinnacle, alter course to port so as to leave it 100 m to starboard on the same course. This leaves **Baxhugen** drying rock 200 m to starboard. Continue to make good 178° True until the chapel of **St Michel Noblet** bears 280° True then turn on to this heading into the anchorage.

From the West

By Day Only   From a position 0·3 mile north of **Ile Vierge** lighthouse, steer to make good 094° True, heading for **Carrec Hir** (dries 8·1 m LAT). When the gap between the two pinnacles of **Carrec Crom** bears 178° True, turn on to this bearing and proceed as in *From the North* above.

Anchorage

Anchor south-east of Penvers Island in 0·6 to 2·9 m sand.

Amenities

Small fishing harbour with sailing school. Dinghy landing at quay.

35 L'Abervrac'h

Tidal Data

Tidal Heights
High Water: approx +0030 Brest, +0540 Dover.
Heights of Tide above Datum: approx MHWS 7·9 m, MLWS 1·2 m, MHWN 6·4 m, MLWN 3·0 m.
Mean Tide Level: 4·7 m. Index 7 B.

Tidal Streams

1. Offshore 5 miles seaward of **Le Libenter** the east-going stream begins at −0300 Brest (+0210 Dover) and the west-going at +0310 Brest (−0405 Dover). Both streams reach 2·8 knots at springs.
2. Off **Le Libenter** and in the **Grand Chenal de l'Abervrac'h** and probably close in to **Ile Vierge** the streams turn earlier. The east-going or ESE-going stream begins at −0500 Brest (+0010 Dover) and the west-going or WNW-going stream begins at +0110 Brest (−0605 Dover). The outer streams attain 3·7 knots and the **Grand Chenal** streams 2·8 knots at springs.

General

L'Abervrac'h is perhaps the best anchorage between Tréguier and Brest, and is much used by yachts bound to or from the Chenal du Four.

The river can be entered by day or night at any state of the tide, but calls for reasonable visibility in order to pick up the leading lines whilst keeping clear of the many off-lying dangers. Approach may be easier by night, but not in bad visibility, as it is necessary to be able to pick up **Lanvaon** light (elevation 55 m, vis 10 miles) at a range of at least 5 miles and **Ile Vrac'h** red light (elevation 19 m, vis 7 miles) at a range of at least 3 miles. By day it is possible to enter in lesser visibility, provided the yacht's position can be fairly accurately plotted whilst looking for the outer marks.

The popular anchorage at La Palue is conveniently near the entrance, but not always fully sheltered. The river above Pointe Cameleut is a snug retreat, sheltered by steep wooded banks.

Approaches

Grand Chenal

By Day   Make a position from which **Ile Vierge** lighthouse, which has a Radiobeacon VG 298·8 kHz range 70 miles (grouped Penlee Point

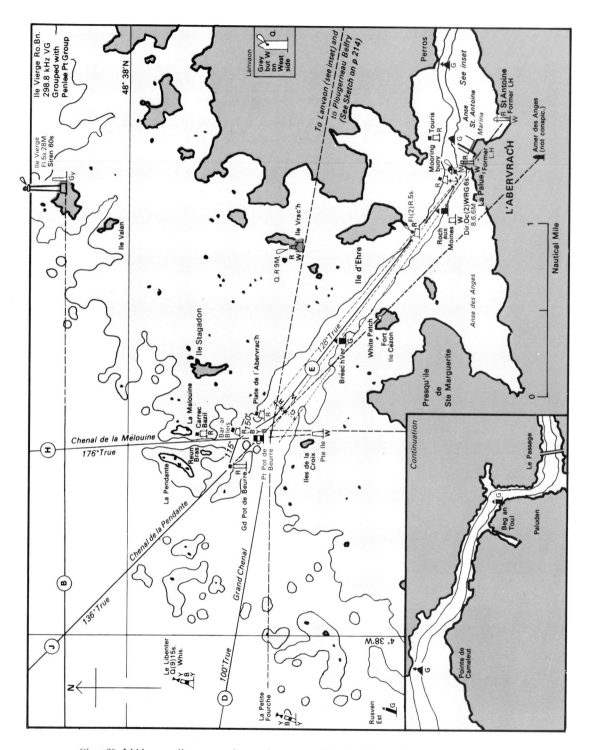

Chart 29. L'Abervrac'h, approaches and entrance. *Based on French Chart No 5772.*

212

Group Seq 5), (elevation 77 m) bears 090° True distant 3 miles, with **Ploudalmezéau** tall steeple on the skyline, open to the westward of **Lampaul** steeple (nearer, below the skyline) bearing 186° True. Alter to follow this line, allowing for strong cross tides, heading for **La Petite Fourche** Cardinal west spar buoy and leaving **Le Libenter** Cardinal west pillar light and whistle buoy with radar reflector 0·17 miles to port. Usually the whistle in this buoy can be heard for over a mile. (Not to be relied on.) See Chart No 29.

Continue making good this course until the leading marks for the **Grand Chenal** come into line; these are **Ile Vrac'h lighthouse** (square white tower with red top on white house elevation 19 m) in line with **Lanvaon** rectangular tower with pointed top painted white towards the transit (elevation 55 m) **Plouguerneau** belfry farther inland is also on this line bearing 100° True. Alter course to follow this line. If visibility is poor, having found the **Libenter** buoy it may then be easier to then identify **Iles de la Croix** which lie 0·2 mile south of line **D**.

This line leaves the following marks on the sides shown:

Libenter Cardinal west pillar light and whistle buoy with radar reflector 0·2 mile to port.

Grand Pot de Beurre Lateral port pyramid 0·1 mile to port. (This mark is deceptive and looks rather like a large pillar buoy from a distance.)

Petit Pot de Beurre Cardinal east beacon tower without topmark 80 m to port.

The yacht pontoon at La Palue.

Plate de l'Abervrac'h Lateral port buoy 150 m to port; but just before this buoy is abeam, alter course to starboard to follow line **E**, **La Palue** former LH (white tower with red top), **St Antoine** former LH (white tower with red top), and the new white light pillar by the lifeboat house, in line bearing 128° True. (line)**E**.)

The line leaves the following marks on the sides shown:

Petite Ile de la Croix white pyramid 0·275 mile to starboard.

Bréac'h Ver Lateral starboard beacon tower 80 m to starboard.

Fort Ile Cézon, a small stone fort with a circular black-and-white mark painted on its northern wall, 0·1 mile to starboard.

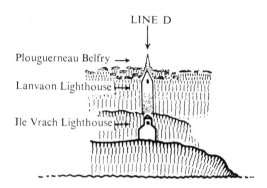

Grand Chenal, L'Abervrac'h, from a position 0·7 mile west of Libenter buoy.

Ile d'Ehre Lateral port buoy 50 m to port.

Roche aux Moines Lateral starboard beacon tower 65 m to starboard. (Towards high water a small yacht working to windward may choose to pass to the SW of this rock, the south-west corner of which is marked by a Lateral port beacon tower. This passage dries 3·0 m LAT, i.e. has 1·5 m of water at half-tide and 3·3 m at MHWN.)

Continuing up the main channel, when the **Roche aux Moines** Lateral starboard beacon tower is abeam to starboard, alter course to 110° True for about 0·2 mile leaving the next Lateral port buoy about 50 m to port. Then alter to port so as to leave **Touris** Lateral port beacon tower 75 m to port. A large round mooring buoy lies to the NNW of the jetty and may be passed on either side. Enter the anchorage or go alongside the pontoon. If bound up the river steer to leave the small Lateral starboard buoy off **Point Cameleut** 50 m to starboard. There is a shoal with only 1 m over it LAT, situated midstream about 0·175 mile SE of **Touris** beacon tower, but there is nearly always enough water over this. Keep close to the lines of moorings off the slipway on the north side of the river at **Perros** and upstream of **Pointe Cameleut** and thereafter keep near the middle of the river all the way to **Paluden**, leaving **Beg an Toul** Lateral

Ile Vierge lighthouse from the northward. The structure is 75 m high and close north west of it is a small square disused light-tower, which makes it unmistakable.

starboard beacon tower close to starboard. It is easier for a stranger to proceed up the river at half-tide, when oyster withies will be seen on each side of the channel.

By Night   Approaching from the north or east, bring **Ile Vierge** light Fl 5 sec to bear 090° True distant about 2 miles and then steer to make good 270° True. Approaching from the west, approach with **Ile Vierge** bearing 090° True. Identify **Libenter** Cardinal west light and whistle buoy, with radar reflector, 0·8 mile to the south of this line (**B**). When this buoy bears 180° True alter to make good this course, allowing for the cross tide, and continue on this course leaving the buoy to port, until the leading lights for the **Grand Chenal Ile Vrach** (*front*) Q R vis 7 miles, in line with **Lanvaon** (*rear*) Q (intensified 090°–110°) bear 100° True. Then alter to follow this transit (Line **D**) until the green sector of **La Palue** Oc GWR directional light comes into view, then stand by to alter course to follow the white sector on a course of 128° True (Line **E**).

Chenal de la Malouine

By Day Only   From a position on line **B**, 1·5 miles west of Ile Vierge lighthouse, identify **La Malouine** a large rock (see photograph), and **La Pendante** a lower rock to the west of it. In the gap between these rocks identify **Le Petit Pot de Beurre** Cardinal east squat beacon tower and the white pyramid on **Petite Ile de la Croix** (see close-up photograph).

Leaving Iles de la Croix to starboard when entering by the Grand Chenal. They are the most conspicuous feature in the approach and at low water the sea breaks heavily on the outlying reef NW of them. The white pyramid to the left is the rear leading mark for the Malouine channel.

Just before Plate d'Abervrach Lateral port spindle buoy is abeam to port alter course to starboard to bring La Palue lighthouse in line with St Antoine lighthouse (rear) at 128° True. Breac'h Ver Lateral starboard beacon tower is left about 80 m to starboard and Fort Ile Cézon (with circular mark) about 0·1 mile to starboard. Fort Ile Cézon is a leading mark for Chenal de la Pendante.

Approaching Chenal de la Malouine. The leading marks are Petit Pot du Beurre Cardinal east beacon tower in line with the white pyramid on Petite Ile de la Croix (see photograph above). It is near low water.

The dangers of the Chenal de la Malouine lie in the approach, but once La Malouine is abeam to port the channel is deep and easy to navigate. The rock is less conspicuous at HW than is shown here. The Lateral port beacon tower to the right is Carrec Bazil (left to port).

A closer view of the leading marks for Chenal de la Malouine, Petit Pot de Beurre Cardinal east beacon tower (front) in line with La Croix (Petite Ile de la Croix) white pyramid at 175° True. The pyramid is not always easy to identify from a distance and in some lights appears dark. Nearer at hand it is masked near low water by Petit Pot de Buerre beacon tower which now is without top mark. The approach is indicated by the broken line, but when Bar-ar-Bleis Lateral port buoy comes abeam, bear to port on the solid line and steer midway between the beacon tower and Plate de l'Abervrach small Lateral port buoy.

217

The Plateau de la Pendante is left to starboard. Here it is seen at LW with a NW swell. In heavy weather broken water is said to extend right across the channel. The leading line brings a vessel very close to an outlier NNE of La Pendante on which the swell is breaking to the right of the picture.

Bring these into line bearing 176° True and steer to follow this line, making allowance for the cross tide. (Line **H**.)

This channel carries a least depth of 3·0 m, but passes very close to the NE end of the **Plateau de la Pendante**, which has a least depth of 0·3 m and over which the sea commonly breaks at all states of the tide. In heavy weather this broken water is said to extend right across the channel, and a yacht should then use the **Grand Chenal**.

This line leaves the following marks on the sides shown:

La Malouine rock 100 m to port.

Carrec Bazil Lateral port beacon tower 90 m to port.

Réun Bras rock (dries 6·4 m LAT) 90 m to starboard.

Bar-ar-Bleis Lateral port buoy 100 m to port.

When the latter is abeam, quit the leading line and steer midway between **Petit Pot de Beurre** Cardinal east beacon tower and **Plate de l'Abervrac'h** small Lateral port buoy. Then bring **La Palue** former LH (white tower red top) **St Antoine** former LH (white tower red top) and the new white light pillar by the lifeboat house into line bearing 128° True and follow this line as for *Grand Chenal*, above.

Chenal de la Pendante

By Day Only   From a position on line **B**, 2·5 miles west of Ile Vierge lighthouse, identify **Fort Ile Cézon**, a small stone fort on an island with a

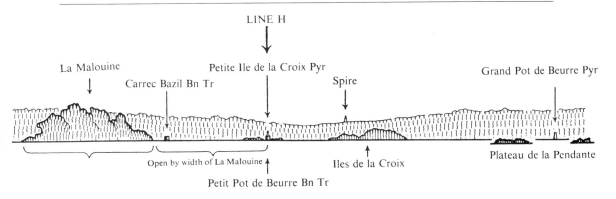

Chenal de la Malouine, L'Abervrac'h, from a position west of Ile Vierge, 1 hour after HWN.

black-and-white circular mark painted on the wall of the fort, and **Amer des Anges** black tower, with a conical top on the skyline. The **Amer des Anges** tower is between a mast to the left and a house to the right and there is a conspicuous water tower about 300 m to the west of it which assists in identification. These marks in line bearing 136° True mark the **Chenal de la Pendante** (line **J**). This channel carries a least depth of 3·6 m, but it passes very close to drying rocks on the NE side of **Le Libenter** and the SW side of the **Plateau de la Pendante**. It should not be attempted, unless the leading marks have been positively identified before approaching, in heavy weather and, still less in poor visibility. The leading marks must be held exactly.

Follow the leading line which leaves:

La Pendante an above water rock 0·1 mile to port.

When **Grand Pot de Beurre** Lateral port beacon bears 175° True, quit the leading line and steer for the **Bar-ar-Bleis** Lateral port buoy, but when **Petit Pot de Beurre** Cardinal east beacon tower comes into line with **Petite Ile de la Croix** white pyramid (line **H**) alter course so as to pass midway between the **Petit Pot de Beurre** Cardinal east beacon tower and **Plate de l'Abervrac'h** small Lateral port buoy. From here follow line **E** and proceed as for the *Grand Chenal* above.

Anchorages

Anchorage is prohibited between Fort Ile Cézon and Ile d'Ehre, owing to telegraph cables. Otherwise:

1. Large yachts usually anchor about 0·2 mile east of **Roche aux Moines** in 10 m LAT, sand, but this position is rather exposed with the wind from the west or

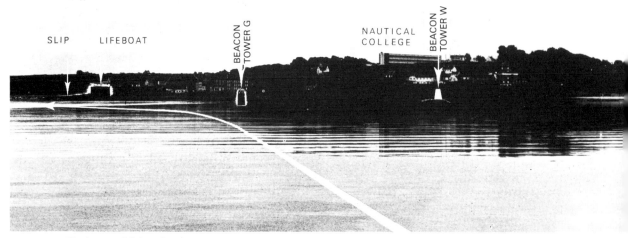

SLIP   LIFEBOAT   BEACON TOWER G   NAUTICAL COLLEGE   BEACON TOWER W

Roche aux Moines Lateral starboard beacon tower is left about 65 m to starboard. The Lateral port beacon tower on the right is at the far end of the rocks.

L'Abervrac'h. Yacht pontoon, village, lifeboat house and landing slip where there is a water tap.

Touris. Lateral port beacon tower is on the left of the picture and the end of the landing slip to the right of it. Rain spoils clarity, but this picture shows the channel at LW and the fishing fleet at anchor.

north-west. There is a foul patch only 100 m north-west of the anchorage position marked on Chart No 29.

2. There is better shelter in the fairway to the south and south-east of **Touris** beacon tower, in 3·0 to 7·6 m, sand. The farther south the better, but the edge of the bank is steep and it is possible to take a sounding in deep water and hit the mud before the next is taken. Much of this anchorage is now taken up by permanent moorings, which are available for visitors with boats over 10 m long.

3. A berth may be available at the yacht pontoon east of the jetty. The outer three berths on each side are available to boats of less than 10 m length, the inner berths are restricted to yachts of 8 m or less. This is very convenient for all purposes. It is possible also to anchor in the adjacent dredged area to the east or north-east of the white buoy, which marks a small area drying 0·5 m immediately west of it.

4. There is perfect shelter anywhere in the fairway above **Pointe Cameleut**, in depths of 4·8 to 6·1 m LAT, mud, as far as **Beg-an-Toul**; and in depths of 1·8 to 3·6 m LAT, mud, from **Beg-an-Toul** to **Paluden**, but space in this reach is limited by local moorings. The position shown on the chart to the east of Pointe Cameleut is a good one. Land on the foreshore (mud at LW) and follow the road over a mile to L'Abervrac'h.

5. There is a good drying berth alongside the small quay on the west bank at **Paluden**, drying 2·4 m LAT, muddy shingle, but this is sometimes required by coasters.

Facilities

La Palue, or Port de l'Abervrac'h. If lying to one of the visitors' buoys, three blasts on the foghorn will bring a harbour launch for free transport ashore. A charge is made for the mooring, boats lying to their own anchors pay half price. Manoeuvring under sail in the port is not allowed. Yachts without engine must hail a harbour attendant. Insurance of yachts is compulsory, although one's word is taken for this, otherwise a premium is charged by the harbour attendant.

Visiting yachts are issued with a temporary membership card for the Yacht Club des Abers which is current for the period covered by the berthing fee.

Water, petrol and diesel are available on the quay.

The yacht club provides wcs, showers (0830–1200 and 1500–1900: not cheap), telephone, sail washing, battery charging, charts, weather forecast, rest-rooms and bar, which has limited opening hours.

Bellevue Hôtel near the quay where travellers' cheques may be cashed, baths and excellent meals obtainable at reasonable prices. Bonded stores may be ordered after arrangements with the Douanier, but only if the yacht is immediately proceeding to another country.

Baie des Anges restaurant, about a quarter mile along the road to the west has been excellent in the past; but was vacant, for sale, in 1982. Créperie

Likewise taken in rain, this picture shows the channel east of Touris at low water if
proceeding up river to Paluden. The channel is indicated by oyster withies on each side and
the direction leads to the landing slip below the white house. Here there are often fishing
vessels at anchor or on moorings. Sail close to them before bearing to starboard to avoid the
long spit of mud on the starboard hand, which is marked by a small Lateral starboard buoy.

To the right is the mud bank extending NW from Pointe Cameleut, on which many yachts
come to grief. The deep water is nearer the north side of the river here, leaving close to port
the local craft on moorings which dry out at LW or are on the edge of the channel. The oyster
stakes are the best indication of the channel.

The anchorage east of Pointe Cameleut is sheltered. The picture faces ESE looking up the
river. It is low water and the oyster withies mark the mud on the north side, after which keep
near the middle of the river.

near quay. Take-away oysters from Belon des Abers. Buses to Brest stop at the café near the root of the mole.

Dinghy landing at the yacht club pontoon or the slip at all states of the tide.

Lannilis, a little over 2 miles SE of L'Abervrac'h and about a mile uphill from Paluden, is a pleasant small town with good shopping facilities and restaurants.

Paluden consists of a few cottages and a good hotel. There are no local shops, but it is possible to obtain milk and other farm produce locally. Simple meal at Café Breton and Relais des Abers, half a mile up the road. Bus to Lannilis.

36 L'Aberbenoit

Tidal Data

Tidal Heights
High Water: approx +0025 Brest, +0535 Dover.
Heights of Tide above Datum: approx MHWS 7·9 m, MLWS 1·2 m, MHWN 6·4 m, MLWN 3·0 m.
Mean Tide Level: 4·7 m.

Tidal Streams

1. Off **La Petite Fourche** buoy the ENE-going stream begins at −0515 Brest (−0005 Dover) and the west-going stream begins at +0055 Brest (+0606 Dover). Both streams attain 2·8 knots at springs.
2. South of **Ile Guenioc** the flood stream begins at −0500 Brest (+0010 Dover) and the ebb at +0100 Brest (+0610 Dover), reaching 2 to 2·5 knots. In the river itself the flood begins 15 minutes earlier and both streams reach about 3 knots.

General

Lying only 2 miles SW of l'Abervrac'h, this little river offers excellent sheltered anchorage in beautiful surroundings. It is known locally as La Rivière de Saint-Pabu.

It can be entered at any state of the tide, but only in daylight and reasonable visibility. In strong westerly or north-westerly winds the Northern Approach described below is said to be dangerous, owing to broken water.

Approaches

Northern Approach

By Day Only   Approach from any direction, make for **La Petite Fourche** Cardinal west spar buoy. From a position 20 m west of this buoy steer to make good 172° True (Line **C**) leaving **Rusven Est** Lateral stbd spar buoy 50 m to stbd. Continue on this course until **La Jument** rock off **Ile Guenioc** is abeam to port, then make good 163° True so as to leave **Poul Orvil** Lateral port buoy 50 m to port (Line **M**). From **Poul Orvil** buoy steer to make good 130° True (Line **N**) to leave **Corn ar Gazel** Lateral stbd buoy 50 m to stbd. Continue this course heading for **Le Chien** Isolated danger beacon tower. This may be left close

225

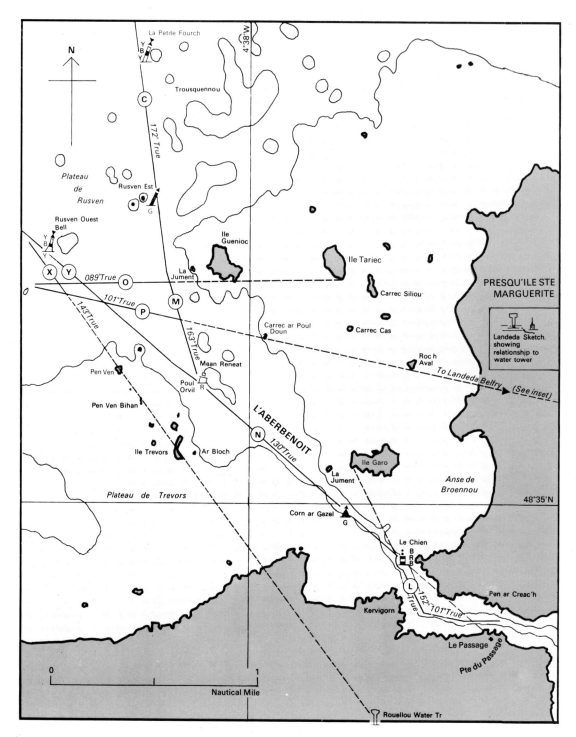

Chart 30. L'Aberbenoit, approaches and entrance. *Based on French Chart No 5772.*

226

Ile Guenioc has ledges of rock on the north and west sides and an outlier named La Jument (not to be confused with the other Jument off Ile Garo, a mile beyond).

A close-up view of La Jument de Garo at low water.

on either hand, except towards LWS when it should be left to port to avoid the 1m patch which lies 50 m to the north. After passing **Le Chien** beacon tower, bring it into line astern with the west edge of **Ile Garo** (line **L**) and hold this course (152° True), leaving the small craft on moorings in the sandy bay of **Kervigorn** to starboard.

When **Pointe du Passage** bears 101° True alter to follow this bearing. There is a rock drying 0·3 m 80 m off the south-east corner of the bay and a drying spit extending 180 m from the point opposite **Kervigorn** bay, outside which there are depths of 0·6 m LAT up to 200 m from the land. After about 0·6 mile, when clear of these dangers keep to midstream, but note that there is an edge of high sand on the south side of the river opposite **Pointe du Passage.** Local shallow draught boats on moorings off that side should be left to starboard. Depths are unpredictable due to dredging.

227

Approach X

By Day Only This is the best approach in bad weather. From the **Rélec** channel (see Chapter 37) with **Rouellou** water tower, which is just below the wood of that name held open to the right of the prominent **Pen Ven** rock at about 143° True (line **X**), follow this line which leaves

Pen Ven as seen from Les Petites Fourches.

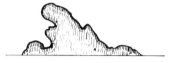

Pen Ven as it appears when on the leading line with the water tower and Ruellou wood.

Rusven Ouest Cardinal west spar bell buoy 50 m to port, after this there are two alternative lines which can be followed:

(a) the South edges of **Ile Guenioc** and **Ile Tariec** in line bearing 089° True (line **O**) or by proceeding about 0·1 mile farther.

(b) **Carrec ar Poul Doun** prominent rock and **Landeda** belfry in line (line **P**) 101° True. These transits lead to line **M** which should then be followed as under *Northern Approach*, above.

Approach Y

By Day Only This is the simplest approach of all but the leading marks must be identified with certainty as the channel lies very close to dangerous underwater rocks.

Le Chien isolated danger beacon tower at low water. The rock covers at high tide and, although a leading mark, it is often difficult to identify at a distance. It may be passed on either side but is best left to port. On the right is Kervigorn bay. Here shallow draft yachts lie on moorings, and the line of moorings can be followed leaving the yachts about 25 to 50 m on the starboard hand and following the bend in the river to port.

After rounding the bend, head ESE towards Pointe du Passage here seen on the right of the picture. Leave to starboard the shallow draft craft moored off it.

From the **Rélec** channel (see Chapter 37) with **Le Chien** beacon tower in line with the high dwelling at **Le Passage** bearing about 130° True (line **Y**), follow this line which leaves:

Rusven Ouest Cardinal west spar bell buoy close to port.
Pen Ven rock outliers which dry 1·8 m and 2·8 m LAT about 80 m to starboard. **Poul Orvil** Lateral port buoy about 50 m to port.
Thereafter proceed as under *Northern Approach* above.

Anchorage

Anchor anywhere in the pool, on either side of the Pointe du Passage. The depths vary due to dredging and there are some patches of rock. There is also anchorage near the entrance in the sandy bay of Kervigorn if the wind is offshore. Anchor in deep water just north of the local yachts and boats on moorings and land by dinghy on the sands. Another anchorage lies off the château on the north side of the river.

Facilities

There is a good dinghy landing at all states of the tide on each side of the river at the Pointe du Passage, especially on the south side. From Le Passage walk a quarter of a mile up the hill where there is a small shop and a modest restaurant Le Valencia. A further quarter mile along the road there is a baker and two garages. Water at Le Passage landing slip or at a pipe in Kervigorn bay. The nearest public telephone is at the first fork up the road from Le Passage.

37 Portsall Inner Passage

Tidal Data

Tidal Streams

The directions and rates of the tidal streams vary in different parts of the channels, between spring and neap tides and are influenced by the formation of the plateaux and rocks between which they run. They are, for example, particularly rapid north of **Ile Verte** where, towards low water the streams are compressed between the island and the shoals northward of the channel. In the more open parts of the channels the streams tend to be more moderate.

The following table shows the approximate rates and directions of the streams in the main channels.

	EAST-GOING STREAM			WEST-GOING STREAM		
Position	*Direction*	*Spring Rate*	*Begins*	*Direction*	*Spring Rate*	*Begins*
Chenal du Rélec	ENE	3·5–4	−0600 Brest (−0050 Dover)	WSW	3·5–4	0000 Brest (+0510 Dover)
Chenal du Raous	E	4·5–5	−0600 Brest (−0050 Dover)	W	4·5–5	0000 Brest (+0510 Dover)
Chenal Méridional	ENE	3·5–4	−0600 Brest (−0050 Dover)	W	4–5	0000 Brest (+0510 Dover)

General

This passage inside Portsall rocks, as well as giving access to Portsall itself, provides a short cut between L'Abervrac'h and L'Aberbenoit to and from the Four channel, together with an interesting exercise in rock dodging. It can be used only in clear weather and, if sailing, with a leading wind. Preferably it will not be used at spring tides as the stream is very strong, especially in the vicinity of Portsall. At low water the rocks are clear, but some of the back leading marks may be masked for a considerable distance by the front marks, standing high above low water. In places the channel between rocks is so narrow that an error would be dangerous, and great care is necessary when navigating through it for the first time, which is best done east

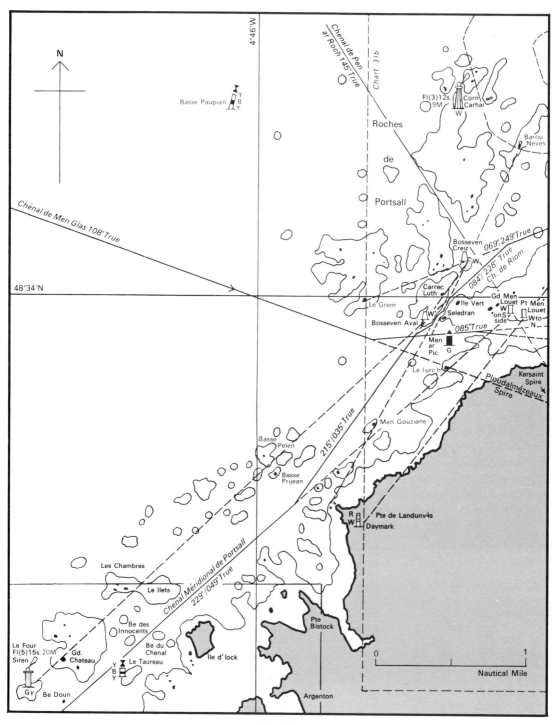

N

Basse Paupian

Chénal de Pen ar Roch 145° True

Chart 31b

4°46'W

Chénal de Men Glas 108° True

48°34'N

Roches

de

Portsall

Fl(3)12s.
9M   Corn
      Carhai
      W

Barou
Neves

Bosseven
Creiz
      W

069°/249° True

084°/228° True
Ch. de Riom

Carrec
Luth

Le Grem

Bosseven Aval

Ile Vert

Seledran

W

085° True

Gd Men
Louet Pt Men
W   Louet
on S   W to
side   N

Men
ar
Pic
G

Le lurc'h

Kersaint
Spire

Ploudalmézeaux
Spire

215°/035° True

Men Gouziane

Basse
Pelen

Basse
Prijean

Pte de Landunvés
R
W
Daymark

Les Chambres

Le Ilets

Chenal Méridional de Portsall
229°/049° True

Be des
Innocents

Be du
Chenal

Ile d'Iock

Pte
Bistock

Le Four
Fl(5)15s. 20M
Siren   Gd.
           Chateau

Y
B
Y

Le Taureau

0   1

Nautical Mile

Gy   Be Doun

Argenton

Chart 31a

232

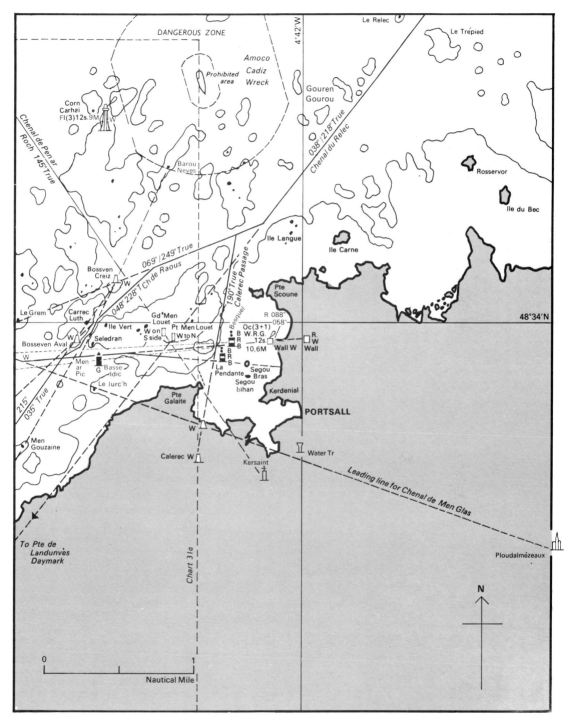

DANGEROUS ZONE

4°42'W

Le Relec

Le Trépied

Amoco
Cadiz
Wreck

Prohibited
area

Corn
Carhai
Fl(3)12s.9M

Gouren
Gourou

Rosservor

038°/218°True
Chenal du Relec

Ile du Bec

Barou
Neves

Chenal de Pen ar
Roch 145°True

069°/249°True

Ile Langue

Ile Carne

048°/228° Ch de Raous

190°True
Calerec Passage

Pte
Scoune

48°34'N

Bossven
Creiz

W

Le Grem

Carrec
Luth

Gd Men
Louet

Pt Men Louet

R. 088°
058°

Bossven Aval

Seledran

Ile Vert

W on
S side

W to N

Oc(3+1)
W.R.G.
12s.
10,6M

R.
W
Wall

Wall W

215°
035°True

Men
ar
Pic

G

Basse
Idic

Le Iurc'h

La
Pendante

Segou
Bras

Segou
bihan

Kerdenial

PORTSALL

Men
Gouzaine

Pte
Galaite

W

Water Tr

To Pte de
Landunves
Daymark

Chart 31a

Calerec W

Kersaint

Leading line for Chenal de Men Glas

Ploudalmézeaux

N

0   1

Nautical Mile

Chart 31b

Chart 31a and b. Portsall Inner Passage, showing entrance to Portsall. *Based on French Chart! No 5772.*

233

water tower | Petit Men Louet | beacon | Grand Men Louet | île Verte | Bosseven Aval | Four lighthouse

The leading marks for the Chenal du Rélec are Petit Men Louet beacon and the beacon, white with red top (on the wrong side and off transit in the picture), which is near the ruins of the old semaphore building SE of the Pointe de Landunves. For a nearer view of the mast and the ruins of the semaphore building on which it stands see photo, p. 238.
NB. All the captions to photographs of marks in the Portsall Inner Passage refer to the westbound passage.

to west. The channels carry 2·1 m LAT (3·3 m MLWS) but as there are rocks in the vicinity of the **Chenal du Rélec** it is sensible to regard them as having 0·3 m LAT (1·5 m MLWS). For reasons which will appear later, it is better to make the passage when the soundings are 3·6 m above Datum. The passage passes through three named and one unnamed channel. From east to west, first there is the **Chenal du Rélec** from La Petite Fourche to Ile Longue; next the **Chenal du Raous** to the rock Bosseven Creiz, with a continuation or unnamed channel to Bossven Aval; finally the **Chenal Méridional de Portsall** which is the passage from Portsall leading south of Le Four lighthouse into the **Chenal du Four** between the mainland and Ushant. This inner passage is known to a number of cruising people, but it would be irresponsible not to emphasise that it is dangerous in strong winds or poor visibility. The overfalls in the narrows with a spring tide against a SW gale, west of **Ile Verte** are said to be as severe as in the famous **Raz de Sein** and the **Chenal Méridional** is described as *extrèmement mauvais* under such conditions.

WESTBOUND PASSAGE

Chenal du Rélec

By Day Only From the **Petite Fourche** Cardinal west spar buoy, situated on the south side of the entrance to **L'Abervrac'h** by the **Grand Chenal** make good 255° True for about 0·6 mile when the leading marks for the **Chenal du Rélec** should be identified on a bearing of 218° True.

The front mark is a tall beacon painted white on its north side (but this may not be obvious if seen against the light), on the north side of the steep **Petit Men Louet** rock or islet. If this cannot be identified from this position it means that the weather is too thick for a stranger to attempt the passage for the first time. The beacon stands on the islet at the east end of the **Men Louet** group of rocks which dry high at low water as shown on the photograph on page 237 though this was taken from the south, the reverse direction. It will not be confused with **Grand Men Louet** beacon standing on the islet a cable west of it, which is squat and painted white only on its south side.

The rear mark, distant 5·5 miles, is a white beacon with a red top on **Pointe de Landunvès** just west of the ruins of a semaphore building, and about 0·2 mile SE of the headland. Do not bring the beacons in line, but keep **Landunvès** beacon just open to the left of **Petit Men Louet** beacon and follow this lead. The transit on French Chart No 5772 is shown as 218° 30′, but few yachts can be steered with such accuracy. According to this chart the line leaves **Queyn-an-Treis** (only 1·3 m LAT) only a few yards to port. As the rock is dangerous at LW springs or in a large swell or rough seas, borrow to the northward temporarily when in its vicinity. The channel next passes between **Le Rélec** (which is an isolated rock on the north side which dries 5·3 m) and **Le Trépied** plateau on the south side (which dries 2·5 m in parts). The next dangers are the line of scattered rocks known as **Gouren Gourou** which lies very close on the starboard hand. When in their vicinity borrow to port where there is plenty of water. The line then leads a little over 0·1 mile off **Ile Longue** which is a low rocky area, mostly covered at HW. Course is altered when **Ile Longue** is abeam to port, to make good 249° True on the transit of the marks for the **Chenal du Raous.**

Chenal du Raous

By Day Only   These are **Bosseven Creiz** (a rock or islet with two apexes and a white beacon), in line with the southernmost high rock (15·8 m above Datum = 8·2 m above MHWS) of **Le Grem** group. At low water the rear rock is hidden behind **Bosseven Creiz** and the track must be held despite the set of the stream. When at least 0·25 mile from **Bosseven Creiz**, make good 228° True with **Le Four** light-house just open south of **Bosseven Aval** (a rock or islet with one apex and a white beacon). The transit on the French chart is shown as 228° 30′. This channel is most difficult between **Men Luth** (also known as **Carrec Luth**, dries 5·2 m LAT) and reefs drying to the NW of **Ile Verte**. At low water it is clearly defined as the rocks can be

Portsall Inner Passage. The next leading marks in Chenal du Raous. They are
Bosseven Creiz and the south rock of Le Grem group in line at 249° True. Le Grem is
opened to the south so that it can just be seen in this picture to the left of the
Bosseven Creiz which masks it at low water.

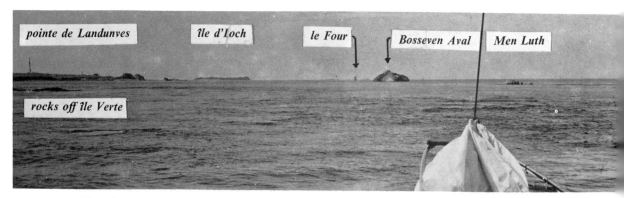

After altering course NE of Bosseven Creiz the next leading marks are Le Four lighthouse
open south (left) of Bosseven Aval. The marks are a little too open in this picture which is
taken in the narrowest part of the channel. The rocks extending from Ile Verte are seen to
port and the rock to starboard is Men Luth which dries 5·2 m LAT and is dangerous when it
is covered. When past this rock steer to leave Bosseven Aval within 50 m except near low
water when refer to the sailing instructions. This picture was taken near low water when the
height of tide at Brest was 6·7 m and the stream in the narrows exceeded 5 knots. With a
strong wind against a spring tide the overfalls here are said to be worse than in the famous
Raz de Sein.

seen. According to the chart the channel is nearly 200 m wide, but at
low water it looks less and the stream attains its maximum rate, so
that a yacht is quickly set off course. **Bosseven Aval** is a steep islet,
but at LAT there is a shoal with only 0·4 m extending 100 m to the
east of it. There is also a rock to the south which dries 1·5 m.
South-west of Ile Verte is **Sélédran** rock which dries 0·8 m LAT and,
to avoid this and the dangers off **Bosseven Aval**, when **Bosseven
Creiz** is in line with **Barou Neves** astern bearing 025° True, alter to
follow this line making good 205° True until **Ile Verte** is abeam then
alter slightly to starboard. When **Men Gouziane** rock touches the
tip of **Pointe de Landunvés** bearing 210° True, alter to maintain
this transit, leaving **Sélédran** rock close to port. Once past **Bosse-**

236

ven Aval and the rock to the south of it navigation becomes easier.

If bound for Portsall bear to port (see *Portsall*) but if continuing in the inner passage when **Men ar Pic** Lateral starboard beacon tower is abeam to port bring **Bosseven Creiz** and **Bosseven Aval** into line astern bearing 035° True and make good the reciprocal 215° True. Identify **Le Iurch** rock which is left about 0·4 mile to port which is one of the next marks. Continue on this line for about 1·5 miles until about 0·1 mile west of **Pointe de Landunvès**. Great care should be taken to keep exactly on the transit when approaching **Landunvès** as many vessels have been lost on the drying rocks of **Basse Pelen** and **Basse Prijean** 0·1 mile north-west of the transit, and there are also dangers to the south-east.

Chenal Méridional de Portsall

By Day Only When the beacon on **Grand Men Louet**, which is painted white on the SW side and is about 0·1 mile west of **Petit Men Louet** beacon, which is grey on this side, is in line with the cleft on the top of **Le Iurch** bearing 049° True alter to make good the reciprocal 229° True. The cleft is like a gunsight and except perhaps at high water, the beacon is lost immediately the yacht deviates to one side or the other, which is easily done on a stern transit. This line leads about 0·1 mile northward of the prominent **Ile d'Iock**, about 0·1 mile south of **Grand Château** rock which is 11 m above datum and which

Le Iurch rock is the essential mark for the Chenal Meridional which is the channel from off Portsall to le Four. The rock has a pronounced cleft in the top and Grand Men Louet white beacon situated east of Ile Verte and a cable west of Petit Men Louet has to be kept in line astern with this cleft at 049° True. At low water the beacon is masked by the rock except when in the cleft. The marks are hazy owing to the weather when the picture was taken. The beacon tower to the left of the picture is Men ar Pic with the Ile Verte group of islets in the background. Le Iurch is also a leading mark (front) for the Chenal de Men Glas. When approaching by this channel Men ar Pic is left to starboard. The picture is taken from about WSW.

237

Portsall Inner Passage. Pointe de Landunvès off which course is altered from 215° with Bosseven Creiz on with Bosseven Aval at 035° True to bring Grand Men Louet beacon in the cleft of Le Iurch at 049° True. The new white beacon with a red top, which is the rear leading mark for Chenal du Rélec, is seen in the middle of the picture just to the right of the ruins of the semaphore building.

Ile d'Iock bearing SW. It is left about 300 m to port.

Grand Château above water rock is left about 0·1 mile to starboard. Here it is seen at high water with Le Four lighthouse to the left of the picture.

has outliers to the south and east which dry 2·2 m and **Le Taureau** Cardinal west beacon tower 0·1 mile to port.

The line then leads into open water about 0·3 mile south of the lighthouse.

EASTBOUND PASSAGE

This passage should not be attempted for the first time with visibility of less than 6 miles since this will be needed for the last pair of leading marks.

Chenal Méridional de Portsall

By Day Only   First identify **Le Grand Château** rock which is 11 m above Datum and which lies about 0·4 mile NE of **Le Four** lighthouse, and **Le Taureau** Cardinal west beacon tower 0·6 mile E by N from the lighthouse. The line runs about midway between these bearing 049° True with **Grand Men Louet** beacon, which is painted white on the SW side in line with the cleft on the top of **Le Iurch**. The cleft is like a gunsight and except perhaps at high water the beacon is lost immediately the yacht deviates to one side or the other. A help is to keep **Men Gouziane** which is easily distinguished, just open west of **Le Iurch**. When **Bosseven Creiz** and **Bosseven Aval** white pyramids come into line, bearing 035° True. Follow this line exactly until **Men ar Pic** Lateral starboard beacon tower is abeam to starboard, then alter course to make good 030° True and keeping the east side of **Men Gouziane** rock touching the tip of **Pointe de Landunvès** on a stern transit bearing 210° True. Follow this line leaving **Sélédran** rock (dries 0·8 m) close to starboard and **Bosseven Aval** 120 m to port. When **Bosseven Aval** is abaft the beam,

Grand Château and associated group of rocks seen at low water.

alter slightly to starboard to bring **Bosseven Creiz** in line with **Barou Neves** bearing 025° True. Follow this transit. Then when **Le Four** lighthouse is just open of **Bosseven Aval** astern bearing 229° True alter to follow this line making good 048° True. Take care to note the cross stream at this point particularly as **Men Luth** (dries 5·2 m) is very close to port.

Chenal du Raous

By Day Only   When the southernmost rock of **Le Grem** is in line with **Bosseven Creiz** on the port quarter bearing 248° True, alter to make good 069° True and follow this line until the white beacon with red top on **Pointe de Landunvès** and the tall beacon painted white on its north side, on the north side of the steep **Petit Men Louet** rock or islet, are in line astern bearing 219° True.

Chenal du Rélec

By Day Only   Then make good 038° True to follow this line, which passes between **Le Rélec** (which is an isolated rock on the north side which dries 5·3 m) and **Le Trépied** plateau on the south side (which dries 2·5 m in parts). It also leaves **Queyn-an-Treis** (only 1·3 m LAT) a few yards to starboard. This line then leaves the **Plateau de Rusven** to starboard and the **Petite Fourche** Cardinal west buoy 0·5 mile to starboard.

38 Portsall and Kersaint

Tidal Data

Tidal Heights
High Water: approx +0010 Brest, +0520 Dover.
Heights of Tide above Datum: approx MHWS 7·6 m, MLWS 1·2 m, MHWN 6·1 m, MLWN 3 m.
Mean Tide Level: 4·7 m. Index 7 B.

Tidal Streams

1. Offshore at **Grande Basse de Portsall** 3 miles NW of Portsall, the NE by E-going stream reaching 3·5 knots at springs, begins at −0515 Brest (−0005 Dover) and the W by S-going stream (reaching 3 knots at springs) at +0100 Brest (+0610 Dover).
2. For **Portsall Inner Passage** see page 23. The streams in the **Chenal de Men Glas** have the same characteristics as **Chenal du Rélec**.
3. In the approach south of **Ile Verte** and in the outer anchorage, the flood stream begins at −0600 Brest (−0050 Dover) in an easterly direction south of **Ile Verte** and ENE in the anchorage, both streams reaching 4 knots at springs. The ebb stream runs west in both positions beginning at −0045 Brest (+0425 Dover) and reaching 3 knots.
4. In the entrance NNW of **Pointe Galaite** the flood (east) begins at −0600 Brest

Ile Verte, which is off to the left of this picture, is a cable on the port hand when entering Portsall on the line of the rectangular white leading beacons. At low water the rocks uncover so that the island is almost continuous with Grand Men Louet (left) and Petit Men Louet (right). Grand Men Louet beacon is painted white on its SW side as a leading mark for the Chenal Meridional and Petit Men Louet is painted white on its NE side as the front leading mark for the Chenal du Rélec. This distinguishes the two beacons as on the correct line the required beacon will be white and the other grey.

(−0050 Dover), 1·5 knots at springs; and the ebb (west) at +0040 Brest (+0550 Dover), 1·7 knots at springs.

General

A pretty drying fishing harbour with one drying berth alongside the quay and good outside anchorages during offshore winds in settled weather. The outer approaches can be very rough with wind against tide.

Approaches

Chenal de Men Glas

By Day   From a position 1·25 miles SW of the **Basse Paupian** Cardinal west spar buoy identify **Ploudalmezeau** church steeple and **Le Iurch** rock (see photograph, page 237) which lies 0·125 mile south of **Men ar Pic** Lateral starboard beacon tower, and bring Le Iurch and Ploudalmezeau steeple into line at 108° 30′. Steer on this transit, allowing for tidal stream, leaving **Portsall** rocks to port (Men Glas, Men Bizina and Le Grem) just over 0·25 mile to port. The channel is wide and there is deep water southwards in this part of the approach.

       When **Le Grem** rocks bear about N (or when the more conspicuous **Bosseven Aval** islet with beacon on top bears 070° True)

Portsall leading marks for the final approach from Chenal de Men Bras are difficult to see owing to white villas built in their vicinity. The rear wall beacon is now painted red and white. The transit is 085° True, but a yacht has to bear to starboard before reaching this position – see sailing instructions. The beacon tower is Besquel Isolated Danger masonry beacon which is left to port when proceeding to the harbour with sufficient rise of tide.

The yacht is in the neap anchorage SE of La Pendante Cardinal north beacon tower. The picture faces about NW by W and the Cardinal north rocks in the background are the Men Louet group. To the left of the fore-halyard is Bosseven Aval with white beacon on its summit and at the extreme left is Men ar Pic Lateral starboard beacon tower. It is near LW and the slick on the surface of the sea to the right of La Pendante indicates below-water rocks. (Pre IALA.)

identify the next leading marks. These are two (white and red-and-white respectively) rectangular beacons on the land bearing 085° True. They are not easy to distinguish among the houses in their vicinity, and should not be confused with a white water tower south of the **Pointe Galaite** which is not a leading mark. The rear wall mark is now RW.

Steer on this transit leaving **Men ar Pic** Lateral starboard beacon tower 150 m to starboard and **Ile Verte** a similar distance to port. The danger on this approach is **Basse Idic** which lies about 300 m east of **Men ar Pic** and has rocks on it drying 0·5 and 2·8 m LAT. The leading line leaves these about 80 m to starboard.

Identify **La Pendante** Cardinal north beacon tower to the right of **Besquel** isolated danger masonry beacon. When **La Pendante** beacon tower is in line with **Segou Bras**, a painted white patch bearing 094° True, follow this line into the anchorage.

If proceeding, with sufficient tide, to the harbour leave **La Pendante** beacon tower about 25 m to starboard and navigate by chart leaving **Segou Bras** and **Segoubihan** and outlying rock to port and **Enes ar Poul Tres**, the rock in the middle of the bay, to starboard.

By Night   The characteristics of Portsall light are: Oc (3+1) 12 s WRG, vis W 10 miles, R 7 miles, G 6 miles. Elevation 9 m. The sectors are

243

green 058°−084° True, thence white to 088° True (4°), thence red to 058° True. The approach may be made in the 4° white sector as far as the outer anchorage. **Portsall** light is more useful for departure at night than for entry by a stranger.

Calerec Passage

By Day Only   When entering from the NE by **Chenal du Rélec** and **Chenal du Raous** instead of proceeding to the **Bossevens** there is a short cut west of **Ile Longue** which can be used with sufficient rise of tide, over a rock which dries 0·6 m LAT and others near which dry 1 m.

About 0·25 mile west of **Ile Longue** when on the **Bosseven Creiz–Le Grem** transit, note two pyramids; **Losquet** white and yellow *(front)* and **Calerec** white *(rear)* bearing 190° True. Alter course and follow this transit precisely for about 0·75 mile heading just west of **La Pendante** beacon tower. Alter course to enter the anchorage as described before.

This channel is very narrow and the leading marks must be held precisely in transit.

This channel is considered better locally, than the pass from **Bosseven Creiz** to **Bosseven Aval**, which involves a detour and where the seas are often more rough.

Chenal de Pen ar Roch

By Day Only   This narrow channel is approached from **Grande Basse de Portsall** Cardinal west pillar light and whistle buoy and leads in between rocks from a NNW direction. It is a deep water channel but passes so close to rocks that it should be treated as drying 1·8 m LAT. The leading marks are **Grand Men Louet** beacon (west of **Petit Men Louet**) on with **Kersaint** church steeple at 145° True. This transit joins **Chenal du Raous** about 0·1 mile SE by E of **Bosseven Creiz** which should then be followed. The channel is subject to cross-streams but these are not so strong as in the **Chenal du Raous.**

Chenal du Bosseven Amont

This approach passes through the *Zone Dangereuse Reglementé* outside the *Zone Interdite* surrounding the wreck of the *Amoco Cadiz*, and its use is therefore not recommended and no directions are given.

Anchorage and Harbour

The recognised anchorage is about 0·1 mile SW of **Petit Men Louet** beacon in 11 to 12 m or in a position where **La Pendante** Cardinal north beacon tower bears SSE 100 m and **Besquel** isolated danger masonry beacon bears E about 100 m in soundings from 4 m LAT to 2·4 m a little to the eastward. Another anchorage nearby with 4 m LAT is on the line of the white leading marks at 085° True, with **Besquel** beacon tower bearing 157° True about 100 m. These anchorages are exposed to all westerly and northerly winds and the streams are strong in the more westerly anchorage. Both anchorages are far from the harbour landing, and the easterly positions are in rather confined waters.

At neap tides, or between neaps and springs, a more convenient anchorage is 100 m south of **La Pendante** beacon tower. Avoid the rocks on which the beacon tower stands and the little rock to the eastward, not shown on chart. This position is used as a temporary anchorage by the lifeboat. On an ordinary spring tide there is 2·1 m at low water, sand bottom. Take soundings as more water can be found a little northward and it shoals to the southward. Distance to the lifeboat slip and harbour is under 0·5 mile. It is probable that moorings will be laid in the vicinity of **La Pendante**, which will be most useful to visiting yachtsmen.

The harbour, all of which dries out, consists of a short breakwater, a quay and a stone slip to the eastward. There is room for one yacht to dry out alongside the outer end of the quay on sand bottom. If she is of 1·8 m draught she will take the ground about 2 hours after HW springs. It has been said that in NW weather a heavy surge reaches the harbour but local opinion varies about this.

The outer breakwater at high water bearing about SE. Pass close off the end of the breakwater and bear to port for the quay.

Facilities

Those of a small fishing village and lifeboat station. Four small cafés at the port including Retour des Pêcheurs run by the wife of the lifeboat coxswain. Restaurant de Famille at Kersaint, about 1 mile distant, where the XIIth century chateau is worth visiting.

39 Argenton

Tidal Data

Tidal Heights
High Water: approx +0010 Brest, +0520 Dover.
Heights of Tide above Datum: approx MHWS 7·6 m, MLWS 1·2 m, MHWN 6·1 m, MLWN 3·0 m.
Mean Tide Level: 4·7 m. Index 7 B.

Tidal Streams

One mile westward of **Le Four** lighthouse the east-going stream reaching 3·5 knots at springs, begins −0545 Brest (−0035 Dover) and the west-going 4 knots at springs at +0100 Brest (+0610 Dover). The inshore streams SE of **Le Four** turn about 10 or 15 minutes earlier.

General

A village with an open anchorage and drying harbour, situated 2 miles east of Le Four lighthouse. At neap tides, during offshore winds and in the absence of swell this is an interesting anchorage. The approach channel is deep but passes close to a 0·9 m LAT rock SE of Brividic Lateral port masonry beacon and passes close to rocks. There is a jetty on the mainland east of Ile Dolvez.

Approach

By Day Only Make a position 0·3 mile south of **Le Four** lighthouse, and heading to make good 083° True, identify three Lateral port beacon towers to port and **Petit Melgorn** rock (17 m above Datum) to starboard. Approach to pass midway between the first masonry beacon, **Le Bélier** and **Petit Melgorn**. Before the latter comes abeam, identify the leading marks on **Ile Dolvez**. The front mark is a small, low, round white beacon tower on the foreshore of **Ile Dolvez** and the rear is a white pyramid on the island itself. (The French chart shows also a white wall mark east of the latter.) Steer in on their transit of 083° True.

Approaching on this line **Petit Melgorn** rock will be left over 100 m to starboard, after which the leading line must be followed exactly, as it passes close to dangers to starboard, including an isolated rock drying 3 m LAT and a shoal to its north with a depth of

247

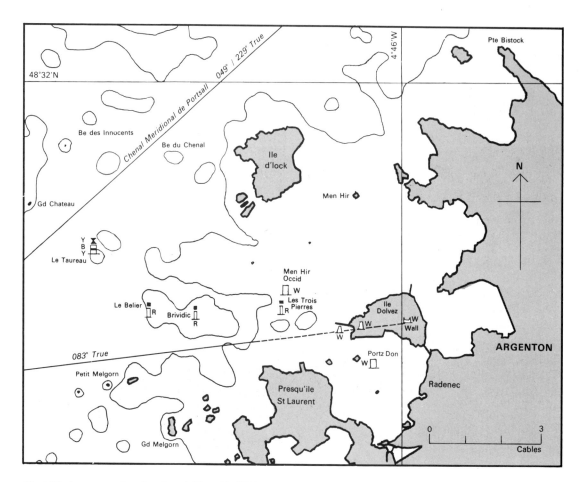

Chart 32. Argenton. *Based on French Chart No 5721.*

248

The picture faces east. The entrance of Argenton is easy to identify. The yacht is just off the leading marks which are two white beacons and rear white mark on Ile Dolvez at 083° True. This leaves Petit Melgorn rock over 100 m to starboard and three Lateral port masonry beacons as bright as pillar boxes to port.

A close-up view of the white leading marks of Ile Dolvez.

Les Trois Pierres Lateral port masonry beacon (the third in the approach) is abeam to port and behind is Men Hir Occidental white beacon, not to be confused with white leading marks on Ile Dolvez.

0·9 m LAT on the leading line. With adequate rise of tide, **Le Bélier** Lateral port masonry beacon will be left to port as also the fat Lateral port beacon tower **Brividic**. The channel is 4 m or more deep as far as **Brividic**, but note the reef shown on the chart, extending ESE of **Brividic** beacon tower. The channel here is at its narrowest, only about 100 m between the extremity of the reef to port and the isolated rock previously mentioned. With sufficient rise of tide, the rest is easy once these dangers have been passed. Hold on to the leading line leaving **Les Trois Pierres** Lateral port masonry beacon tower about 100 m to port, and so to the anchorage – see under *Anchorage*. If proceeding to the jetty, with sufficient rise of tide, navigate to the northward round **Ile Dolvez** by chart, noting the rock which dries 12 m near the breakwater on its northern tip.

Anchorage

There is anchorage on the leading line off the **Ile Dolvez** about 100 m off the outer white beacon in 0·9 m LAT (2·1 m MLWS or 3·9 m MLWN), or the same distance SW of the beacon. A mooring buoy moored between **Les Trois Pierres** and **Ile Dolvez** is reserved for the lighthouse tender. There is 1·7 m depth 120 m north of the end of the lifeboat slip, with **Men Hir** white beacon tower in line with **Le Four** lighthouse and with the east side of **Presqu'île St Laurent** just open bearing 180° True. The French chart shows about 2 m LAT south and east of **Les Trois Pierres** Lateral port masonry beacon and SE of the mooring buoy. This has not been verified and the bottom may be rock.

The anchorage is partially sheltered from the north by **Ile d'Iock** and rocks, and from E through S to SSW by land. It is exposed to all westerly winds and swell (which is said to be enormous) so even the approach would be dangerous in strong onshore winds. Under suitable conditions the anchorage is pleasant, though far from the jetty and the village.

Shallow draught yachts will find better anchorage in the bay NE of **Ile Dolvez** which dries 2 m LAT so would have 0·1 m at neaps. It is said locally that there is 1·8 m.

The harbour consists of a short west jetty against which a yacht can dry out on the south side on sand bottom – not rock as shown on the charts. The west jetty dries about 3·0 m but is covered at high water springs. Another jetty and slip to the east is used by racing dinghies. There is less water there and it is not recommended for berthing, although it might be possible. The west jetty is stated locally to be safer than Portsall jetty, and is protected from all directions except north, by the mainland and Ile Dolvez. It used to be stated that there was a violent surge in the harbour in strong westerly weather, and this may well be possible, despite the breakwater on the north side of **Ile Dolvez**. A north-west sea or swell could penetrate between **Ile d'Iock** and the mainland when the rocks are covered. A yacht might be weather-

A yacht can dry out alongside the south side of the quay on sand near the crane. The picture faces NW towards Ile d'Iock.

Facing south across the inner slip which is used by dinghies.

bound alongside the jetty and unable to beat out of the approach channel in the event of an unexpected westerly gale or the swell in advance of one, but under ordinary weather conditions, the harbour is snug enough, which is why it has been adapted as a centre for dinghy sailing.

Facilities

Water at jetty. Yacht club and small shops. Photograph processing. Bus to Brest.

251

40 Melon

Tidal Data: See under Argenton, above.

General

A small drying harbour lying between the island and the village of the same name, about a mile north of Laberildut. The island is 14 m high and bordered by low cliffs. The port offers good shelter except at high water and with a NW wind.

Approaches

The main approach is from the NNW. First identify **Le Compère** rock 7·2 m above Datum, from which **Le Four** lighthouse bears 334° True distant 1·25 miles. Pass about 0·1 mile to the SW of this rock, then bring it into line (astern) with **Le Four** lighthouse. Steer to make good 154° True keeping on the transit. This line leads to the anchorage over a least depth of 6·2 m, but passes very close to drying rocks on either hand.

The approach from the south, inside the **Ile Melon**, is intricate, and no adequate directions can be given.

Anchorages

1. In easterly weather, a yacht may anchor in 6·7 m sand with **Le Compère** rock in line with **Le Four** lighthouse, and the north end of **Ile Melon**, distant 0·2 mile. In this position the north end of the small **Ile Mazou-Bras** bears about 050° True, but be sure to anchor clear of the rocky shoal to the SW of the anchorage.
2. The port has no quays or facilities, and dries from 2·5 m to 5 m LAT.

41 Laberildut (Lanildut)

Tidal Data

Tidal Heights
High Water: approx +0005 Brest, +0515 Dover.
Heights of Tide above Datum: approx MHWS 7·6 m, MLWS 1·2 m, MHWN 5·7 m, MLWN 3·0 m.
Mean Tide Level: 4·6 m. Index 4 B.

Tidal Streams

1. About 3 miles west of Laberildut the NNE-going stream begins at −0520 Brest (−0010 Dover) and the SSW-going at +0030 Brest (+0540 Dover). Both streams reach 2·8 knots at springs. Close inshore the coastal streams probably turn earlier.
2. The ebb tide from Laberildut near the entrance sets to the NW on the offlying rocks, reaching 3 knots at springs.

General

This small natural harbour is shown on most charts as drying right out, but for many years ballast boats have been taking sand off the entrance and from the bed of the harbour for use at Brest. As a result, it provides an attractive and sheltered anchorage in which small craft can lie afloat at LW springs.

The bar, which is stony, lies immediately to seaward of Le Crapaud, the prominent rounded rock close off the light structure and joined to the northern shore by a jetty. The bar dries about 1·5 m LAT (i.e. has 2·7 m at half-tide and should permit a vessel of 1·5 m draught to enter at LWN). It cannot be dredged and a stranger would be well advised to take soundings when entering at half-tide or below.

Approaches

By Day   The recommended approach for a stranger is to keep **Brélès** church spire (see Chart No 33) in line with **Lanildut** church spire bearing 079° True (Line **P**). These marks are not easy to identify from a distance, and the most prominent feature in the approach is **Le Lieu** Lateral port beacon tower. This line passes about 100 m north of **Laberildut** light structure, and carries a least depth of 1·2 m LAT (i.e. 2·4 m MLWS) as far as the bar. It leaves **Pierre de Laber** Lateral starboard beacon 200 m to starboard and **Le Lieu** Lateral

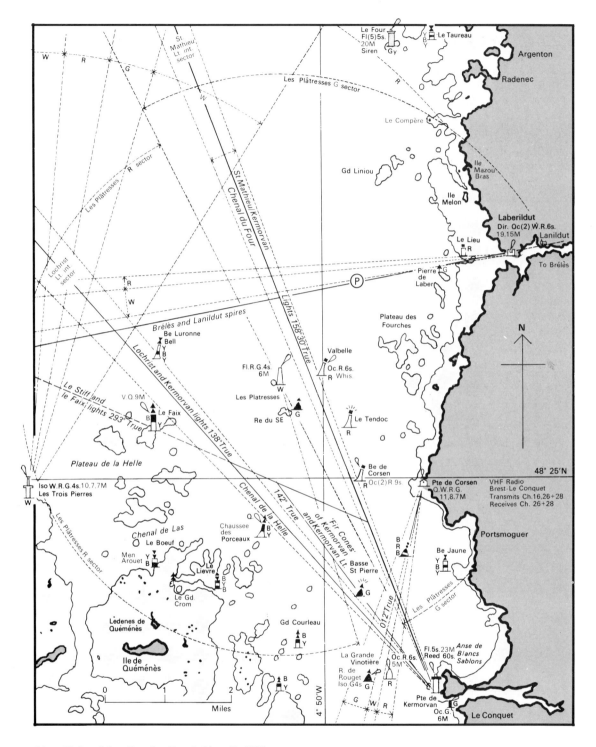

Chart 33. Lanildut. *Based on French Chart No 5721.*

254

Le Lieu Lateral port beacon tower bearing about NE near low water. This beacon tower is easiest means of identifying the entrance of Laberildut, and is left about 0·125 mile on the port hand.

On the left is the light structure. In the outer approach this structure is about 100 m south of the leading line which consists of Breles church spire in line with Lanildut church spire at 079° True. The sand barge in the entrance has passed close to Le Crapaud rock and is bearing sharply to starboard to the south side of the channel. The picture is taken from No 2 anchorage facing about east. The tide has risen but it is still below half-tide.

port beacon tower 140 m to port. The front wall of the light structure has an aperture, the right hand half being open and the left hand part with a red window. The light itself shines through a window to the rear of this aperture. On closer approach steer so as to centre the window through which the light shines in the open part of the aperture bearing 083° True. Keep clear of the red sector as there are drying rocks east of **Le Lieu** beacon tower.

To find the best water over the bar proceed as follows:

Enter as above until the right edge of the wood seen on the skyline is in line with the left edge of the quay on the south side of the entrance. Now make good a course directly towards **Le Crapaud**.

LINE P

Brélès Spire

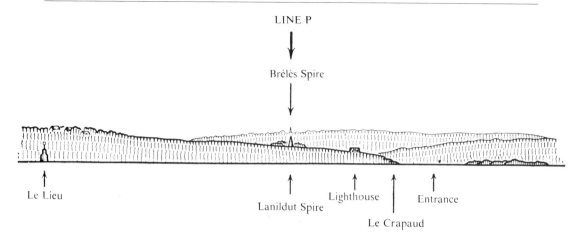

Le Lieu

Lanildut Spire

Lighthouse

Le Crapaud

Entrance

Laberildut, from a position on line **P**, and just westward of Pierre de Laber Lateral starboard beacon 1 hour after HWN.

When past **Le Crapaud** steer for the west end of the quay and on approaching bear to port so as to pass leaving it about 50 m to starboard and avoid the rocky spit which extends from the northern shore. When off the eastern end of the jetty bear to port again heading towards **Laber** landing slip leaving the many permanent moorings and moored boats close to starboard and the larger mooring buoys approaching **Laber** close to port.

By Night   If in doubt as to the general position of the entrance bring **Keréon** (Oc (2+1) WR 24 s) into line (astern) with **La Jument** Fl (3) 15 s (see Chart No 36). This line crosses the centre of the white sector of **Laberildut** light Dir Oc (2) WR 6 s, vis W 19 miles, R 15 miles. White sector from 081° to 085° True, red 085° to 087° True. Keep in this white sector until very close to the entrance, then proceed as above if visibility permits; otherwise bring up in one of the outer anchorages.

Anchorages

1. With **Le Lieu** beacon tower bearing about 285° True distant 0·15 mile. The least depth here is 7 m.
2. With the light structure bearing about 075° True distant about 0·2 mile in about 3·6 m sand. There has been considerable dredging in the vicinity of this anchorage and, with the help of soundings, it is possible to anchor further to the south of the position marked on the chart.
3. The harbour is now very crowded with moorings for local boats and there is very

The landing slip at Laber bearing about NE by N.

little, if any room left to anchor. The moorings are close together and care should be taken to make sure there is swinging room if picking up a vacant buoy.

Surroundings

The shores of the harbour are of sand and rock, with landing slips at the villages. There is a public fresh water pump near the slip at **Laber**. Repairs to wooden vessels can be undertaken and there is a marine engineer. There are fair shopping facilities and hotels and restaurants in the vicinity. The nearest restaurant Hôtel Rec Melen east of the slip is inexpensive. The great disused quarry on the right bank of the river once supplied stone for the construction of many of the ocean harbours of France and for several works in England, including the Thames Embankment.

257

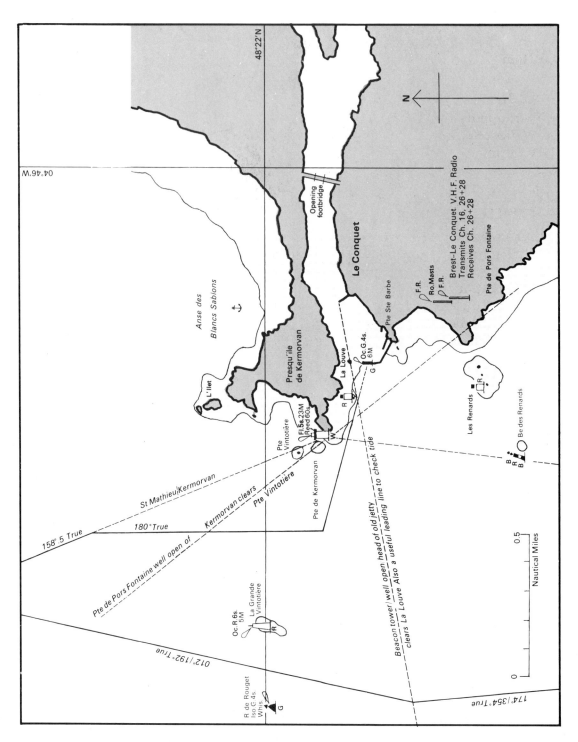

48°22′N

04°46′W

N

Opening
footbridge

Le Conquet

Brest-Le Conquet, V.H.F. Radio
Transmits Ch. 16, 26+28
Receives Ch. 26+28

Pte Ste Barbe

F.R.
Ro.Masts
F.R.

Pte de Pors Fontaine

Anse des
Blancs Sablons

Presqu'île
de Kermorvan

L'Îlet

Oc.G.4s.
6M
G

La Louve

R.

R.

Be des Renards

Les Renards

R
B

Pte
Vintotière

Fl.5s.23M
Reed 60s.

W

St Mathieu/Kermorvan

Pte de Kermorvan

Kermorvan clears
Pte Vintotière

158°.5 True

180° True

Beacon tower/ well open head of old jetty line to check tide
clears La Louve Also a useful leading
Pte de Pors Fontaine well open of

012°/192° True

Oc.R.6s.
5M
R

La Grande
Vintotière

174°/354° True

R de Rouget
Iso.C. 4s.
Whis.
G

0   0.5

Nautical Miles

Chart 34. Le Conquet. *Based on French Chart No 5159.*

258

42 Le Conquet

Tidal Data

Tidal Heights
High Water: approx −0005 Brest, +0505 Dover.
Heights of Tide above Datum: approx MHWS 7·6 m, MLWS 1·5 m, MHWN 5·7 m, MLWN 3·0 m.
Mean Tide Level: 4·6 m. Index 4 B.

Tidal Streams

1. In the northern approach to the **Chenal du Four** about west of **Laberildut** the NNE-going stream begins at −0520 Brest (−0010 Dover) and the SSW-going stream at +0030 Brest (+0540 Dover). Both streams attain 2·8 knots at springs.
2. Off **St Pierre** Lateral starboard buoy some 2 miles NW of **Pointe de Kermorvan** the streams turn earlier. The north-going stream begins at −0615 Brest (−0105 Dover) and the south-going stream at +0015 Brest (+0525 Dover). Both streams attain 2·5 knots at springs, but note the sharp increase in rates to the southward which are referred to below.
3. In the southern end of the **Chenal du Four**, between **Grand Vinotière** Lateral port beacon tower and **Basse du Chenal**, west of **Pointe de St Mathieu**, the north-going stream begins at −0550 Brest (−0040 Dover) attaining 5·6 knots at springs and the south-going at +0015 Brest (+0525 Dover) attaining 4·7 knots at springs.
4. At the anchorage there are eddies on the flood stream, sometimes setting towards the entrance but on the ebb the stream is very weak.

General

Le Conquet is on a lee shore in most westerly winds, but is well spoken of by yachtsmen and receives a measure of protection from **Ile de Beniquet** and the fierce offlying tidal streams. The anchorage is sheltered from north through east almost to south and, with the building of the new breakwater shelter from the south and SSW is improved with limited space to lie afloat in its shelter.

Approaches

By Day   From the north, this is by the **Chenal du Four** which is entered between **La Vabelle** Lateral port pillar light buoy and **Les Platresses**

Pointe de Kermorvan and lighthouse on the northern side of the entrance. When approaching
Le Conquet there is a cross stream at 5 to 6 knots SW of the lighthouse. La Louve Lateral
port beacon tower is seen to the right of the lighthouse. There are rocks between the
lighthouse and the beacon tower. The yacht from which the photograph was taken had been
swept by the stream to northward of the correct approach and the picture faces ESE.

white beacon tower, on the transit of **Kermorvan** lighthouse
(*front*) square white tower, and St Mathieu lighthouse (*rear*) square
white tower bearing 158° True. Steer to make good this course.
When **L'Ilet** is abeam steer 180° True so as to pass 0·2 mile west of
Pointe de Kermorvan and to avoid **La Petite Vinotière** and other
drying rocks to the north of the point. When **Pointe de Kermorvan**
lighthouse is abeam alter course to port leaving **La Louve** Lateral
port beacon tower to port. **Les Renards** Lateral port beacon tower is
left 0·5 mile to starboard. The only feature of navigation to this easy
approach is allowance for the cross tidal streams which may attain
5·5 knots. On a spring flood a yacht is set rapidly towards **Pointe de
Kermorvan** and the stream only relaxes when it gets under the tidal
lee of **Pointe St Barbe** at the entrance. Avoid the rock which dries
2·8 m LAT which is situated about 0·15 mile east of **La Louve**,
beyond the outer breakwater.

By Night From the north, identify **Kermorvan** light Fl 5 s, and **St Mathieu**
light Fl 15 s (there is a fixed red light on a radio mast 1·7 miles ENE
of the latter). Make a position from which **Les Platresses** Fixed
Green light bears 190° True distant one mile when the leading lights
will be in line bearing 158° 30′ True. Steer to make good this transit
and if visibility permits proceed as *By Day* above, otherwise when
Pointe de Corsen light changes from green to white bearing 012°
True alter course to make good 192° True and keep in the white
sector and pass between **La Grande Vinotière** beacon tower Oc R
6 s, and **Rouget** Lateral starboard pillar buoy Iso G 4 s. When
well past these steer for the Oc 4 s G light on the new breakwater,
making due allowance for the cross tide.

2

1

5

The lifeboat house on with the most westerly house gives a rough indication of the 2 m low water line at MLWS, but it is necessary to take soundings and calculate the tide of the day. At neaps a yacht can anchor nearer the harbour.

The inner harbour of Le Conquet is protected by a breakwater. Yachts can dry out alongside, but the berths are often crowded by coasters, fishing and other craft.

Anchorage and Harbour

The building of the new breakwater provides deep water mooring under its lee at all states of the tide but this is largely occupied by fishing boats which have moorings secured to ground chains and buoying the anchor is essential. Room must be left for the ferry which berths alongside the end of the jetty and it arrives with considerable élan.

The inner harbour has merely a jetty alongside the eastern side of which vessels can lie, with fair protection from offshore winds. The jetty dries about 2·4 m and berths alongside are often occupied by commercial vessels.

In southerly weather an alternative anchorage is in the Anse des Blancs Sablons, which can be approached direct from the leading line, and is useful whilst waiting a fair tide or clearance of fog. Gradually shelving shore and good sands for bathing. Sometimes a swell finds its way in. There are many fishermen's floats in the SW corner. Short walk over the Kermorvan peninsula to Le Conquet.

Facilities

Many shops and restaurants. Hôtel de Bretagne is well spoken of. Water from tap by wall in inner harbour. Petrol, etc. available half a mile along main road.

43 Ile de Molène

Tidal Data

Tidal Heights
High Water: approx +0010 Brest, +0520 Dover.
Heights of Tide above Datum: approx MHWS 7·6 m, MLWS 1·2 m, MHWN 5·7 m, MLWN 3·0 m.
Mean Tide Level: 4·4 m. Index 5 B.

Tidal Streams

1. In the **Chenal de la Helle** at the northern entrance the ENE-going stream begins at −0520 Brest (−0010 Dover) reaching about 3 knots at springs and the SW-going at −0045 Brest (+0425 Dover) reaching about 4 knots at springs. At the SE end where the channel joins the **Chenal du Four** the streams are 2·5 knots only.
2. In the middle of the **Passage du Fromveur** the ENE-going stream reaching 7·5 knots at springs begins at −0520 Brest (−0010 Dover) and the WSW stream, reaching 6·5 knots at +0045 Brest (+0555 Dover). Near **Kéreon** lighthouse streams attain the same rates but they start earlier and the directions differ. The NNE-going stream begins at +0550 Brest (−0125 Dover) and the SSW-going stream at −0030 Brest (+0440 Dover).
3. Between **Ile de Molène** and **Plateau de la Helle** the north-going stream begins at +0605 Brest (−0110 Dover) and the south-going at −0015 Brest (+0455 Dover). Both streams reach 2·8 knots at springs.
4. In the channel NW of **Ile de Molène** the streams turn at the same times as in 3 above but the directions and rates differ. At the west end of the channel NNE and SSW reaching 3·8 knots; at the east end ENE reaching 5·6 knots and WSW attaining 3·8 knots
5. In the **Chenal des Las** the north-going stream begins at +0605 Brest (−0110 Dover) and the south-going at −0200 Brest (+0310 Dover). Both streams reach 2·8 knots at springs.

General

Molène is a small island situated half-way between Le Conquet on the mainland and Ushant. Viewed on a small scale chart the approach looks difficult, being beset by rocks and fierce tidal streams. Under the right conditions, however, it is easily approachable from northward, easier, for example, than Ushant or Ile de Sein. There is an anchorage, usually sheltered from east through south to WSW. The tiny island has a character of its own, less rigorous than Ushant or Ile de Sein.

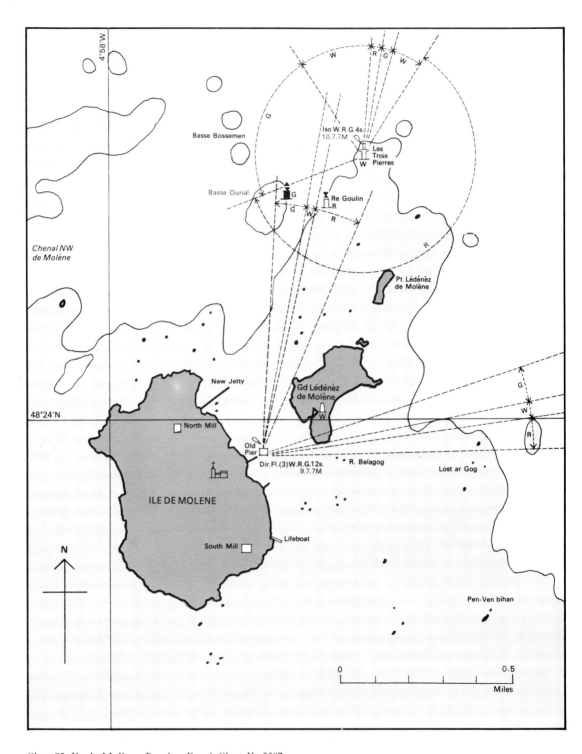

Chart 35. Ile de Molène. *Based on French Chart No 5567.*

264

Approaches

Northern Approach

By Day First make a position about 0·5 mile to the north of **Le Faix** Cardinal north lighthouse situated on the north side of **Plateau de la Helle**. From here steer to make good about 270° True leaving about 0·5 mile to port a distinctive solitary rock 15 m above Datum named **La Helle**. When just over 0·5 mile west of this rock identify the first leading marks which are the North Mill (a stumpy stone tower, painted day-glo red, at NW of **Ile de Molène**), on with **Les Trois Pierres** (white light tower, situated about 0·75 mile NE of **Ile de Molène**). At 2 miles distant, the mill appears lower than **Les Trois Pierres** and therefore, to be seen, can be opened to either side, but preferably to the west (see sketch A). The transit is 215° True which should be followed.

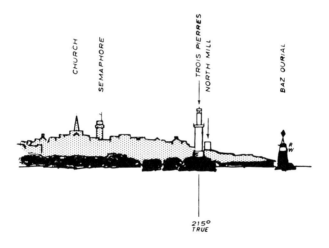

North Mill just open west of Les Trois Pierres lighthouse.

When within 0·1 mile of this light tower, make a detour round it to the west, leaving it about 0·1 mile to port and then take up the second leading marks which are, the South Mill tower (with no sails) in line with the white patch at the end of the north breakwater bearing 190° True (see sketch B).

Note that at spring tides the streams will be strong off **Les Trois Pierres**. Only a mile westward in the channel between **Ile de Molène** and **Ile de Balanec** they attain 5·6 knots at springs. Follow this transit which leaves **Basse Ourial** Cardinal east beacon tower

Les Trois Pierres lighthouse is the front leading mark on with the North Mill at rear at 215° True. When within a cable of the lighthouse steer to starboard to bring the next marks in line.

The North Mill. This is the rear leading mark for the eastern approach (Passe des Las) as well as for the northern. It is painted Day-glo red at the top only, and at a distance looks like a house with a red roof.

Note: Photographs and sketch refer to the northern approach.

South Mill on transit with white patch at end of north breakwater at 190° True. The leading lights are 191° True.

North Mill just open west of Les Trois Pierres lighthouse.

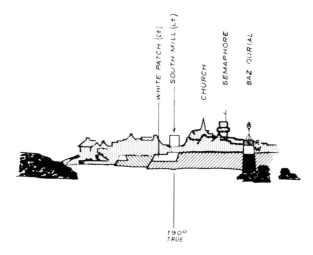

100 m to starboard and **Roche Goulin** Cardinal west beacon tower the like distance to port, continue for 0·5 mile to the pool.

By Night   **Les Trois Pierres** lighthouse to the NE of **Molène** has the following characteristics: Iso WRG 4 s, vis W 10 miles, R 7 miles, G 7 miles; elevation 15 m. Sectors green 070°–147°, thence white to 185°, thence red to 191°, thence green to 197°, thence white to 213°, thence red to 070°.

Approach in either white sector, preferably on the northern edge of the narrow NE white sector at 191° True. When 0·25 mile off **Les Trois Pierres** alter course to enter the narrow white sector of **Molène** light from 190° to 192° True, which from this direction is Fl (3) 12 s. Steer in this sector until 0·1 mile after passing between

266

Basse Ourial and **Roche Goulin** beacon towers (unlit) when bear to starboard and continue in the green sector.

Southern and Eastern approach

By Day Only   Follow the leading marks for the **Chenal de la Helle** which are **Kermorvan** lighthouse (*front*) (square white tower, elevation 20 m) and **Lochrist** (*rear*) (octagonal white tower, red top, elevation 49 m) by making good 318° True. When about 0·5 mile NE of **Chaussée des Pourceaux** Cardinal north pillar buoy, bring the white beacon on **Grand Lédénèz de Molène** to bear 264° True and steer to make this good as a course, allowing for cross stream. As soon as the **North Mill** (a stumpy stone tower, painted day-glo red, at NW of Ile de Molène) is identified, bring the two in line and steer to follow this transit strictly bearing 264° True. Not before the west end of **Ile de Quéménès** bears 170° True alter course to 300° True heading 0·25

The next marks are the South Mill in transit with the right of the white patch at the end of the breakwater at 190° True. The South Mill is often difficult to identify and appears dark when the light is behind it. This picture was taken on a hazy day and the marks have been touched up in white.

Baz Ourial Cardinal east beacon tower bearing about SE. It is left to starboard. North Mill is seen on the left of the picture. (Pre IALA.)

On nearer approach the leading marks are clearer, but the fishing boat will need to bear a little to starboard as she enters the anchorage.

mile north of **Les Trois Pierres** lighthouse and bring **Men Arouet** Cardinal south beacon tower, **Le Grand Crom** Cardinal north beacon tower and **Le Lièvre** Cardinal east beacon tower on a stern transit of approximately 120° True. Steer to make good 300° True to follow this transit until approaching **Les Trois Pierres** lighthouse, which leave 0·25 mile to port as there are shoals east and ENE of the lighthouse. Before turning to circle the lighthouse, join the northern approach to **Ile de Molène** *By day* as before. Be alert for tidal sets.

Anchorage and Harbour

In the pool about 0·1 mile north-east of the new jetty, there is about 1·9 m at LAT. Depths decrease to the southward but with soundings it will usually be possible to find a berth to the south of this and at neap tides to anchor between the new jetty and the old pier. The shelter in the outer position depends on tidal conditions and at springs is pretty well open from WSW through north to east. The holding ground of sand and rock is said to be poor and the anchor should be buoyed.

Much of the harbour has a rocky bottom but there are positions where a yacht could dry out alongside, if local advice is obtained.

The French chart shows there to be an anchorage ENE of the northern tip of **Grand Ledenez de Molène** in 9 m sand and mud, but this would appear to be exposed to the west at high water and unprotected from all easterly sectors.

Facilities

There are a post office, small shops, a co-operative where some chandlery can be obtained and three small restaurants. Water is scarce and there is no fuel.

Molène is an oval-shaped island, about 0·75 mile from north to south and 0·5 mile from east to west. The houses above the harbour are dense, so that viewed from a distance it looks like a town. The principal buildings are the semaphore tower and the church. The clock tower on the latter was a gift from England in recognition of the services of the men of Molène when the *Drummond Castle* was wrecked on Les Pierres Vertes. The bodies of twenty-nine of the passengers are buried in the cemetery. A local industry is gathering kelp from nearby islets and rocks. It is just a remote windswept island with magnificent views over the islets and rocks standing in the fierce tidal streams towards Ushant.

The harbour showing the white patch on the northern breakwater. The harbour dries out and as the bottom is rocky local advice is needed before drying out alongside.

Facing NE from the land across the anchorage and over Petit Ledenes and rocks towards les Trois Pierres lighthouse.

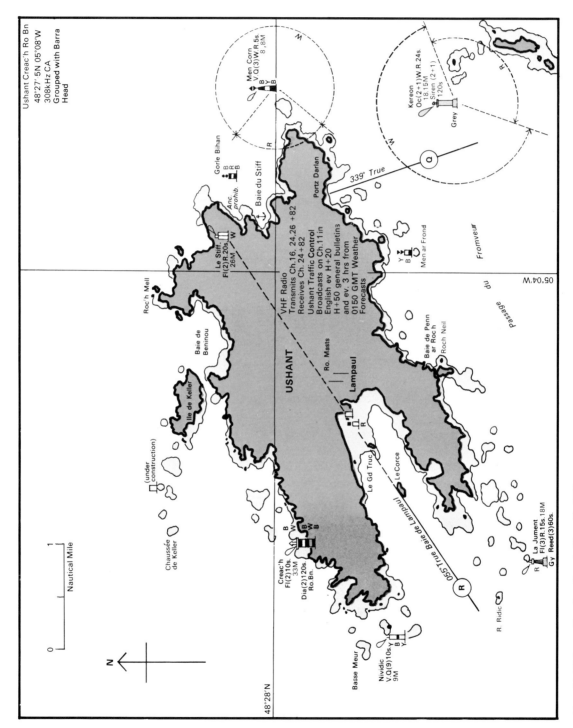

Chart 36. Ushant. Based on French Chart No 5567.

44 Ushant

Tidal Data

Tidal Heights
High Water: approx −0005 Brest (+0505 Dover).
Heights of Tide above Datum: approx MHWS 7·6 m, MLWS 1·2 m, MHWN 5·7 m, MLWN 3·0 m.
Mean Tide Level: 4·5 m. Index 5 B.

Tidal Streams

1. For streams between Ushant and the mainland and in the Passage du Fromveur see page 263.
2. At **Basse Meur** (0·75 mile NNW of **Nividic** lighthouse at the west end of the island) the NNE-going stream begins at −0550 Brest (−0040 Dover) and the SSW-going stream at −0045 Brest (+0555 Dover). Both streams reach 5·6 knots at springs.
3. The streams south and SW of the entrance of **Baie de Lampaul** vary in direction, time and rate within a relatively small area of sea.
    (a) Off **La Jument** lighthouse and **Ar Ridic** 0·5 mile NW of the lighthouse, at springs the NW-going stream begins at +0350 Brest (−0325 Dover) and the south-going at 0000 Brest (+0510 Dover) both streams reaching 4·7 knots at springs. At neaps the NW-going stream begins at +0435 Brest (−0240 Dover) and the south-going stream at −0045 Brest (+0425 Dover); both streams reaching 1·8 knots.
    (b) About 3 miles westward of the entrance of **Baie de Lampaul** the streams differ again and are sometimes quite clearly defined by overfalls in one tidal area and smooth water in the other. Here the NW-going stream begins at +0535 Brest (−0025 Dover) and the south-going at +0030 Brest (+0540 Dover).

General

The island of Ushant (Ile d'Ouessant or in Breton Enez Eussa), although one of the most important milestones on the world's sea traffic lanes, is not often visited by yachts. This is partly due to its lack of good anchorages, and partly to a general feeling that the extreme NW corner of Brittany is no place for loitering, whether outward or homeward bound. It also has more days when visibility is less than 1 km than any other north French port, with a maximum in July.

Approaches

Provided account is taken of the strong tides, particularly in the **Passage du Fromveur**, of the overfalls which these can create especially with adverse winds, and of the possibility of a deterioration in visibility, approach to the island from the mainland is straightforward whether direct from the east or from the south via the **Chenal de la Helle**.

Anchorages

(1) BAIE DE LAMPAUL

In spite of being open to the SW this bay is the chief anchorage at Ushant.

Approach

A line (**R**) formed by **Le Stiff** lighthouse (white tower shaped like a vertical figure of eight, 28 m high, elevation 85 m) open to the north of **Le Corce** (a rock about 34 m high) by a distance equal to the width of the latter and bearing 055° True, clears all the outer dangers comfortably.

Pass either side of **Le Corce**, which has drying rocks extending about 100 m on its northern side, then keep well over to the eastward to avoid the shoals which fill the northern corner of the bay. If proceeding to the harbour alter course when the Lateral port beacon tower bears north, and steer between this beacon tower and the Lateral starboard beacon tower.

Anchorage and Harbour

In the approach anchor near the mooring buoys in 5·7 to 9·1 m, sand and mud, good holding ground, or secure to a vacant buoy.

Entrance of Passage du Fromveur. Le Stiff lighthouse with the Baie du Stiff between the near and far headlands. To the right is Men-Corn lighthouse. The picture is taken from a SE direction.

The port of Lampaul (or Port de Portzpaul) consists of what may be termed the outer harbour with 1·8 to 2·1 m LAT near the entrance and a quay for the mail steamer, and the inner harbour which dries out and is almost closed by two short jetties leaving a gap about 7·9 m wide through which small vessels may pass when the tide serves.

There is room to anchor in the outer harbour, in the channel, roughly on the line from the Lateral port beacon tower to the quay. There are three mooring buoys on this line and soundings should be taken if deviating to the north or south of them, as

After leaving Le Corce to starboard a good line of approach to Lampaul harbour is with the outer Men ar Blank Lateral port beacon tower in line with the church spire or a little to the south of the line. The barge is beginning to turn to port to enter between the Lateral port and Lateral starboard beacon tower. See also photo on page 276.

The picture is taken facing about WSW across the entrance of the outer harbour and shows Men ar Blank Lateral port beacon tower. The white motor vessel is on the outer moorings, and the yacht Cohoe III is on the second one. To the left is Le Corce. It is near low water.

Lampaul harbour. In the centre is the lifeboat slip and to the left of it the new pier where the Brest steamer berths. There is about 1·8 m MLWS off the pier, more water to the west but the water shoals rapidly eastward off the lifeboat slip. On the right is the narrow entrance to the inner harbour. The picture is taken from drying rocks (see extreme right) facing NW at about half-tide.

Facing to the south the picture shows the entrance of the inner harbour at Lampaul at HW viewed from the land. The bottom is steeply shelving but a yacht could dry out on the west side near the entrance.

the basin is only a little over 100 m wide with drying rocks on each side. There is 2·3 m LAT between the beacon towers with rock bottom 2 m north of the Lateral starboard beacon tower and about 0·6 to 0·9 m LAT off the steamer jetty. The water shoals rapidly beyond the lifeboat slip. If one adds 1·2 m at MLWS, or 3·0 m at MLWN, it will be seen that there is usually plenty of water for a yacht in the anchorage. This is protected from north and east by land and from the southward there is a fetch of less than 0·5 mile. From the west the anchorage receives some protection from rocks which dry out north of the Lateral port beacon tower, but at high water it might be dangerous with strong winds blowing into the bay. Yachts can secure to a mooring buoy, if vacant, but these are used by the lifeboat when she is launched, so if one is picked up it is best to enquire at the lifeboat house whether it is in order to remain there.

The best dinghy landing is at the lifeboat slip, which dries out at low water, when land at a ladder to the west of it.

Facilities

Water from pump at head of drying harbour. Petrol, etc. from garage a quarter of a mile from harbour. Post office, several small shops. Small hôtel and restaurants. Excellent table d'hôte lunch at the Hotel Roch-ar-Mor where one can hire a taxi.

(2) BAIE DU STIFF

This bay is sheltered from south through west to NW, but heavy weather from any quarter sends in a huge swell which makes the anchorage untenable. The holding ground is only moderate.

Approach

Straightforward but avoid **Gorle-Bian** rocks in the middle of the bay, marked by an isolated danger beacon tower. The small bay 0·2 mile south of **Le Stiff** lighthouse receives the submarine cable from **Laberildut**, and is a prohibited anchorage.

Anchorage

There are white mooring buoys, which are heavy and unsuitable for yachts. What appear to be lighter mooring buoys are markers for the fishermen's keep boxes. Room to anchor can be found but avoid a rocky patch in the south corner of the bay. Avoid also the end of the jetty which is used by *vedettes*. It is possible to land by dinghy at all states of tide at the lifeboat slip which is behind the jetty.

The jetty and landing place in Baie du Stiff near HW. The picture faces across the bay to the SE.

The anchorage in Baie de Pen ar Roch is easy of access from the Passage du Fromveur in settled weather. It is sheltered by Ushant from west, NW and north winds.

(3) PORTZ DARLAN

This consists of a small drying inlet partly protected by a jetty on its SW side. The end of the jetty dries 1·5 m.

Approach

Approach with **Le Stiff** lighthouse (white tower shaped like a vertical figure of eight 28 m high. Elevation 85 m in line with the right edge of the beach, east of the jetty, bearing 339° True. (Line **Q**).

Entrance of Baie de Lampaul. Stiff lighthouse at 055° True is held just open to the north of Le Corce island, seen here on the right of the picture. Alternatively if the visibility is poor the church can be held open on the north side of Le Corce which will clear dangers to the southward in the approach. Neither landmark shows in this picture owing to haze over the land.

276

Anchorage

There is a temporary anchorage in 3·6 m LAT, sand, with the end of the jetty bearing about NW distant 0·1 mile. There is also a mooring buoy near this position which may be used if vacant but in northerly winds it is used by the mailboat.

There is a landing slip on the north side of the jetty.

(4) BAIE DE PEN AR ROCH

This bay offers very little shelter, but is used by the mail steamer during strong westerly winds.

Approach

Approach is straightforward and the dangers can be seen on Chart No 36.

Anchorage

There is a temporary anchorage in about 12 m LAT, sand, with **Roc'h Neil** bearing about 200° True, distant 0·15 mile. There is a landing slip which can be used at all states of the tide.

Nautical Terms

English–French

aboard – *à bord*
afloat – *à flot*
aft – *arrière*
aground – *à terre*
anchor – *ancre* (f.)
to anchor – *mouiller*
anchorage – *mouillage* (m.)
ash (wood) – *frêne* (m.)
awash – *à fleur de l'eau*

baler – *écope* (f.)
ballast – *lest* (m.)
bank (of river) – *digue* (f.), *rive* (f.)
bar (of river) – *mascaret* (m.)
barge – *chaland* (m.)
basin – *bassin* (m.)
battery (electric) – *batterie* (f.)
baulk (of wood) – *tin* (m.)
bay – *baie* (f.)
beach – *plage* (f.), *grève* (f.)
beacon – *balise* (f.)
beacon tower – *tourelle* (f.)
beam (width) – *largeur* (f.)
bearing (direction) – *relèvement* (m.)
to beat to windward – *louvoyer*
to belay – *frapper une amarre*
belfry – *clocher* (m.)
bell – *cloche* (f.)
below – *en bas*
bend (of a channel) – *coude* (m.)
to beware of – *se méfier de*
black – *noir*
block (pulley) – *poulie* (f.)
to blow – *souffler*
boat – *bateau* (m.), *canot* (m.), *embarcation* (f.)
boat-building shed – *chantier* (m.)
boathook – *gaffe* (f.)
bollard – *bitte d'amarrage* (f.)
boom – *bôme* (m.)
bore (tidal) – *mascaret* (f.)
bottom (sea bed) – *fond* (m.)
bows – *avant* (m.)
bowsprit – *beaupré* (m.)
breaker (surf) – *brisant* (m.)
breakwater – *brise-lames* (m.)

breeze – *brise* (f.)
bridge (of river) – *pont* (m.)
broken down – *en panne*
buoy (navigational) – *bouée* (f.)
buoy (mooring) – *corps mort*
burgee – *guidon* (m.)

cabin – *cabine* (f.)
calm – *calme*
can buoy – *tonne* (f.)
canal – *canal* (m.)
canvas – *toile* (f.)
cape – *cap* (m.)
to capsize – *chavirer*
to cast off – *larguer*
to caulk – *calfater*
chain – *chaîne* (f.)
channel – *manche* (f.), *chenal* (m.), *canal* (m.), *passage* (m.)
chart – *carte* (*marine*) (f.)
to clean – *nettoyer*
to clear (an obstacle) – *franchir*
cliff – *falaise* (f.)
close-hauled, to come – *ranger le vent*
clump of trees – *bouquet de bois* (m.)
coast – *côte* (f.)
coaster – *caboteur* (m.)
coasting, coasting trade – *cabotage* (m.)
cockpit – *baignoire* (f.)
compass – *boussole* (f.), *compas* (m.)
copper – *cuivre* (m.)
corrected time – *temps compensé* (m.)
course – *route* (f.)
cove – *anse* (f.)
crane – *grue* (f.)
creek – *crique* (f.), *anse* (f.)
crew – *équipage* (m.)
cruise – *croisière* (f.)
Custom house, Customs – *douane* (f.)
Customs officer – *douanier* (m.)
current – *courant* (m.)
cutter (rig) – *côtre* (m.)

daymark – *amer* (m.)

deck – *pont* (m.)
depth – *profondeur* (f.)
diesel oil – *gasoil* (m.)
dinghy – *canot* (m.), *annexe* (f.)
to disembark – *débarquer*
diver – *plongeur* (m.)
dockyard – *chantier* (m.)
downstream – *aval*
to drag (anchor) – *chasser*
draught – *tirant d'eau* (m.)
to dredge – *creuser*
dredger – *gabarre* (f.), *dragueur* (m.)
to dry out – *échouer*
dyke – *digue* (f.)

east – *est* (m.)
eastern, easterly – *oriental*
ebb tide – *marée descendante*, *jusant* (m.)
eddy – *remous* (m.)
elapsed time – *temps réel*
to embark – *embarquer*
engine – *machine* (f.)
English Channel – *la Manche*

fathom (French) – *brasse* (f.) (5 ft 4 in.)
fender – *défense* (f.)
ferry – *bac* (m.)
fish – *poisson* (m.)
fish hook – *hameçon* (m.)
fish pond – *vivier* (m.)
fisherman – *pêcheur* (m.)
fishing boat – *bateau pêcheur* (m.)
fire – *feu* (m.)
flag – *pavillon* (m.)
flood tide – *marée montante*, *flot* (m.)
fog – *brouillard* (m.), *brume* (f.)
forward – *avant*
fresh water – *eau douce*

gaff – *corne* (f.)
gale – *coup de vent* (m.)
galley – *cuisine* (f.)
galvanised – *zingué*
gangway – *passerelle* (f.)

279

graving dock – *forme de radoub* (f.)

grease – *graisse* (f.)

grid – *gril de carénage* (m.)

grounding – *echouage*

gunwale – *plat-bord* (m.)

to gybe – *empanner, gambeyer*

halftide – *mi-marée* (f.)

halyard – *drisse* (f.)

harbour – *darse* (f.), *havre* (m.)

harbourmaster – *capitaine du port* (m.)

hard astarboard! – *tribord tout!*

hard (adj.) – *dur*

to haul – *haler*

to heave the lead – *jeter la sonde*

to heave-to – *mettre en panne*

high water – *haute marée, haute mer, pleine marée*

to hoist – *hisser*

holding ground – *tenue* (f.)

horse power – *chevaux* (pl.)

hose (pipe) – *manche* (f.)

to hug (pass close to) – *rallier, ranger*

hull – *coque* (f.)

hydrant – *prise d'eau* (f.)

insurance – *assurance* (f.)

iron – *fer* (m.)

island – *île* (f.)

jetty – *jetée* (f.)

jib – *foc* (m.)

keel – *quille* (f.)

kelp – *goémon* (m.)

ketch – *ketch* (f.)

knot – *noeud* (m.)

ladder – *échelle* (f.)

landfall – *atterrage* (m.)

landing slip – *cale* (f.)

to lash – *amarrer*

launching – *mise à l'eau* (f.)

lead (sounding) – *sonde* (f.)

lead (metal) – *plomb* (m.)

to leak – *faire eau*

to leave (to port, etc.) – *laisser (par babord, etc.)*

legs (of a boat) – *béquilles* (f.)

length – *longueur* (f.)

to let go – *larguer*

lifeboat – *canot de sauvetage* (m.)

lifebuoy – *bouée de sauvetage* (f.)

lifejacket – *ceinture de sauvetage* (f.)

lighter – *chaland* (m.), *gabarre* (f.)

lighthouse – *phare* (m.), *feu* (m.)

lightship – *bateau feu* (m.)

lock (of canal, etc.) – *écluse* (f.)

low water – *basse marée, basse mer*

low water mark – *étiage* (m.)

lubricating oil – *huile de graissage* (f.)

lugger – *lougre* (m.)

mahogany – *acajou* (m.)

mainsail – *grande voile*

to make fast to – *amarrer sur*

mast – *mât* (m.)

masthead height – *tirant d'air*

methylated spirits – *alcool à brûler* (m.)

mile – *mille* (m.)

mizzen – *tapecul, artimon* (m.)

mole – *digne* (f.)

to moor to – *amarrer sur*

mooring dolphin – *Duc D'Albe*

mooring ring – *organeau* (m.)

moorings – *corps morts*

mouth (of river) – *bouche* (f.)

mud – *vase* (f.)

muddy – *vaseux*

nautical mile – *mille marin*

neap tide – *marée morte, morte eau*

net – *filet* (m.)

north – *nord* (m.)

oak – *chêne* (m.)

oar – *aviron* (m.), *rame* (f.)

offing – *large* (m.)

oilskin – *cirés* (m.) (pl.)

open sea – *pleine mer, large* (m.)

owner – *propiétaire* (m.)

oyster bed – *parc à huitres* (m.)

painter (rope) – *bosse* (f.)

paraffin – *pétrole* (m.)

to pass to the westward of the beacon – *laisser dans l'est la balise*

passenger – *passager* (m.)

passengers – *embarcation* (f.)

passport – *passeport* (m.)

pebbles – *cailloux* (m.) (pl.)

peninsula – *presqu'île* (f.)

petrol – *essence* (f.)

pier – *jettée* (f.)

pierhead – *musoir* (m.)

pilot – *pilote* (m.)

pine (wood) – *pin* (m.)

pool – *fosse* (f.)

poop – *dunette* (f.)

port (harbour) – *port* (m.)

port (side) – *bâbord* (m.)

pump – *pompe* (f.)

to pump – *pomper*

quay – *quai* (m.)

quicksands – *sables mouvants*

race – *course* (f.)

radio – *T.S.F.* (f.)

rain – *pluie* (f.)

ready about! – *paré à virer!*

to recaulk – *calfater*

red – *rouge*

reef (of rock) – *écueil* (m.)

reef (of sail) – *ris* (m.)

to reef – *riser*

to reeve – *passer*

to refit, to repair – *remettre à neuf*

riding light – *feu de mouillage* (m.)

rig – *gréement* (m.)

river – *rivière* (f.)

roads – *rade* (f.), *anse* (f.)

rock – *rocher* (m.), *roche* (f.), *écueil* (m.)

rope – *cordage* (m.), *corde* (f.)

rough (of sea) – *dur*

to row – *nager*

rowlock – *dame de nage* (f.)

Royal Navy – *marine de l'état* (f.)

rudder – *gouvernail* (m.)

runnel – *ruisseau* (m.)

sail – *voile* (f.)

sail loft, sail-making – *voilerie* (f.)

sailmaker – *voilier* (m.)

sand – *sable* (m.)

sandbank – *banc de sable* (m.)

sandy – *sableux*

schooner – *goëlette* (f.)

screw (propeller) – *hélice* (f.)

to scrub – *nettoyer à labrosse*

sea (ocean) – *mer* (f.)
sea (wave) – *coup de mer* (m.)
seaweed – *goémon* (m.)
to seize – *amarrer*
shackle – *maillon* (m.)
sheet – *écoute* (f.)
shells – *coques*
sheltered – *abrité*
shingle – *cailloux* (m.) (pl.)
ship – *navire* (m.)
shoal – *haut-fond* (m.)
shrouds – *haubans* (m.) (pl.)
side light – *feu de navigation* (m.)
sill (of lock) – *radier* (m.)
slack (stream) – *étale*
sluice – *pertuis* (m.), *vanne* (f.)
soft – *mou* (m.), *molle* (f.)
to sound (depth) – *sonder*
south – *sud* (m.)
speed – *vitesse* (f.)
spinnaker – *spinnaker* (m.)
splice – *épissure* (f.)
spring tide – *grande marée, vive eau*
standing rigging – *gréement dormant* (m.)
starboard – *tribord* (m.)
stay – *étai* (m.)
staysail – *voile d'étai* (f.)
steel – *acier* (m.)

steeple – *clocher* (m.)
to steer for – *gouverner sur, mettre le cap sur*
steps – *escalier* (m.)
stern – *arrière* (m.)
stove – *étuve* (f.)
straits – *pertuis* (m.)
stream – *ruisseau* (m.)
surf – *ressac* (m.)
surge, swell – *houle* (f.)
to swim – *nager*
swinging room – *évitage* (m.)

tackle – *palan* (m.)
teak – *teck* (m.)
tidal – *de marée*
tide – *marée* (f.)
tide-gauge – *échelle de marée* (f.)
tide-mill – *moulin a l'eau* (m.)
tide-race – *raz* (m.)
tiller – *barre* (f.)
timber yard – *chantier* (m.)
ton – *tonne* (f.)
topping lift – *balancine* (f.)
topsail – *hunier* (m.)
to tow – *remorquer*
towage – *touage* (m.)
towpath – *chemin de halage* (m.)
trawl – *chalut* (m.)
trawler – *chalutier* (m.)

trysail – *voile de cape* (f.)
tug (boat) – *remorqueur* (m.)

upstream – *amont*

wall beacon – *amer* (m.)
warp – *aussière* (f.)
warping – *touage* (m.)
water (fresh) – *eau douce*
water point – *prise d'eau*
wave – *vague* (f.)
way, to get under – *appareiller*
weather (met) – *temps* (m.)
weather forecast – *la metéo* (f.)
to weigh anchor – *appareiller, lever l'ancre*
well (water) – *puits* (m.)
west – *ouest* (m.)
western, westerly – *occidental*
wet dock – *darse* (f.), *bassin à flot* (m.), *bassin* (m.)
wheel (steering) – *roue* (f.)
white – *blanc*
wind – *vent* (m.)
wire – *fil* (m.)
wireless – *T.S.F.* (f.)
wreck – *naufrage* (m.)

yacht – *yacht* (m.)
yawl – *yawl* (m.)

281

French–English

abrité – sheltered

acajou – mahogany

acier – steel

alcool à brûler – methylated spirits

amarrer (sur) – to moor, make fast (to), to tie, to seize

amer – daymark, wall beacon

amont – upstream

ancre – anchor

annexe – dinghy

anse – creek, cove

appareiller – to weigh anchor, get under way

arrière – aft, stern

artimon – mizzen

assécher – to dry out

assurance – insurance

atterrage – landfall

aussière – warp

aval – downstream

avant – forward, bows

aviron – oar

bâbord – port (side)

bac – ferry

baie – bay

baignoine – cockpit

balancine – topping lift

balise – beacon

banc de sable – sandbank

barre – tiller

basse marée, basse mer – low water

bassin – basin, dock

bassin à flot – wet dock

bateau – boat

bateau feu – lightship

bateau pêcheur – fishing boat

batterie – battery (electric)

beaupré – bowsprit

béquilles – legs (of a boat)

bitte d'amarrage – bollard

blanc – white

bôme – boom

à bord – aboard

bosse – painter

bouche – mouth (of river)

bouée – navigational buoy

bouée de sauvetage – lifebuoy

bouquet de bois – clump of trees

boussole – compass

brassee – French fathom (5 ft 4 in.)

brisant – breaker (surf)

brise – breeze

brise-lames – breakwater

brouillard, brume – fog

cabine – cabin

cabotage – coasting, coasting trade

caboteur – coaster

cailloux – pebbles, shingle

cale – landing slip

calfater – to caulk

calme – calm

canal – channel, canal

canot – boat, dinghy

canot de sauvetage – lifeboat

cap – cape

capitaine du port – harbourmaster

carte (marine) – chart

ceinture de sauvetage – lifejacket

chaîne – chain

chaland – lighter, barge

chalut – trawl

chalutier – trawler

chantier – timber yard, boatbuilding shed, dockyard

chasser – to drag (anchor)

chavirer – to capsize

chemin de halage – towpath

chenal – channel

chêne – oak

chevaux – horse power

cirés – oilskins

cloche – bell

clocher – belfry, steeple

compas – compass

coque – hull

coques – shells

cordage, corde – rope

corne – gaff

corps morts – moorings

côte – coast

côtre – cutter (rig)

coude – bend (of a channel)

coup de mer – sea (wave)

coup de vent – gale

courant – current

course – race

creuser – to dredge

crique – creek

croisière – cruise

cuisine – galley

cuivre – copper

dame de nage – rowlock

darse – wet dock, harbour

débarquer – to disembark

défense – fender

digue – bank, dyke, mole

douane – Custom house, Customs

douanier – Customs officer

dragueur – dredger

drisse – halyard

Duc d'Albe – mooring dolphin

dur – hard (adj.), rough (of sea)

eau douce – fresh water

échelle – ladder

échelle de marée – tide gauge

échouage – grounding

écluse – lock (of canal, etc.)

écope – baler

écoute – sheet

écueil – reef, rock

embarcation – small boat, passengers

embarquer – to embark

empanner – to gybe

en bas – below

épissure – splice

équipage – crew

escalier – steps

essence – petrol

est – east

étai – stay

étale – slack (stream)

étiage – low water mark

étuve – stove

évitage – swinging room

falaise – cliff

faire eau – to leak

fer – iron

feu – lighthouse, fire

feu de mouillage – riding light

feu de navigation – side-light

fil – wire

filet – net

à fleur de l'eau – awash

flot – flood (tide)

à flot – afloat

foc – jib
fond – sea bed
forme de radoub – graving dock
fosse – pool
franchir – to clear (an obstacle)
frapper une amarre – belay
frêne – ash (wood)

gabarre – lighter, small dredger
gaffe – boathook
gambeyer – to gybe
gasoil – diesel oil
goëlette – schooner
goémon – seaweed, kelp
gouvernail – rudder, helm
gouverner sur – to steer for
graisse – grease
grande marée – spring tide
grande voile – mainsail
gréement – rig
grève – beach
gril de carénage – grid
grue – crane
guidon – burgee

haler – to haul
hameçon – fish hook
haubans – shrouds
haussière – (see aussière)
haut-fond – shoal
haute marée, haute mer – high
water
havre – harbour
hélice – screw (propeller)
hisser – to hoist
houle – surge, swell
huile de graissage – lubricating
oil
hunier – topsail

île – island

jetée – jetty, pier
jeter la sonde – to heave the lead
jusant – ebb

ketch – ketch

laisser dans l'est la balise – to
pass to the westward of the
beacon
laisser par bâbord – to leave to
port
large – offing, open sea
largeur – beam (width)

larguer – to cast off, let go
lest – ballast
lever l'ancre – to weigh anchor
longueur – length
lougre – lugger
louvoyer – to beat to windward

machine – engine
maillon – shackle
manche – hose (pipe), channel,
English Channel
marée – tide
de marée – tidal
marée descendante – ebb tide
marée montante – flood tide
marée morte – neap tide
marine de l'état – Royal Navy
mascaret – bore
mât – mast
se méfier de – to beware of
mer – sea (ocean)
metéo – weather forecast
mettre en panne – to heave-to
mettre le cap sur – to steer for
mi-marée – half tide
mille – mile
mille marin – nautical mile
mise à l'eau – launching
molle (f.), *mou* (m.) – soft
montée d'eau – height of tide
morte eau – neap tide
moulin à l'eau – water mill,
tide-mill
mouillage – anchorage
mouiller – to anchor
musoir – pierhead

nager – to swim, to row
naufrage – wreck
navire – ship
nettoyer – to clean, to scrub
noeud – knot
noir – black
nord – north
noroit – northwest

occidental – western, westerly
organeau – mooring ring
oriental – eastern, easterly
ouest – west

palan – tackle
en panne – broken down, hove
to
parc à huitres – oyster beds

paré à virer! – ready about!
passage – channel
passager – passenger
passeport – passport
passer – to reeve
passerelle – gangway
pavillon – flag
pêcheur – fisherman
pertuis – straits, sluice
pétrole – paraffin
phare – lighthouse
pilote – pilot
pin – pine (wood)
plage – beach
plat-bord – gunwale
pleine marée, pleine mer – high
water
plomb – lead (metal)
plongeur – diver
pluie – rain
poisson – fish
pompe – pump
pomper – to pump
pont – deck, bridge (of river)
port – port (harbour)
poulie – block
presqu'île – peninsula
prise d'eau – water-point,
hydrant
profondeur – depth
propriétaire – owner
puits – well (water)

quai – quay
quille – keel

rade – roads
radier – sill (of lock)
rame – oar
rallier, ranger – to hug (pass
close to)
ranger le vent – to come
close-hauled
raz – tide-race
relèvement – bearing (direction)
remettre à neuf – to refit, repair
remorquer – to tow
remorqueur – tug (boat)
remous – eddy, dead water
ressac – surf
ris – reef (of sail)
riser – to reef
rive – bank (of river, etc.)
rivière – river
rocher, roche – rock

roue – wheel (steering)
rouge – red
route – course
ruisseau – runnel, stream

sable – sand
sables mouvants – quicksands
sableux – sandy
sas – lock (of canal, etc.)
sonde – lead (sounding)
sonder – to sound (depth)
souffler – to blow
spinnaker – spinnaker
sud – south
suroit – southwest

tapecul – mizzen
teck – teak

temps – weather (met)
temps compensé – corrected time
temps réel – elapsed time
tenue – holding ground
à terre – aground
tin – baulk of wood
tirant d'eau – draught
tirant d'air – masthead height
toile – canvas
tonne – ton, can-buoy
touage – towage, warping
tourelle – beacon tower
tribord – starboard
tribord tout! – hard astarboard!
T.S.F. – radio

vague – wave
vase – mud

vaseux – muddy
vent – wind
vitesse – speed
vive eau – spring tide
vivier – pond or enclosure for
   live fish
voile – sail
voile de cape – trysail
voile d'étai – staysail
voilerie – sail loft, sail-making
voilier – sailmaker

yacht – yacht
yawl – yawl
youvou – dinghy

zingué – galvanised

Charts

French Official Charts

(a) Small-scale and Medium-scale Charts

5400. La Manche.
5069. La Manche, partie Ouest.
4587. Atterages de l'Entrée de la Manche et de la Côte Nord-Ouest de France.
 878. De l'île de Bréhat à Barfleur.
 880. Du cap Fréhel au havre de Carteret.
 879. De l'île Bréhat au cap Fréhel.
 970. De l'île de Bas à l'île Bréhat.
6031. De Brest à l'île de Bas.

(b) Large-scale Charts

 844. De cap Fréhel à Cancale; abords de Saint-Malo.
5645. De la pointe du Décollé à la pointe de Rothéneuf; rade de Saint-Malo.
4233. La Rance, de Saint Servan au Chatelier.
5646. Du cap Fréhel à la pointe du Décollé.
5724. D'Erqui au cap Fréhel.
 833. De Portrieux au cap Fréhel; baie de Saint Brieuc.
5725. De la pointe du Roselier à la pointe de Plouba.
 832. De l'île de Bréhat aux roches de Saint Quay; partie de la baie de Saint-Brieuc.
 831. Des Héaux de Bréhat à Paimpol; plateaux des roches Douvres et de Barnouic.
3670. Port et anse de Paimpol.
 882. Ile de Bréhat et ses environs.
2845. Rivière de Pontrieux.
 967. De l'île Grande aux Heaux; les Sept îles; rivière de Tréguier.
 972. Passes de la rivière de Tréguier.
 973. Rivière de Tréguier.
 974. Entrées de Perros et du Port Blanc.
5950. De l'île de Bas aux Sept îles.
6056. Mouillage de Trébeuden.
5827. Baie de Morlaix.
5828. Ile de Bas.
 966. De Pontusval à l'île de Bas; Port de Pontusval.
 964. Des roches de Porsal à Pontusval; l'Aberbenoit, l'Abervrach, Correjou.
5772. Du phare du Four à l'île Vierge.

5721.   De la pointe de Kermorvan à l'île d'Iock; Chenal du Four.

5567.   De l'île de Molène à l'île d'Ouessant; passage du Fromveur.

5287.   De Porsal à la pointe de Saint Mathieu; chenal du Four et environs de l'île d'Ouessant.

5159.   De la pointe de Saint-Mathieu à l'île de Molène; chaussée des Pierres Noires.

'C' Charts

Published by Imray, Laurie, Norie & Wilson Ltd, Wych House, St Ives, Huntingdon.

C33A. The Channel Islands (North) and adjacent coast of France.

C33B. The Channel Islands (South) and adjacent coast of France.

C34. Cap d'Erqui to Morlaix Bay.

C35. Point de Primel to Cap de la Chèvre.

The above charts are in colour with insets of harbours.

Navigational Publications

British Admiralty Publications

Channel Pilot.
List of Lights, Vol. A.
Tidal Streams, European Waters.
Tide Tables, European Waters (annual).
Pocket Tidal Atlas for the English Channel.
Pocket Tidal Atlas for the Channel Islands and Adjacent Coast of France.

Other British Publications

The Cruising Association Handbook.
Tidal Streams North Coast of France between Cape Barfleur and Pointe de Penmarch. Imray, Laurie, Norrie & Wilson Ltd.

French Admiralty Publications

Instructions Nautiques, No. C 11A, Côtes Nord et Ouest de France.
Phares et Signaux de Brume, No. 11–210, Série C.
Annuaire des Marées and supplement *Tables des Hauteurs d'Eau pour les Côtes Françaises de la Manche et de L'Atlantique.*

Other French Publications

Almanach de Marin Breton (Roux, Le Fret, Finistère, France).

Guide du Yachtsman en Manche–Atlantique by P. M. Bourdeaux
(Edition 'Eole', Boulevard Malesherbes, Paris 8e),
Tome III. Du Raz de Sein aux Héaux de Bréhat.
Tome IV. Des Héaux de Bréhat à Cherbourg.

Guide de Petite Croisière, du Raz de Sein au Havre, by Jean Merrien (Libraire Nautique du Yacht, 55 rue de Châteaudun, Paris 9e).

Guide de la Croisière Bretagne, by Le Berne Guillemot, Edition Neptune.

Index

Chart references are shown in bold type